Daisy And The Reluctant Alchemist

A Romantic Screwball-Comedy-Adventure
By John Mark Oates

CHAPTER ONE:

In Which Fred Is About To Take The Plunge

But Not In The Usual Sense.

"Ollie!"

The name came out as a shriek of last-ditch desperation. Startled, Fred was momentarily aware of a vision bearing down upon him that could quite possibly have been an angel. Big, blue eyes. A halo of golden hair. Stone-washed denim. Long, bright pink legs. Possibly an angelic, denim-clad flamingo. He was also aware of an irate duck; although his attention was mainly focused on the Old English sheepdog that had leapt into his arms to escape the aforementioned duck. Lastly, he was conscious of the fact that he had lost his balance. He remembered the park boating lake behind him, and suddenly found himself underwater.

The lake was not all that deep; being more of a pond with ideas above its station. Once he had remembered that, and the dog had used his face as a stepping stone for vacating its perch on his chest, Fred stopped drowning and stood up. The water came up to his pockets, swirling murkily with the mud from the bottom that his unexpected dip had stirred up. The duck that had been initially responsible for his downfall was careering across the water towards the far bank, quacking hysterically.

With exasperated fingers, Fred scraped his wet hair back. Just two hours to his wedding and he was saturated in brown, muddy water; covered in pond weed, algae and a

3

not inconsiderable assortment of aquatic life. He wondered vaguely if the day could possibly get any worse...?

-oOo-

The wedding was set for ten in the morning and at half-past seven, Frederick Longfield had been standing in the front room of his parents' house watching Charlie Newton, his best friend and lab technician colleague, fiddling self-consciously with the ring. Charlie, a gangling creature with a shock of spiky ginger hair that made him look like a lit match when he stood up straight, was proving a less than ideal choice of Best Man.

Charlie had tried putting the little box with the ring in every pocket of his suit at least twice. He had tried carrying the ring in every pocket of his suit *out* of its box. He had tried knotting his handkerchief through the ring to make its location more obvious and still he could never simply stick his hand in his pocket and retrieve it when required. As ring-bearers went, if he had got the job of taking it to Mount Doom, he would have been toast before he got out of the front door.

"How's he going to pass for best man?" asked Fred's mother, staring at Charlie with an expression that was a mixture of alarm and exasperation. "He looks like shop-soiled would be stretching a point." She turned her attention to her son's appearance, and realising something drastic had to be done, wandered away to the sideboard for the tools to rectify the situation.

As bridegrooms went, Fred Longfield was not the most inspiring specimen. In his mid-thirties, he presented an owlish aspect. An absent-minded inclination to untidiness gave the impression he had been sleeping in his best suit, even though it had been carefully pressed a matter

4

of moments before he had put it on. The collar of his new shirt felt like a surgical neck-brace and his trousers showed an alarming tendency to descend round his ankles in spite of his belt. He hoped cleaning his spectacles might improve matters, but having carefully dusted the lenses with the handkerchief from his top pocket, he was forced to admit it did not.

Fred straightened his tie and gazed forlornly at himself in the mirror. His face had taken on the expression of a habitual lemon-sucker. The look in his eyes was that of something small and furry being hunted by big men with guns and sticks. He was in trouble. Big trouble. And he knew it.

He had been a Chemistry teacher at St. Norbert's R.C. High School in Chayne Abbas for the best part, (or was that worst part), of three years and teaching at the school was more fraught with terrors than his time as a spotty pupil there. Genghis Khan and his Mongol hordes would have asked for danger money to even come near the heathen masses under his charge. The pupils now occupying the school were a far cry from the mere yobs and hooligans that had been his contemporaries when he was a pupil at dear old St. Norbert's. The current intake was the worst collection of hoodlums, thieves, neo-Nazis and perverts he had ever come across, and they were the least of his problems. He did not find them remotely as terrifying as the Headmaster, his prospective father-in-law.

Professor Masters was a large, bear-like man in his mid-fifties who had been teaching at the school in Fred's school-days, and still scared the living daylights out of him. A man of such fine furies, it was easy to believe the school folklore that he had been known to kill rats with his teeth. Whether in anger or for his own entertainment, Fred had never been able to ascertain. Initially opposed to the union of Fred and his darling daughter Melissa with the last molecule of his dying breath, the Headmaster was now responsible for the indecent haste with which the impending nuptials were bearing down juggernaut-like upon Our Hero.

Fred gave a grunt of surprise as his mother grabbed him in a half-nelson and started to attack his hair with a brush. "You might at least comb this mop occasionally," she observed through teeth gritted in determination. Fred was used to his mother treating him like a five-year-old, and said nothing.

Once she was satisfied she had at least slightly improved her son's appearance, his mother released him and checked her reflection in the mirror. "Hickory sticks!" she exclaimed suddenly, "The buttonholes!" She raced into the kitchen where she had left the blooms in the sink.

His father was sprawled comfortably in the armchair, leafing through the previous evening's Gazette. Actively terrified of Melissa, the Longfield patriarch took every opportunity to voice his own reservations towards the union. He turned the newspaper to face Fred and tapped the headline. *Daisy Does It Again.* Below it, a slightly blurry picture showed a slender, flaxen-haired figure wrapped in a policeman's tunic being led away by the tunic's owner from what appeared to be a re-enactment of the Battle of Bosworth Field by two cricket teams. At the very least there was a lot of mud and blood, but Fred was concentrating on the startled-looking blonde.

Fred's father peered through his half-frames at the print. *"Warmhamptonshire's answer to Lady Godiva, local celebrity Daisy Chayne* (pictured, with arresting officer PC James Wodehouse,) *was escorted from the grounds of the Royal Warmhampton Cricket Club following an incident at the annual charity cricket match in aid of the Chayne Abbas Hospital Trust. A fight broke out after Ms Boadicea Ballcock accused the Captain of the winning team of deliberately tearing off Ms Chayne's dress as she presented him with the cup. Seventy-two arrests were made..."* He tapped the picture meaningfully with a forefinger. "Now *that's* the sort of girl you should have been looking for." He shook his head in wonder. "Crazy as a bucket of squirrels, that one."

"Chance would be a fine thing." There was considerably more gloom in Fred's voice than he might have intended.

The Chayne family was a mainstay of the Warmhamptonshire community, and the factory out on the Down was one of the area's main employers. Youngest Chayne daughter Daisy had acquired a certain notoriety in Warmhamptonshire society for a line in adventures that less kind-hearted souls might have described as hare-brained. Whether by design, sheer bad luck or the machinations of others, these adventures almost inevitably resulted in her being escorted stark-naked to safety by police officers. Fred had often read of her exploits in the Gazette, but to date had never been present in the flesh, as it were.

The Chayne fortune had been made in bathroom and sanitary fittings; the current patriarch of the dynasty Sir Roland was one of the governors of the school but Fred had only ever seen him once, and only then from a distance at a school prize-giving ceremony.

He checked his watch and turned to Charlie with the air of a condemned man. "Got the ring?"

Charlie rummaged obscenely in his trouser pockets and triumphantly held up the thin band of gold.

"Very good, Charlie." Fred chose his words carefully. "But to avoid a scene at the church, I would strongly advise you to keep it somewhere that isn't going to get you arrested for indecency when the priest asks you for the ring." Charlie shrugged and tucked the ring into his breast pocket, which would almost certainly be the last place he looked when asked for it.

"Fred," enquired his father quietly. "What do I say when I give you away?"

Fred shot his father a don't-you-start look and accepted a white carnation buttonhole from his mother. He made a half-hearted attempt to attach it himself and allowed her to take over. She flicked a piece of fluff off his shoulder and stood back. "It'll have to do," she said at length.

-oOo-

The morning seemed to be speeding by. Fred's Mum looked up at the clock and realised that the thing that was rushing was Fred. He was almost ready to go to the church, and there were still two-and-a-half hours to go before the ceremony. If he kept on at the rate he was going, he would be waiting at the reception for the rest of the wedding party before *they* set out for the church. She grabbed Fred by the arm and steered him into the corner before he did some damage. "Fred, love, it's only half-past seven. There's ages to go yet. You'll work yourself into a frazzle if you keep on this way!"

Fred looked at the clock, and only half-believing it, double-checked his watch. He looked ready to take off at a sprint at any moment. "Nerves," he said apologetically. "You know how it is when there's something you want to get over and done with — dentists' appointments, tax inspector interviews. Firing squads..."

His mother nodded understandingly. "Take a couple of deep breaths and sit down. Try to relax. I know you're anxious, but try to calm down before you drive the rest of us bananas."

Fred stared down at the toes of his shoes, which he had polished and re-polished at least three times that morning. "Sorry."

"Are you sure you're doing the right thing, Fred? You can still back out, you know." The idea of having Melissa as a daughter-in-law filled Fred's Mum with dread. The two women had not got on from the day they met, having diametrically opposed opinions as regards the successful upkeep of a Frederick Herbert Longfield. She tried not to think about being grandmother to Melissa's children at some time in the future, as the doctor had warned her about her blood pressure. "It's not too late if you're having doubts," she observed. There was a hint of hopeful desperation that Fred did not miss.

Fred was beginning to appreciate his mother's standpoint, although for completely different reasons. "I can't back out now," he said uncertainly. Those important two little words, '*can I?*' remained unspoken.

Fred's betrothed, Melissa, did *not* take after her mother, a small softly spoken woman who gave the impression she might wilt if breathed on too heavily. Rather she shared her father's build and somewhat ferocious nature. Unkind souls tended to use terms like "sturdy" or "rugby prop forward" in describing her, but

Fred had taught himself to think of her as "healthy", in the same way that hippopotamuses were healthy. On the hockey field, she was a terror to behold, and Fred suspected that she would probably class a husband as a member of the opposing team.

Well-scrubbed of features and brisk of demeanour, Melissa had taken up the position of head of girls' PE at St Norbert's straight from teacher training college. Her appointment was nothing to do with her father's position in the school, rather a demonstration of her own single-mindedness. She had voiced such an ambition while a junior pupil at the school and that had taken her through the positions of Head Girl, Captain of the hockey team at both the school and University, and ultimately to playing for England while at teacher training college. She was "sporty" in the Biblical sense, a personality trait not remotely shared by Fred. His mother had hit the proverbial nail on the head when she observed that Melissa was one of that athletic breed of young woman who could happily crack walnuts with her thighs.

The relationship had been founded eighteen months earlier in a blind double-date with Charlie Newton and his then-girlfriend Karen. Distinctly pro-active in matters of the heart, Melissa had refused to let the date be a one-off affair and Fred had found himself a permanent fixture on Ms. Masters' social calendar. Initially, she had demonstrated a starry-eyed romantic side that prompted her to address him as "Captain Snuggly," but of late she had been more inclined to use his full Christian name, delivered in her most strident tones, which Fred would readily admit was not a good sign. A distinctly old-fashioned sort of girl, she insisted that they should reserve their passions for each other until they were married; and even then only a few years down the line when they started planning a family.

The first cracks in the relationship had emerged when they realised they had little if anything in common. She liked horse riding. He preferred a good read. She enjoyed tropical beach holidays; he preferred more temperate climes. She wanted a flat in Warmhampton. He was happy where he was. At first any differences of opinion had not seemed to matter. She would suggest her father arbitrate in the matter and he would hastily concede the point.

He had hoped for a nice lengthy engagement, where any problems would have been sorted out at the living-together stage, or she would have got bored with him and left. He had not been granted that luxury. It only seemed like a few days since Melissa had announced their engagement, rather than three months, yet here he was being thrust headlong towards married life, propelled by a rocket up the seat of the pants courtesy of Melissa's darling daddy. He was increasingly of the suspicion that what was in store for him was what might be termed a 'marriage of convenience,' although he was sure none of it was for his.

Nothing short of a visit by the four horsemen of the apocalypse appeared capable of deflecting Melissa and her father from their sinister intent. Any sane person who believed in ill omens would have cancelled the wedding after the month he'd had, thought Fred. There had been various mishaps and disasters that could only be construed as the Gods or Fates looking on the union as a Bad Idea. Things had kicked off with the plans for their honeymoon, which had virtually bankrupted him. His usual idea of a holiday was a fortnight pottering around the garden, so two weeks smearing himself with zinc oxide and watching Melissa breeding freckles was something of a departure for him in more ways than one. The honeymoon was a moot point, however, as Foreign Office guidelines issued in the past couple of weeks advised against being on the same continent since the civil war had broken out. On television he had seen the hotel where they had the honeymoon suite booked reduced to a pile of smouldering concrete by artillery fire, and he suspected that the golden sands where Melissa had planned to do her famous beached whale impression were now littered with mines.

In the last couple of days, the bakery where the wedding cake was being prepared had been consumed by a blaze rumoured to have been started by the Masters' family secret recipe for rich Dundee cake and the volatile liquids it contained. Fred had sampled the recipe at Christmas, handed a slab of fruitcake of the weight and consistency of bog-peat with a warning not to smoke or stand too close to the fire. It was no stretch of the imagination that the mixture had virtually exploded upon insertion into the bakery oven and resisted all attempts to extinguish the conflagration.

His stag-night would remain indelibly etched on his memory for the rest of his days. Organised in Charlie's inimitable style, at first it had gone reasonably well. His work colleagues had dragged him off to a club in Stretcham, where they had got a reasonable glow on. One of the strippers had covered him in lipstick kisses and nearly smothered him with her ample bosom (an experience he would recommend to anyone). Then things had started to go wrong. His prospective father-in-law had invited himself to the revels, and proceeded to get himself quite outrageously inebriated — with a little mischievous engineering from Messrs. Law and Lasseter, the French and Art teachers respectively, who were the school's foremost anarchists.

The two men had helped the Headmaster back to his

house across the road from the school, and had helped him through a window at the back of the house so as not to wake his wife. It would have helped if they had opened the window first, and the good Professor, wearing only his string vest and Y-fronts had not decided that at three in the morning it was the perfect time to teach the entire household to belly dance...

For his own part, Fred had not enjoyed waking up duct-taped stark-naked to the roof rack of the Chief Constable's Daimler. Fortunately, it had been the wife of that most senior police officer who had discovered him in that predicament, otherwise he suspected he would have still been answering questions at the local police station.

What was supposed to be the happiest day of his life, and Fred felt as though he would rather simultaneously face root canal work unanaesthetised, a tax assessment and maybe wrestle a couple of crocodiles for good measure instead. The thought of marrying into the headmaster's clan filled him with terror.

If nothing else, he was a man of his word, and he had responsibilities to Melissa, her father, and the dozens of wedding guests counting on his presence as the groom. Ultimately, neither Melissa or the Headmaster were forgiving types, and were most likely to come after a reluctant bridegroom with a rusty pair of garden shears to deprive him of part of his anatomy. He had meditated on the contingency of fleeing the country, but in the end he knew he had only one Sydney-Carton-style course of action available.

"Why don't you go for a nice, long walk," suggested his mother. With him out of the way, they could get ready for the church in their own time. She smiled at him kindly. "Get a bit of fresh air."

13

Fred looked at his mother, then at his father and Charlie, and realised he had better get out of the house before they organised a lynch mob between them. He gave them an embarrassed smile. At least he would be able to sort out his thoughts on his own.

-oOo-

Chayne Park was a matter of a five minute walk from his parents' front door. The bright morning sunshine had brought out a handful of joggers, three people walking fast-overheating dogs, and a couple of mothers wheeling their tots through the park in pushchairs. Fred strolled through the East gate of the park and down the winding path through the copse towards the boating lake, wrestling with his thoughts. Two falls and a submission to decide the winner. The doubts that had been nagging him since his stag-night had grown steadily worse.

He walked down the gravel path to the side of the park boating lake. The ducks regarded him with passing interest in case he had a bag of bits of bread with him. To ducky eyes, he looked the sensible sort of chap who would toss morsels of unwanted sandwiches in the water so the bread was nice and soggy when they ate it. He looked a better proposition than those toddlers in the push chair, who threw stale bread to maim.

Deep in reflective thought, Fred stood at the water's edge his hands wedged in his pockets, wishing a bolt from the heavens would come down and finish him off.

"Ollie!!!"

CHAPTER TWO:

In Which Fred Meets The Girl Of His Dreams

And She Takes Him To The Cleaners.

As has been previously established, careering completely out-of-control towards him down the slope from the crazy golf course to the boating lake, was a figure - details of which he only had a matter of a split-second to register. Then the fleeing Old English Sheepdog at the other end of the leash had jumped into his arms. A crazed duck had shot into the safety of the boating lake behind him using the shortest route between his legs. Before Fred could express anything more than mild surprise, the dog's weight and impetus had propelled him backwards into the water.

There was, Fred reflected as he surfaced, some kind of tedious inevitability in the incident. He should have known that going anywhere near the boating lake in his best suit and on his wedding day that the fates would conspire to deposit him in the deepest, muddiest part of that body of water. Finding his feet on the bottom, he stood up.

The Angel had disappeared without trace.

He gave a whoop of fright and floundered in the water as a nightmarish creature of mud and weeds surfaced explosively in front of him, waving its arms and spraying him with more foul-smelling sludge. He was momentarily convinced the Swamp Thing was there to drag him under to a watery grave, when he realised that Creatures from the

15

Black Lagoon seldom had blonde hair. The Beast From Twenty Thousand Fathoms was about to go under again when Fred suddenly galvanised himself into action and seized the apparition under the arms, hauling the young woman to her feet. Coughing and spluttering, she spat out a mouthful of murky water and clawed strands of long, blonde hair and pond weed out of her face. Fred froze as he took in the vision in front of him.

The long, blonde hair framed a face that held him entranced. A visage that could only be described as angelic - hence the initial impression. Flawless skin (in spite of the streaks of mud), high cheekbones, an expressive and sensual mouth, and eyes so big and blue they put the sky to shame. Those startlingly blue eyes focused on Fred as he held her up, then widened. "You rescued me!" she gurgled. "My hero!!" The incredible beauty threw her arms around Fred's neck and kissed him passionately.

In his time, Fred counted himself lucky to have been on the receiving end of a wide variety of kisses, ranging in intensity from the chaste to the incendiary. He put his arms around the stunning beauty, losing himself in an embrace that would have to be classed under an entirely new order of magnitude.

The angelic creature broke the kiss self-consciously and took a step back in the water, regarding him bashfully. She gave a little gasp as she remembered that she had an Old English Sheepdog with her when she fell in the boating lake. "Ollie?" she squeaked in dismay, casting around for the beast. She peered into the murky water, trying to part the surface with her hands. "Ollie??" Satisfying herself that the dog was not still underwater, she waded around in a circle, calling the name. Then she caught sight of the animal on the far side of the boating lake. A dripping mass of matted fur, mud and twigs was hurtling away across the crazy golf course as if the devil himself were after it. "Ah well, he'll find his own way home," she reassured herself. "He usually does." She sneezed explosively and the treacherous nature of the bottom of the boating lake manifested itself once again.

Fred was forced to sweep the dazzling young woman up in his arms to prevent her sinking once more. She regarded him with those impossible to overlook big, blue eyes and gasped in horror. "Oh! You're all wet!" She picked a strand of slimy, green weed out of his hair. "I'm terribly sorry about this. Your suit's ruined!" she gushed.

"No problem. Accidents will happen." Fred shrugged absent-mindedly. He was in a state of some abstraction from the kiss that had been bestowed on him. At that moment he realised he would do anything for another.

"It's Ollie, he's scared stiff of ducks," apologised the incredible beauty by way of explanation.

"Ollie?" Fred looked even more puzzled.

"The dog," she elucidated. "I was walking him for a friend, and a duck went for him and...." She treated Fred to a helpless smile that made him forget where he was.

"Oh." For some bizarre reason it all made sense to Fred.

"He's a chicken-hearted old pooch, that one," she observed chattily. "Neurotic as they come, but a real sweetheart." Fred continued to stare, captivated. The young woman seemed unconscious of the effect she was having on him as she picked bits of pond weed out of her cleavage. "Ducks, sheep, cats, postmen; anything a normal dog would woof at terrifies him. I reckon it's all Bouncy's fault. Bouncy's the friend, by the way."

Fred nodded dumbly.

Suddenly self-conscious, the angelic creature ventured: "Uh, you can put me down now."

"Oh, sorry." Fred set her down on the steep grassy bank below the path.

The flamingo-like aspect that had impressed itself upon Fred moments before their collision was down to a pair of fluorescent-pink tights on the longest, shapeliest, most impeccably-turned legs he had ever seen in his life. Now he had the opportunity of closer examination he realised his initial impression had been woefully inaccurate. The limbs were singularly un-flamingo-like. Emerging from under the hem of a quite breathtakingly short denim mini-mini skirt, they terminated in a pair of white leather ankle boots which were caked with slime from the primeval depths of the boating lake. Lifting one long limb up in the air, she drained water of a bilious green hue out of the boot, wrinkling her nose in disgust as most of it ran back up her leg. She drained the other boot in the same manner.

"I wasn't planning on taking a dip this morning, but considering the weather recently, it's been quite enjoyable. I just wish I had a towel with me," she commented.

Fred patted his pockets, nodding dumbly. Mesmerised by the sight of the incredible beauty adjusting the hem of her mini-mini skirt. He tried to look elsewhere lest he be accused of impropriety, patting his pockets absent-mindedly. The girl arranged her long legs with the mien of a pedigree cat. "They probably frown on

18

swimming here, anyway." She scraped her long, blonde hair back from her face and treated him to a dazzling smile, leaning back on her elbows. She cocked her head on one side and the big, blue eyes that were still her second-most striking feature regarded him thoughtfully. "Are you enjoying it in there?" she enquired.

"Mmm?" In spite of himself, Fred continued to stare, an enraptured smile on his face.

"It can't be all that pleasant. You really ought to get out of there before you catch something nasty," ventured the incredible beauty. She knelt on the edge of the bank and extended a hand to help Fred out of the water.

Fred took the proffered hand uncomprehendingly. He held it, marvelling at the slimness and coolness of that most delicate extremity. Then the beauty's words sank in. From the midriff down, he was cold and wet. He looked around vaguely and suddenly noticed he was standing up to his pockets in the boating lake. That snapped him out of it. He swarmed up the bank to her side with a breathless "thanks".

Fred flopped down on the grass beside the young woman. "I shouldn't worry about your friend's sheepdog. I had a dog once. Pedigree pick'n'mix. Daft as a brush. Every time we let him off the lead in the park, he shot off like a rocket. When we got home, he was always sitting on the front step waiting for us."

"You're probably right," nodded the water nymph sagely. She had found her handbag in the reeds at the water's edge where it had fallen during the impact and was extracting the last few tendrils of pond weed from her hair with a brush. She was about to return it to her handbag when she looked inside the bag and grimaced. Fred jumped as she evicted a small, green frog from her bag, gently releasing it back into the water. She wiped her hand on her thigh and extended it to him. "Incidentally, my name's Daisy. Duh as in Delectable, Ay as in Astounding, Zee as in Zestful."

"Fuf... Fuf... Fred Longfield. F-R-E as in Freezing-to; D as in Death." Fred was starting to feel the cold. In spite of the warm day, the waters of the boating lake were still at their customary sub-arctic temperature. His teeth were chattering faster than a flamenco dancer's castanets.

"Pleased to meet you." Daisy treated him to possibly the sunniest smile he had ever seen.

"Pleasure's all mine." Warmed by the smile, Fred was completely bewitched again. He knew exactly where he had seen the dazzling blonde before. On the front page of the Gazette that morning. Crazy Daisy Chayne. Suddenly self-conscious he was staring, he gazed ruefully down at his own legs. They were caked with black mud which smelt, unsurprisingly, like the bottom of a pond. "I'd say that just about puts paid to these trousers." He gingerly eased his shoes off, trying not to get his hands covered in foul-smelling sludge. Then resigning himself to the inevitable started to scrape the mud away with his fingertips from what had been impeccably polished shortly before.

Daisy could not help feeling sorry for the pitiful sight in front of her. His white shirt covered in muddy paw prints from where Ollie had clambered over him in his flight from the duck and coated from crotch down in the most spectacularly unpleasant pond silt, Fred presented an image of semi-drownedness that could do nothing but elicit sympathy.

His best suit - his only reputable-looking suit - looked as if he had fallen in a stagnant pond, which indeed he had. It would probably take boiling to get clean, which could prove a problem as the label inside distinctly said 'dry clean only'.

"You'll catch your death of cold in those," she opined. "You'd better take them off."

"Pardon?" Fred looked as though he had been dealt a stealthy blow with a freshly-caught trout.

"Your trousers," reiterated Daisy. "You'd better take them off." Without being invited, she attacked the buckle of the belt helpfully.

Fred floundered momentarily. "I.... er... ooo!" In a matter of seconds, in spite of his protestations and attempts to slap hands away, his mud-encrusted trousers had been extricated from his person. So, almost, had his Marks-and-Sparks last line of defence but he had wrestled them back from his blonde attacker. Daisy stood up with her consolation prize and carefully draped the muddy trousers to dry over the nearby bushes that were the only cover between them and the casual foot-traffic between the playing fields and the park café.

"*Oi!!*" An irate voice drifted across the park to them and Daisy looked around. Her eyes narrowed as she took in the spindly figure in the peaked cap stalking towards them. "Can't you read the signs?" the park-keeper was shouting indignantly. "A) No swimming!" He started counting off the contraventions to the park bye-laws on his fingers. "B) Keep Off The Grass. C) No Heavy Pettin'…"

"Knickers, it's the parkie!" she grumbled, and Fred had the distinct feeling there was some history of animosity between the dazzling blonde and the approaching council employee. She grabbed him by the sleeve, squeezing brown water out of the material. "Come on, Fred." She bounced to her feet, dragging him bodily across the grass on to the path and sprinted in the direction of the park gates.

Fred had the presence of mind to snatch up his shoes and trousers in passing, but otherwise could do nothing but keep up with her as the beautiful creature took off at a sprint in the direction of the park gates. Wondering why he was running away from the park-keeper, he did his best to match the pace set by the slim, willowy blonde, who was quite literally streaking along with gazelle-like grace. He juggled the damp bundle of muddy clothes, trying not to lose anything along the way.

He staggered as he ran into the back of the beautiful blonde, who had in her turn collided with a figure on the footpath coming in the opposite direction. He caught her deftly under the arms before she landed on her backside, but his shoes rained down painfully on his toes.

"Constable Wodehouse!" squeaked Daisy, recognising the immovable object her irresistible force had collided with.

The police officer gazed down at Daisy with an air of expectations routinely met. "Oh, it's you," he growled. He touched the peak of his helmet, "Miss," and carried on down the path towards the boating lake.

Daisy stared after the retreating back of the police constable, a pretty frown creasing her forehead. "I get the impression he doesn't like me."

"No accounting for taste," mumbled Fred, still

having some difficulty assimilating the morning's events. He had expected them to wind up in the cells, charged with behaviour likely to cause a breach of the peace at the very least. Steadily getting more confused, he quickly gathered up the clothing again from where it had fallen and hurried after Daisy as she strode off up the path.

She slowed her pace as they reached the park gates and headed straight for a battered black Mini parked with consummate carelessness on the grass verge. She slid elegantly behind the steering wheel and leaned across to open the passenger door. "Get in." Fred was too confused to do anything else. He flopped into the passenger seat and had just pulled the car door shut when Daisy stamped an elegantly booted foot on the accelerator and floored it. The Mini tore out into the flow of traffic passing the park. Leaning on the horn, she skilfully steered the car round an oncoming juggernaut. Later that day, Fred would have sworn that the Mini actually passed between the wheels of the articulated trailer. Daisy looked round to speak to Fred and looked startled as he had disappeared. "Fred?" She discovered him crammed into the foot well of the passenger seat, where he had slid when she braked to avoid the cat. "What are you doing down there?"

Fred surfaced breathlessly. After all, squeezing a thirteen-and-a-half-stone man into such a small space had not been the easiest of manoeuvres. "Your guess is as good as mine," he growled. He slumped back in his seat and just managed to fasten his seat belt when the Mini took a corner on two wheels. He crossed himself and closed his eyes. Houses, shops and other cars whipped past at a sickening rate as the Mini wove drunkenly through the traffic. Daisy was hunched over the steering wheel, cursing under her breath at her fellow road users. Fred did the wise thing and kept his eyes tight shut.

-oOo-

Fred flinched as he was prodded in the ribs. He had decided the best line of defence was to shut out everything and had stuck his fingers in his ears and screwed up his eyes. He cautiously opened his eyes and found that the Rolls was parked on the tarmac forecourt of a country house of the variety normally inhabited by minor members of the Royal Family. He looked around in confusion. "Where are we?" he squeaked. He began to wonder if Daisy was some kind of mad kidnapper. Perhaps the Headmaster had hired her to get him out of the way by taking him on a day-trip to Longleat.

"This is Mum and Dad's place," Daisy informed him genially. "I thought I'd better get you dried out before you caught pneumonia, and the Manor's better equipped for that than my flat."

Old-monia, pneumonia, it made no difference to Fred. If he caught his death of cold it suited him down to the ground, a sentiment he communicated to Daisy in no uncertain terms. Daisy replied that he could not be so down-in-the-dumps if he could still make rotten jokes. Fred unfolded himself from the passenger seat of the Mini and leaned on the roof to straighten out his back.

Fred was thoroughly intimidated by his new surroundings, but Daisy led him inside as if she owned the place.

CHAPTER THREE:

In Which Fred Takes A Shower

And Meets The Parents.

They were confronted in the cavernous, marble-tiled hall by a small, ancient, amiable-featured man in the livery of a butler. He did not bat an eyelid in spite of the picture they must have presented - a tall, spectacularly damp blonde, and a walking mud-pie. This was it, thought Fred. Now they would get thrown out.

"Dear me, Miss Daisy," quavered the ancient retainer solicitously. "Did you fall in the boating lake again?"

Good guess, thought Fred.

Daisy beamed, sweeping the butler up in a conspiratorial huddle. "Wilkins," she wheedled. "This is Mr Longfield. He's had a slight accident. Is there any chance Mrs Sowerberry could get his suit cleaned?"

"I'm sure that could be arranged, Miss Daisy."

"You're an angel." Daisy planted a kiss on the old man's forehead and Fred saw the man straighten visibly as if rejuvenated. Fred wondered what strange powers this beautiful, willowy creature possessed, and if falling in the boating lake was a regular occurrence. "You'll find his suit in a bin bag in the boot of the Rolls," she added.

"Very good, Miss."

25

Daisy turned her attention back to Fred. "You'd better have a nice, hot shower before you catch your death. We can use my bathroom." She had him half-way up the grand staircase when she remembered: "Oh, Wilkins, are Mum and Dad in?"

"Lady Marigold is in the conservatory, Miss," replied the butler. "I believe Sir Roland is in his workshop, endeavouring to improve the efficiency of the motorised lawnmower. Something about a turbo-charger, Miss." The last observation was made with a hiked eyebrow.

"Dad's a great one for tinkering with things, Fred." Daisy offered a helpless shrug. "I'm sure you two will get on like a house on fire. Come on."

Fred allowed himself to be led through the warren of passageways of the upper floor of the grand old house. Many of the rooms were either empty, used for storage, or had been pressed into service as makeshift workrooms. There was an air of cosy dilapidation that bordered on neglect.

Daisy kept up a running commentary that included anything that happened to pop into her head. "Lovely old fellow, Mr Wilkins," she breezed. "He's been with the family for centuries - at least it seems that way. Dad inherited him with the house and business when Grandpa passed away. There's only him and Mrs Sowerberry the housekeeper on the staff these days. They have an 'understanding' you know, which is sort of sweet... Here we are!"

Fred looked startled.

"My room." Daisy indicated a door in the far corner with a slim finger. "Bathroom's in there. Once you've got your kit off, we can get it down to Mrs Sowerberry for cleaning."

"Ah... uh... thanks." Fred looked nonplussed. He attempted to undo the knot of his tie, but the material refused to come undone. Without waiting to be invited, Daisy took over, picking the knot open with slim fingers. She turned her attention to unbuttoning the shirt. "Thank you. I can..." Fred started to say, but Daisy was already peeling the wet shirt from his person.

"What was that, Fred?"

"I was saying I can... um... undress myself, thanks all the same."

"No problem, Fred," chirped Daisy. She had knelt on the floor in front of him and as she spoke, she yanked his boxer shorts down round his ankles. "Good heavens, Fred, you could put somebody's eye out with that!" she commented mildly. Fred made a noise like a hippopotamus surfacing and flailed momentarily trying to salvage his modesty. The only thing that came to hand was his tie which he clutched to himself while making indignant but largely incoherent noises.

"Come on, Fred, a nice hot shower will put the life back in you!" Daisy breezed. She grabbed the end of the tie clutched in Fred's hand and whipped it back out of his grasp with a whine of silk against skin. Fred jumped and went bright red.

Daisy bundled him into the bathroom, having put his clothes out in the hall for the butler to have cleaned.

The bathroom was dominated by an enormous Victorian shower and bath. One end of the bath was enclosed on three sides by a cage of heavy brass piping crowned by a foot-wide shower rose. Daisy perched on the side of the bath and turned the brass taps at the head of the bath, testing the water gushing from the single outlet with her fingers. Once she was satisfied with the temperature, she threw an ivory handled lever above the taps. The entire device gave a powerful shudder. Then a rising *hiss* heralded powerful jets of water squirting from nozzles attached to points on the cage of brass piping. Finally, with a low *whoosh*, a deluge of water issued from the huge shower head. Daisy extended an arm into the mist of water, smiled satisfactorily and said : "Okay, Fred, you can hop in."

Fred regarded the shower unit in wonderment. There was an air of H.G. Wells' Time Machine about the design. Holding on to the brass superstructure for support, he climbed into the bath. He was enveloped in a hot spray as the nozzles of the brass cage squirted him from multifarious and frequently embarrassing angles.

"Need somebody to do your back?" enquired Daisy mischievously.

As much as the prospect of sharing a shower with her appealed, and would feature in the most universal fantasies of red-blooded males, Fred was first and foremost a schoolteacher and as such was firmly stuck-in-the-mud. "Don't!" His voice shot up an octave unintentionally. "...take this the wrong way. I honestly can take a shower without any assistance. I've been doing it for years."

"Shy," commented Daisy, quite charmed.

"Under the circumstances, yes." Fred nodded.

Daisy pouted. "If that's the way you feel..." There was a hurt-feelings tone in the dazzling blonde's voice. "It's... ah... all yours," smiled Daisy over her shoulder to Fred.

She sauntered out of the bathroom, leaving Fred with his shattered nerves. He let out a shaky breath of relief, then caught sight of himself in the half-steamed-up mirror over the washbasin. "Wimp," he muttered.

-oOo-

Fred peered round the door of Daisy's bedroom, an expression of mounting embarrassment on his face. Finishing his shower, he had only managed to find a hand towel, but it was woefully inadequate for the task in hand.

It was while completing his ablutions on his own that he had finally put together where he was. The enamelled plaque on the shower surround had the legend *Wilberforce Coleridge Chayne and Sons - 1893 - Excelsior Spa Bath* in half-inch letters. Chayne Abbas had been founded by the family in the seventeenth century, and there were references to the Chaynes all over the county - it had been the boating lake in Chayne Park that Daisy and the Old English Sheepdog had knocked him into.

Fred could remember the articles in the local Gazette about the trouble faced by the Chayne factory a few years back. The Avocado Bathroom Suite Fiasco, as it was known, had nearly ruined the company. A famous designer-cum-television-fashion-pundit had made the claim that such fixtures were about to explode back into vogue, and huge orders had been placed with the factory. The orders evaporated overnight when the designer was proved entirely incorrect and quite possibly certifiably delusional. The factory had been stuck with a production run it could not give away, at which point one of Sir Roland's oldest friends and major rivals, Lord Sydney Ballcock of the high street plumbing giant *Flushes 'R Us* had made an unprecedented offer for the Chayne business. The attempted takeover had been thwarted at the last moment by an injection of capital organised by a workforce syndicate, but Lord Ballcock had still been able to acquire a thirty-five percent share in the company and Sir Roland had found himself with an unwanted junior partner. With the junior partner came his darling twin daughters, Boadicea and Britannia, who had been terrorising the eligible bachelor population of Warmhamptonshire ever since.

Using the hand-towel to dry his hair with, he took a few tentative steps back into the large, well-appointed bedroom. There was no sign of Daisy or the butler, in fact the place seemed deserted. "Hullo?" he called. "Is there anybody there? I need a towel. A bath towel. Hullo?" Maintaining what little was left of his modesty with the hand towel, he stepped out on to the landing in search of help. "Hullo?" he called. He turned round to call the other way and dropped the towel in shock.

"Hullo, young feller." The figure standing in front of him was a short, untidily-dressed man in his mid-sixties. The laboratory smock he wore over a tweed suit that had seen better days, was dotted with chemical burns and stains. A spanner projected from his top pocket and there were streaks of oil on the pockets of the smock and the lapels of the suit underneath. Receding, heavily pomaded hair, a pencil moustache of the variety favoured by 1930s leading men, his wrinkled face gave off an air of absent-minded amiability as he fixed Fred with an unwavering, blue-eyed stare that Fred recognised. "Been taking a shower in Daisy's room?"

"I... er... I... er..." Fred's mouth worked, but nothing intelligible came out.

"You'll catch your death of cold wandering around the house like that," opined the old man. "There's a fierce wind comes off the heath some times, you know. What you need is a towel or something."

"Mmm." Fred nodded, still too embarrassed to say anything sensible.

"I've got a robe in my room you can borrow."

"Dad! I see you've met Fred," breezed Daisy, strolling along the landing towards them. She was in a similar state to Fred, stark naked but possessed of a slightly larger hand towel that was barely adequate to the task. For his part, Sir Roland didn't bat an eyelid. Fred was doing all of the batting. "This is Fred Longfield. Fred, this is my Dad."

"Suh... Sir Roland??" stuttered Fred.

"Pleased to meet you, young feller," chortled Sir Roland, shaking Fred's free hand, the one that was not engaged in concealing his embarrassment.

Daisy turned to Fred and raised an eyebrow at his chronic state of undress. "I met him in the park when we fell into the boating lake. I had a slight accident with Bouncy's dog."

"Fell in the boating lake?" Her father nodded sagely, and Fred got the distinct impression that kind of thing happened to Daisy all the time.

"I was out walking Ollie for Bouncy and Britt. A

duck went for him and Fred and I both fell in the water," Daisy explained. "I brought him back here to dry off. I thought it was the least I could do."

"Capital, capital," beamed Sir Roland. "Well, I won't get in your way." He shuffled off down the passage towards the grand hall.

"I think he likes you," Daisy smiled. She opened a concealed panel on the wall and took out two white, towelling robes from the airing cupboard that had been revealed. She handed one to Fred and without a moment's consideration shrugged into the other, casually discarding her towel. The robe sported an embroidered "D" on the breast and was, in common with her usual choices of wardrobe, exceptionally short. She tied the belt with consummate carelessness and the ensemble gave every impression of being on the verge of slipping completely from her slim form. "Incidentally, you're dripping on the carpet."

-oOo-

Fred descended the grand staircase into the hall, considerably cleaner than he had been when he arrived. Daisy had supplied him with Sir Roland's monogrammed, white terry-cloth bathrobe. The letter "R" was picked out on the breast in gold embroidery along with the family crest of a squirrel rampant and the family motto: *"In Balneum Cantare"*. Daisy's father was of a considerably smaller build, and Fred had not only to be careful not to put too much strain on the seams, but the robe was more than a little on the short side and he was in constant jeopardy of attracting a charge of indecent exposure. When Daisy had given him the garment in place of his hand towel, it had taken a long, pointed look on his part to communicate to her that he was not about to treat her to the Full Monty again. She had sauntered off downstairs, leaving him with explicit directions for finding his way back. Her comment that occasionally, lost house guests could wander around the Manor for days calling out plaintively for assistance did not exactly fill him with confidence.

Daisy popped her head round one of the panelled oak doors that led off the entrance hall. "Ah, there you are, Fred," she beamed. "I thought I heard you coming down. We're all down here in the drawing room."

"Whoops!"

Fred had nearly collided with a tall, attractive, middle-aged woman coming round the foot of the stairs. She had been completely engrossed in the vase of flowers she was carrying and had jumped back with a lady-like squeak of fright when confronted with him in his woefully inadequate robe. Suddenly she was surrounded with flowers, fragments of pottery and a pool of water.

"It's all right, Mum, he's with me." Daisy hurried over to them.

It had been a toss-up who had been the more startled, Fred or Lady Marigold. Recovering, Fred darted forwards apologetically to help Daisy's mother clean up the mess.

"It's all right, dear," Lady Marigold reassured him with as sunny a smile as anything her daughter could manage. "Nothing that can't be fixed." It was obvious to Fred where Daisy got her looks and demeanour. Lady Marigold was a mature version of Daisy, with the same, striking bone structure. Her eyes were as startlingly blue as Daisy's, and she regarded him with a kindly expression.

Fred offered Lady Marigold a sickly smile and handed her the carnation he had picked up. The stalk had been broken an inch below the head, so the scarlet flower lolled at a pathetic angle. Lady Marigold deftly turned the casualty into a buttonhole which she pinned to the lapel of his dressing gown.

Momentarily upstaged by her mother, Daisy came forwards to make proper introductions, then took Fred by the sleeve with the intention of leading him away. "Come on, Fred, before you demolish the place completely."

"I hope you'll stay to lunch, Fred," Lady Marigold smiled graciously. After such a charming invitation, Fred felt it would be churlish to turn her down.

Daisy linked arms with him. "That's two of the Chayne women you've charmed," she smiled. She gave him an approving once-over. "Great legs, Fred," she purred admiringly.

"They're not a patch on yours." Fred said what he was thinking, but Daisy took the compliment for what it was and beamed.

"Oh Bugger!"

The exclamation ripped through the hall like a smallish explosion. Fred nearly jumped out of his skin, thinking momentarily he might be the cause. Fortunately he was not. He rearranged his robe to make some concession to propriety as Daisy moved to investigate whatever had elicited the outburst.

Daisy went over to the door of her father's study, the source of the verbal pyrotechnics, and peered round with an eyebrow hiked at her father's uncharacteristic explosion. "Something up, Pops?" Fred followed her through the doorway.

-oOo-

CHAPTER FOUR:

In Which Sir Roland Gets Bogged Down

And Fred Gets Punched

Sir Roland's study was large and comfortably appointed. In front of the huge, leaded picture-window that presented a panorama of the grounds of Chayne Manor stood a technical illustrator's board. On the board was pinned a detailed schematic of what looked suspiciously like a lavatory pan. In front of that was Sir Roland's imposing, antique, carved oak desk; the sort of desk where naval treaties were signed. A Chesterfield settee, armchair and a low coffee table had been pushed to the margins of the room, obstructing the bookcases lining the walls, to free an area of floor in the middle of the room. Flexible piping snaked across the floor from an adjoining room to that area, which had been prepared against the eventuality of a deluge with sandbags and heavy, black PVC sheeting. The old man himself was standing in the middle of the improvised dam, peering down the bowl of a white, porcelain specimen of what his factory produced and what Fred suspected was illustrated on the plans.

"Feeling a little under the weather, Dad?" enquired Daisy playfully.

Her father, his features an alarming shade of puce from the exertion, straightened up sharply as he realised the image he must have been presenting. He blustered a little until he noticed his daughter's mischievous expression. He indicated the lavatory pan with the right lug of his reading spectacles. "Damn thing's stuck!" he offered as explanation. Fred followed Daisy over for a closer inspection.

"Is this the new Deluxe 500?" Daisy brushed a long lock of hair out of her face as she leaned over the object.

The old man looked very proud and nodded. "First moulding off the line." He patted the prototype loo. "Built in bidet, the lot." He looked Fred squarely in the eye. "Got to save trees somehow." Fred looked confused until Daisy whispered "Loo paper," in his ear.

"So what's the problem?" asked Daisy, peering into the bowl to see what damn thing was stuck.

"The spigot's stuck."

"That sounds painful," chirped Daisy facetiously.

"Longfield," mulled Sir Roland, rolling the name round his mouth like a boiled sweet. "Any relation to Professor Plum Longfield over at Grisley End?"

Fred nodded. His late Grandfather's youngest brother and the mad scientist of the family. An additional pall over the proceedings of the last couple of weeks had been the old man's funeral. Ninety-six and had finally managed to blow himself up. "My Great-Uncle, Sir."

"Really?" Sir Roland beamed at Fred. "Small world, small world. Your Great-Uncle was a dear friend and a close collaborator on a number of projects for the firm. We have great hopes for his cyclonic flush patent. May well revolutionise the industry."

Fred could only nod wistfully. To him, the old fellow had been simply "Uncle Plum." Always had time for him and was always up to something weird, wonderful and possibly extremely dangerous. Encouraged by his similarly-minded father, he had always dreamed of following in the Professor's footsteps but had wound up sidetracked into education by a desperate shortage of research opportunities.

"There's a problem with the spigot, Dad?" Daisy asked brightly.

Fred craned his neck and spotted a small, metal fitting in the rear wall of the pan. The old man pressed a button on the control box wired up to the pan and there was a low grinding noise, the porcelain vibrating alarmingly. "You see, if something happens to the spigot gearing assembly, it won't extend, and there's no way to get at the mechanics without taking the bowl out." Sir Roland rubbed his chin thoughtfully. "I've cut away this one to see if I can spot the problem, but I'm blowed if I can."

By a happy coincidence, this was Fred's favourite territory - tinkering with anything electrical or mechanical. From the age of three he had demonstrated the same fondness as his own father for dismantling toys and household appliances, and to be fair he had always enjoyed a higher success rate than his father for putting the same toys and household appliances back together again afterwards. Daisy leaned on the top of the cistern and gazed indulgently down the back of the unit at her father and Fred as they probed the workings with screwdrivers. She had no idea what they were up to, but it seemed to keep them entertained. Standing over the bowl of the Deluxe 500, she was blissfully unaware of the bidet spigot surreptitiously extending, until a jet of ice cold water shot up under the hem of her robe and hosed down part of her anatomy she would have preferred not to be squirted suddenly with cold water. She bounced into the air with a squeak of alarm.

As he stood up from the workings of the Deluxe 500, Fred suddenly found his arms full of stunning blonde. He caught Daisy deftly and she threw her arms around his neck. Sir Roland looked up and raised an eyebrow as he saw his daughter in the young man's arms.

Fred offered Sir Roland an embarrassed smile as he lowered Daisy self-consciously to the floor. "Have you considered two or three small jets aimed from the side of the bowl?" Fred tried to change the subject. He shuffled as Sir Roland stared at him intently.

"Say again?"

"Rather than having a single vertically firing spigot that has to extend and retract, you could use two or three small, fixed, directional jets aiming in from the sides of the bowl," ventured Fred. "They wouldn't have to clear the rim of the pan, and they'd cover the same... er... target area as the centrally firing spigot jet." He looked taken aback as Sir Roland handed him a pencil and pointed at a clear area of the plan on the drawing board. Offering Daisy and her father an apologetic smile, he quickly drew what he had in mind, explaining as he drew. Talking off the top of his head, he hoped he was not talking out of the back of it. He put the pencil down on the ledge along the bottom of the drawing board self-consciously, as Sir Roland was staring hard at the sketch, his head cocked on one side like a West Highland terrier.

"There's a thought," Daisy's father chortled enthusiastically. "Well played, young feller!" He slapped Fred heartily between the shoulder blades. "Smart thinking."

"Was it?" Daisy looked genuinely startled. She looked at Fred with new eyes.

"Half the production costs," Sir Roland sounded impressed. "No moving parts, no need for wiring, and the whole unit can be machined at the factory without having to order out." He shook Fred's hand and turned to Daisy. "This one's brighter than most of the ones you've brought home. Don't let him get away."

Daisy acquired a bright pink hue. "Dad!" she exclaimed shyly. She hid her embarrassment by moving over to the window and staring out across the croquet lawn. Fred matched Daisy's hue pretty accurately. He hurried over to the window to join her and they both gazed out across the sun-drenched grounds of Chayne Manor. It was certainly a glorious day. The sun was shining, the birds were twittering in the trees and a wiry figure in a sharp, Armani suit was strolling towards the house with the air of a conquering hero, a large, cuddly effigy of the Pink Panther tucked under his arm. "Oh knickers!" muttered Daisy. She ducked out of sight of the window and flattened herself against the curtains as if avoiding an enemy sniper.

"What is it?" Fred was startled at this new turn of events. He darted after her into the cover of the curtains.

"It's Julian," replied Daisy.

"Julian?" Fred was confused.

"Julian Ballcock. He's Lord Ballcock's slimy nephew. He's the company's senior sales rep. He seems to think I'm engaged to him, but I'm not." She folded her arms and frowned. "He keeps showering me with presents. Boxes of chocolates, bouquets, teddy bears. That sort of thing." She stared through the window. "There was a time I thought he was...." She trailed off self-consciously and shuddered. "One date with him shattered my illusions. He's still trying to butter me up in the hope of a 'reconciliation', but I'd rather have extensive dental surgery than get friendly with him again. C'mon!" Visibly agitated, she grabbed Fred's hand and hauled him across the room towards the door.

"Where are you taking young Fred?" asked her father, who had been in the process of getting the plans for a new shower unit out to show him.

"Back up to my room," replied Daisy.

"Oh. Jolly good." Sir Roland nodded cheerfully. Fred looked startled.

-oOo-

As Fred had discovered earlier, Daisy's "room" was in fact a suite of three adjoining rooms to the rear of the rambling, old house. She had been at pains to point out that she lived most of the time in her own flat on the other side of town.

"We'll be safe up here," Daisy said reassuringly, although Fred had the feeling she was the person who needed reassuring. As far as Daisy was concerned, Julian was bad news, and that made him an enemy in Fred's eyes.

"Sir, you can't go up there!" The protesting voice of Wilkins the butler rose up the stairs.

"Nonsense, man," a voice drawled condescendingly. "Daisy will see me. I've got a present for her."

"Nevertheless, Sir."

Daisy gave a squeak of alarm as she heard Julian's lizard-like tread as he ascended the stairs. She looked around for somewhere to hide. Then she had a brainwave. Fred would have called it a brainstorm. She grabbed Fred by the lapels of his dressing gown and threw herself backwards on the bed, dragging him after her. They rolled across the counterpane, kissing as if their lives depended on it.

Later in the day, Fred would expend considerable thought trying to figure out Daisy's reasoning behind the move, but at that precise moment he was too busy enjoying the situation to complain. Suddenly there seemed to be an awful lot of bare skin in close contact. Similarly, in retrospect, Daisy would wonder what on Earth had possessed her to do such a thing, but at the time it had seemed like the proverbial good idea. A very good idea, in fact.

Making the sort of noise two people would make eating the same peach, they kissed passionately. Suddenly Daisy was undoing the belt of Fred's robe, and he was reciprocating by pushing her robe from her shoulders. All of this was done without breaking lip contact for even a split second. They only finally broke contact to come up for air. "Oh, Fred!" Daisy exclaimed, raining kisses on Fred's face. Their hands were all over each other, inside and outside what little they were wearing in a show of sheer animal passion. Fred was kissing every square inch of Daisy's bare skin that he could locate, and as she worked her way out of her robe, that area was getting steadily greater.

"Daisy!" gurgled Fred in between passionate kisses. "We shouldn't be doing this... We hardly know each other..."

"I know," gasped Daisy, reciprocating each kiss.

"We shouldn't... start... what we can't... finish!" gulped Fred. He devoured her lips. "We should... we should..."

Daisy started kissing all over his face. "We should... what?"

Fred sucked her earlobes. "Can't remember..." He kissed her neck fervently. "Can't have been important..."

Daisy put a hand against his shoulder to give herself breathing space. "We're getting carried away!" she panted, gathering together her robe before it slipped beyond the bounds of modesty. It was a bit late for that.

The door opened and Daisy, who had ended up lying on top of Fred, looked around with a squeak of alarm. She had completely forgotten about Julian in those few moments. Whatever the pros and cons of the situation, Daisy was later to admit to herself that kissing Fred could well turn out to be a whole new pastime for her.

Recovering brilliantly she offered the interloper an innocent smile. "Hullo, ferret-features. What brings you round here?"

"Daisy," whined the newcomer, a look of abject dismay on the noble features. "Wh-wh-what's going on??" He took in just how much of Daisy was visible - more of her than he had ever been privy to previously - and just how much Fred was visible also.

Up close, Fred could see what Daisy found so

objectionable about young Mr Ballcock. In his early thirties, perhaps a couple of years or so younger than he was, Julian Ballcock was the personification of the modern-day rake - corporate raider in the morning and lady-killer at night. In spite of a sharp suit and expensive haircut, he looked like most people's idea of a 19th Century romantic poet. A thin, boyish face with bedroom eyes and a Byronic (or would that be *mor*onic?) air. He gave the arrogant impression he laboured under the misapprehension he was a knock-out with the ladies. He was the result of generations of inbreeding among the Ballcocks of Warmhamptonshire. Public school, a nanny who had trained with the SS and a small personal fortune inherited from a potty maiden aunt had conspired to produce a soul so self-centred, mean-spirited and callous that he was guaranteed a great future in either the City or politics.

Daisy rearranged her dressing gown and helped Fred off the bed. She made the introductions. "Julian Ballcock? I'd like you to meet Fred Longfield. We're engaged."

Fred stared at Daisy. Engaged? He could not remember proposing. He goggled at her momentarily before falling down as Julian punched him squarely in the nose. She had dropped him right in it again, he observed as the back of his head thudded into the thick pile carpet.

Julian was beside himself. He pointed at Fred, making indignant little squeaking noises. "*We're* engaged already, Daisy!" he exclaimed. "Engaged! As in 'to be married'!" He put an immaculately manicured hand to his forehead as if trying to ward off a migraine attack. "I must say, I wouldn't have expected this kind of behaviour from you, of all people!"

Daisy stared at Julian in disbelief. This was too

much. She prodded him angrily in the chest with a fingernail. "We are *not* engaged, Julian," she shouted. "I've told you we're not engaged hundreds of times, but you never listen. I don't want to be engaged to you. I'd *hate* to be engaged to you. I would *loathe* the very thought of being engaged to you. I would rather be engaged to Vlad The Impaler than you, but you're too stupid to get the message!"

"Now, now, Daisy, you're just overwrought." Julian tried to calm her, backing up as she advanced on him threateningly.

"No, Julian. I'm sick of you turning up and making out that we're engaged!" shouted Daisy. "Any possibility of any continued relationship between us ended on that first date when you suggested dressing me as a nun, tying me to your bed and licking marmalade from every inch of my body."

"I said we could have used Marmite if you'd preferred." Julian had backed out on to the landing.

"Call me old fashioned, but I'd have thought a goodnight kiss would have sufficed on the first date."

"We'd have done that after I'd licked off all the marmalade." Julian sounded defensive.

"Julian, you are the sleaziest individual it has ever been my misfortune to encounter. Why don't you take your cuddly toys and try and get yourself arrested in the park? *Again.*" Daisy's baby-blue eyes had a steely aspect to them.

"Does this mean the engagement's off?"

Daisy screamed in exasperation and gave Julian a hard shove. Unfortunately for Julian, he had retreated as far as the top of the Grand Staircase under the onslaught of Daisy's tirade, and there was nowhere else to go but down. He teetered on the top step for what seemed like an eternity, like Martin Balsam in *Psycho*. The Pink Panther had somehow become entangled in his stick-like legs, so that ultimately his descent to the entrance hall was made the hard way.

Bump bump bump bump bump-bump-bump-bump crash.

CHAPTER FIVE:

In Which Fred Remembers What Day It Is

And Gets Punched Again.

"Oh, your poor nose!" Daisy squatted beside Fred, who had decided it was safer to stay on the floor of her room where he had fallen. "I didn't think he was going to wallop you. Does it hurt?"

"It does, rather," admitted Fred.

Daisy raced into her personal bathroom and emerged moments later with a towel of the variety he failed to locate earlier, dampened with cold water. She applied it gently to Fred's swollen beak. "I'm sorry I got you involved in all of this," she apologised. "It was the only thing I could think of on the spare of the moment to get rid of him." She showed him the towel. "See? No bleeding."

"Just like my opportunity to defend myself," growled Fred.

Daisy went over to the window and looked down at the gravel forecourt outside. She could hear Julian ranting and raving below. She opened the window and leaned out. Her eyes narrowed. Julian was in the process of picking a fight with Wilkins the butler, presumably over what had just gone on. She knew the poor man could not very well stick one on the repellent young Ballcock, but there was nothing to stop her coming to his aid. She ducked back inside. Standing on the dressing table was a nasty old green vase she had been given as a birthday present by a maiden aunt. She had never liked it much, and it would be perfect for the job. She leaned out of the window. Fred hurried over to join her, a puzzled look on his face.

Daisy took careful aim. "Three, two, one... zero."

The vase hit Julian squarely on top of the head, shattering spectacularly. He sank silently to the ground and the butler looked up to see where the missile had come from. He spotted Daisy and Fred before they could duck back inside. "I'll just find Mrs Sowerberry to help me throw this back over Lord Ballcock's wall, Miss," he called.

Fred gazed at the spread-eagled form on the driveway, not quite able to believe his eyes. He ducked back inside. Daisy had stepped away from the window and was dusting off her hands in satisfaction. "Just because his family owns most of Warmhamptonshire," she muttered in disgust. She shrugged her shoulders and offered Fred a cheery grin. "Fancy a spot of breakfast?" she enquired.

-oOo-

Half-past nine arrived, and there was no sign of Fred. His mother stared at the clock on the wall, wondering where on earth he had got to. One thing was for sure, if he did not turn up within the next few minutes, they would have to leave for the church without him. He would just have to catch up with them. She was sure it was *brides* that were supposed to be late for weddings, not *bridegrooms*. She just hoped he had not got his suit in a mess. He might be a thirty-something-year-old schoolteacher, but to her he would always be a querulous toddler with a marked tendency to topple over into puddles.

Daisy's internal body clock, Fred was in the process of discovering, was based around meal times and was in that respect highly accurate. Breakfast; ideally a second breakfast or brunch; elevenses; lunch itself; a-little-something-to-tide-one-over-in-the-afternoon; high tea; dinner and supper divided the day into pleasant, bite-sized pieces and yet in spite of having the appetite of a smallish stampede of horses, she remained wonderfully slender.

Fred looked round as the door of the drawing room opened again and Daisy entered, laden down with a large, silver serving tray. She put down her burden on the small table near the fireplace and put a plate down in front of him piled high with the biggest fry-up Fred had ever seen. Bacon, eggs, sausage, tomato, mushrooms and fried bread, all prepared by Daisy's own fair hand. The sort of meal truck drivers set themselves up for the day with. She returned with two steaming mugs of strong, hot, sweet tea and sat down opposite Fred to attack her matching plateful with gusto. Fred suddenly remembered that he had not eaten since teatime yesterday, and his stomach was making noises like a caged tiger.

Fred could not help staring at her. He had never met a woman like her. She simply took his breath away. He committed every detail of her face and body to memory in case it was all a dream. If it were a dream, he hoped he would never wake from it. He had nothing better to do that day as far as he could remember, and intended to revel in every moment he could spend in the stunning creature's company.

So far, he had discovered that Daisy was the youngest of three daughters, Buttercup and Bluebell being the elder siblings. Their father, the affable Sir Roland, had up to her birth resisted the obvious choice of name for a Chayne girl, and she had narrowly escaped being called Cowslip. Buttercup was married to the firm's legal advisor. Bluebell had toyed with a career dancing in cabaret in Paris and Las Vegas and was now working as a veterinarian's assistant just outside of Los Angeles. Single, free-spirited and willing to try anything, Daisy had attempted a variety of would-be careers before ending up working for her father: A year alongside her elder sister as a showgirl in Las Vegas; photographic model; dolphin trainer; would-be author; aerobics instructor; would-be painter; clairvoyant... Daisy seemed to be intent on telling him everything there was to know about herself and the family and he was desperately trying to commit it all to memory.

Daisy impaled a sausage with her fork and paused with it half-way to her mouth, continuing the story she had been in the process of telling him before her fit of domesticity. "...So there we were. South of France. Just out of finishing school and completely unprepared for the real world. Bouncy had this idea of spending the summer on the beach before we headed home. Ran out of money the first week, of course, so we spent the rest of the holiday making doughnuts at night and selling them on the nudist beach during the day. Great fun. Made a lot of friends and quite a tidy profit." She picked up one of the plates. "Can I press you to another slice of fried bread?"

"You can press me to anything you like," Fred replied.

Daisy giggled girlishly. "Why Fred, that's the most romantic thing anybody's ever said to me." She regarded him shyly from under her fringe. "Are you normally this romantic?"

"When the mood takes me, I can be even more romantic," Fred replied, leaning forwards so that their faces were only a matter of inches apart.

"I'd like to be around to see that."

Fred stared at the stunning blonde. "I've never met a girl like you before, Daisy. You're quite incredible," he said in awed tones.

Daisy preened herself. "I'll take that as a compliment," she smiled.

"It's intended as one," Fred said gallantly. "I don't think I've ever had a day as eventful as this one, and it's only half-past nine in the morning."

"I hope we can find something as entertaining for the rest of the day," smiled Daisy.

"I sincerely hope so," agreed Fred.

-oOo-

"There you are!"

Daisy started violently. She glared over to the door. Two, tall, voluptuous, raven-haired young women of fashion-plate demeanour that Daisy knew only too well, but Fred had yet to make the acquaintance of were standing on the threshold. Sharply-tailored business-suits with short, pencil skirts hung on tanned figures ideally suited to Paris catwalks or the pages of society magazines. Both regarded him with eyes as startlingly green as Daisy's were blue, but Fred suddenly had the suspicion that unlike Daisy, they were the sort of young lady that would eat a schoolteacher such as himself as an entreé.

"Where's Ollie?" demanded one of the brunettes. "Where's my dog??" She looked closer at Daisy. "Where are your clothes?"

"Sorry, Bouncy. I had an accident. We fell in the boating lake and Ollie just took off."

"If anything happens to that poor ol' pooch, I'll tie those crazy legs of yours in a knot!" The brunette's jaw set. She indicated Fred. "Who's this?"

Daisy rolled her eyes in exasperation. "Fred Longfield, I'd like you to meet my best friends. Boadicea and Britannia Ballcock."

"B... B... Boadicea," stuttered Fred. "As in Queen of the Iceni, wife of Prasutagus, who led a revolt against the Roman occupation in AD61 and trashed Colchester, London and St. Albans?"

"That's the chick," beamed the brunette. She extended a delicate hand for a surprisingly firm handshake. "I'm the brains of the outfit. What are you? You sound like a teacher."

"It's a job."

"This is my twin sister Britannia. We're identical." Boadicea continued the introductions.

"Britannia?" gurgled Fred.

"As in 'Rule,...' ," smiled Britannia.

"Fred rescued me from the boating lake," continued Daisy. "I fell in." The two brunettes regarded her with identical expressions which said *so what else is new?*

"Well, I..." started Fred modestly.

Boadicea had not let go of Fred's hand and used it to pull him towards her. "In that case..." Before Fred knew what was happening, a simultaneous kiss was planted on either cheek by Boadicea and her sister. "Bravery should always be rewarded."

Daisy obviously knew some very friendly people, Fred thought, reeling slightly from being kissed in stereo. "Pleasure's all mine," he said faintly.

Boadicea perched on the arm of Daisy's chair and helped herself to a sausage uninvited. "I thought Julian was never going to leave. We saw Wilkins and Mrs S slinging him over the kitchen garden wall and realised the coast was clear, although I don't think they realised the cold frames were the other side. By the way," she enquired politely. "What did you hit him with?"

"Vase," replied Daisy.

"That nasty green one off the dressing table?"

Daisy nodded.

"Good choice." Boadicea turned her attention to Fred. "Did that nasty ol' Julian take a poke at you?" she pouted as if sympathising with a small child or pet. Fred suspected he might be classed under the latter by Ms Ballcock. "Jule's awfully possessive about our Daisy," she smirked. "He just won't take no for an answer."

"I've even considered having it tattooed on his forehead in his sleep," grumbled Daisy, irked at being upstaged by the Ballcock twins who were draping themselves across Fred.

Fred was squirming, as both sisters' hands were wandering inquisitively. "You were engaged?" The query came out pitched considerably higher than he had intended and he coughed to clear his throat, which given the location of Boadicea's hands would reveal much about his physical condition.

"It was never anything official," blustered Daisy defensively.

"Pfft!" exclaimed Boadicea. "Dad had the wedding invitations printed and the Cathedral booked the day you and Jules went off on your first date."

"And last date," Daisy pointed out.

"Two great sanitaryware dynasties coming together like a couple of ancient Royal families," chortled Boadicea mischievously. She tugged the belt of Fred's robe experimentally. "So tell us, Fred. Are you the Crown Prince of some European principality in disguise? An eccentric billionaire? Are you a good catch?"

"Noooo…" Fred shook his head, wide-eyed. "I'm just a secondary-school Chemistry teacher."

Daisy interceded before Boadicea could unfasten the belt of Fred's robe, intent on mischief. "Just out of curiosity, Fred. What were you doing wandering around the park this morning dressed like a dog's dinner?"

"I was... um... getting married." The thought flitted into Fred's mind like a butterfly. A butterfly armed with a tactical thermonuclear weapon. He sat bolt upright as the enormity of what he had just said sank in. "Married??" He looked at his watch, a sickening feeling entering the pit of his stomach. A quarter-to-ten!

A quite tragic look of disappointment had crossed Daisy's face as this piece of news was imparted. She tucked her feet out of the way as he bounced out of his chair, and regarded him with a solicitous expression.

"Hell's bells!!" Fred had woken from his dream, and found himself in the middle of a nightmare. "Hell's bells!! Hell's bloody bells!"

"Are congratulations in order, Fred?" his dream-girl enquired brightly.

"I'm supposed to be getting married in fifteen minutes!" Fred paced up and down the room, beginning to panic. He must have been out of his mind to accept Melissa's proposal; but then, it was a lady's prerogative to propose to the man during a leap year, and how could he have refused when she did it in front of three hundred other hotel guests?

"Now, just a cotton-picking minute!" Boadicea stepped in front of him, her jaw set indignantly. "Correct me if I blacked out momentarily just then, but did you say *married?*"

"As in 'Do You Take This Woman, etc. etc.??'" Britannia appeared at her sister's side and prodded him accusingly in the chest with a forefinger. "And was there, or was there not, mention of 'in fifteen minutes'?"

"I...er..." Fred floundered helplessly.

"You mean to say you've cynically led Daisy on –

letting her knock you into a boating lake, bring you home, clean you up, and dry you out, all out of the goodness of her heart? And all the time you've had a bride waiting for you at the altar?" Even to the untrained eye, it was obvious Boadicea was heading for an explosion, yet Fred was taken completely unawares by the well-aimed slap that whistled in from the right. He was spun back the other way by Britannia's smart backhander which rattled his fillings more than the first blow. As falling down seemed to be the done thing under the circumstances, he landed in a heap at Daisy's feet.

Fred's mouth worked noiselessly like a startled goldfish's. Leading anybody on had been the last thing on his mind. The only thing that had been on his mind was Daisy, who had somehow eradicated thoughts of everything else, not least any thought of his impending nuptials.

"And what about the poor bride-to-be?" Britannia was not letting him off the hook. "Who is this unfortunate girl, anyway?"

"My... er... the... er... the Headmaster's daughter." The real world was flooding back into his consciousness like a tide of crude oil from a ruptured tanker. "You probably don't know her. Melissa Masters."

The Ballcock sisters drew back in alarm. "Not *Malicious* Melissa Masters, aka 'Crusher' Masters, Captain of the St. Norbert's hockey team?" Boadicea exchanged a horrified look with her sister.

"Big girl," Britannia filled in the details. "Ginger hair. Nasty temper. Matching sense of humour. Built like a brick sh..."

"You know her."

The shift in perceptions was almost audible. In a split second, Fred went from heartless philanderer to hapless, pitiful victim. "Oh, you poor thing!" Boadicea Ballcock dropped to her knees at his side, clutching him to her bosom like a lost waif and making sympathetic noises. Kneeling down on his other side, Daisy yanked him out of the warmth and Chanel-fragranced depths of Boadicea's cleavage and clutched him to *her* bosom like a lost waif. "Oh, you poor thing!" Melissa's idea of a show of affection was a hefty thump of approbation between the shoulder blades, so for Fred the experience was a distinct improvement.

"Were you doing it for a bet, or were you drunk?" enquired Britannia brightly, adding herself to the equation.

As much as Fred would have loved to spend the rest of the day under a pile of beautiful women, certain that it would be the last place on Earth that Melissa would have looked for him, he knew he had to go back to the real world eventually.

Daisy leaned over to the fireplace and tugged the cord to ring the bell for Wilkins the butler, then peered at him solicitously. "You look like someone who's been given a life sentence," she observed.

Fred knew the haunted look on his face betrayed his emotions. "That's the problem," he confirmed quietly. "I can't help wondering if that's what I'm letting myself in for."

Daisy perked up at this admission. "You're not having doubts, are you?"

Fred considered the question long and hard. If he broke off the wedding at such short notice, Melissa and her father would probably flay him alive and the results donated to the science lab. He realised with a jolt of horror that any feelings for Melissa had not come into the argument. Was he only marrying the girl because it was expected of him? Of course not. He was marrying her because he was terrified of her father, and quite possibly her as well. He swallowed audibly. Whatever he did, he realised he would probably almost certainly regret it. It was probably too late for second thoughts, though. "No, no doubts," he replied doubtfully.

"Is there anything we could do to help?" asked Boadicea. "We could hide you out at the Hall," she suggested. "There are priest-holes all over the place. You could hide out there for years."

"Or at least until we could organise plastic surgery to alter your appearance," added Britannia.

Fred had to admit he was tempted, but he had been over every contingency and realised that he had little option but to surrender to his fate. Resistance Was Useless. Given the choice, quite honestly he would have preferred to face an entire Martian invasion fleet complete with giant killer robots at that moment.

"Ahem. Miss Daisy?"

Wilkins the butler, demonstrating a startling prescience, had arrived carrying Fred's freshly laundered and pressed suit on a hanger and behind him came Mrs Sowerberry the housekeeper with the rest of Fred's clothes similarly all neatly pressed. His shoes had been restored to their pre-wedding shine and the only thing not to have survived the morning's adventures had been his buttonhole.

Within moments of the butler and housekeeper

withdrawing from the room, Fred found himself being dressed again by three sets of hands. It occurred to him that he could have informed them that like the process of undressing earlier on, he had been doing the job for himself for over thirty years. It occurred to him that he really should make some kind of indignant show once more. Then it occurred to him that he was fully dressed and the three women were standing back and looking at him critically. "It'll do," said Britannia at length.

Fred was amazed. He would hardly have known he had ever fallen in the boating lake, as his appearance certainly showed nothing of his adventures. Daisy cocked her head on one side and gave a low, admiring whistle. "C'mon, Fred, I'm going to get you to the church on time."

-oOo-

Fred hurried down the front steps of the Manor after Daisy, who was still wrapped in her towelling robe. The one concession to going out she had made was to pull on a pair of high-heels. "Aren't you going to get dressed?" Fred asked.

"I didn't want to delay you," replied Daisy, twirling her car keys on one finger. "I reckoned you wouldn't appreciate waiting half-an-hour for me to pick an outfit out of my wardrobe."

"Very considerate of you." Fred was touched. If he was honest with himself, he wasn't sure he wanted to go back to the real world. He liked the way things were on this side of the rainbow…

CHAPTER SIX:

In Which Daisy Gets Fred To The Church On Time

And Fred Gets Punched Again.

The Mini arrived at the church in a matter of minutes, leaving a trail of strained nerves and near collisions behind it. Daisy executed the perfect parallel-park as a half-handbrake-turn, spraying up gravel and narrowly missing the gravestones nearest the entrance of the church. Fred leapt out of the car almost before it had fully come to rest, but an urgent cry of "Fred!" from Daisy stopped him in his tracks. She raced round the front of the car and arranged the collar of his suit for him. She straightened the white carnation that her mother had provided to replace the one he had lost at the park boating lake.

He could hear in the distance old Mrs. Bell the organist gingerly picking her way through *Jesu, Son Of Man's Desiring* as though crossing a live minefield. She was of the old school of church organist and adhered to the philosophy of all the right notes, but not necessarily in the right order. The church would already be packed with relatives and friends, there to see sentence carried out."Best of luck, Fred," Daisy sighed sadly and gave him a kiss that made him forget what day it was. Fred was so busy revelling in the sensation, that he was only vaguely aware of Melissa Masters' BMW screeching to a halt at the gates of the church and the Titian-haired hockey-player that was his bride-to-be leaping out of the vehicle.

"Frederick Herbert Longfield!!"

Fred surfaced for breath. "Mm?" he enquired dreamily.

Daisy could see trouble coming, and slammed the passenger door of the Mini. Intending to race round the other side of the car and dive in, driving off before any damage was done, she neglected to notice the hem of the towelling robe had caught in the door.

"Whoops!!" The husband-to-be floundered pathetically discovering that suddenly he was in the company of a naked girl. "That always seems to be happening to me," chortled Daisy self-consciously.

The bride-to-be was conspicuously not dressed for the occasion. Fred had, in spite of his own misgivings, thought she might have made an effort. Something white and impractical along the lines normally worn by brides. Instead, she was attired in the sort of garb that her pupils and her victims on the hockey field were familiar with. Striped jersey in the school team colours and shorts that showed off her sturdy legs. Hockey was Melissa's personal fighting style. She had it elevated almost to a Martial Art, untroubled as it was with anything resembling the Marquess of Queensberry rules. The expression on her face was not one either he or an opposing player would wish to see.

"Mur... mur... mur..." bleated Fred.

Daisy had managed to salvage her modesty and turned one of her dazzling smiles on the bride-to-be. "Melissa." She held out a hand in greeting.

Melissa Masters ignored the proffered hand, beside herself that her plan to theatrically dump her would-be-husband-to-be at the altar had been upstaged by the

61

presence of this... this... *blonde*. She rounded on Fred, suddenly proving she was indeed her Daddy's girl as she revealed just how much of her father's mercurial nature she had inherited. "I didn't have to come to the church, you know!" she screeched. "I could have just left you standing here like a lemon in your best suit, but I didn't because I foolishly thought you'd be devastated. I came here out of the goodness of my heart to let you down gently, and what do I find? You canoodling in the grounds of the church where we were going to get married with some floozie."

"Floozie?" Daisy looked insulted, which was exactly what she had been.

"The wedding is off, Frederick Longfield." Melissa made a vehement sweeping gesture with both hands that would have demolished anybody standing either side of her. "I realised last night that I couldn't face married life with you, and I was only going through with this fiasco for Daddy's sake. I just thank goodness I saw sense in time," barked Melissa. "I tried to call, but all I got was your stupid answering machine."

"But... but... but..." Fred floundered helplessly.

Evidently tiring of the conversation, Melissa pulled a scented pink envelope out of the pocket of her shorts. "It's all in here," she snapped, ramming the envelope into the breast pocket of his suit and tearing the lining. With some difficulty, she pulled the engagement ring from a stubby finger and threw it at him. "I just thank goodness I saw sense in time."

Fred flinched as the twenty-four carat band ricocheted off his forehead. (Daisy fielded the ring and dropped it into the pocket of her robe as she was sure Fred would want it at some later date.) He stared, stunned, as

62

the girl he had been resigned to spending the rest of his life with rounded on Daisy, who took an apprehensive step backwards. "How long has this deception been going on?" demanded the fiery-haired amazon. "Is this," she indicated Daisy's state of undress, "how you've been spending your time away from me? Poodlefaking?"

"Poodlefaking?" Daisy and Fred looked at each other.

"I've never faked a poodle in my life!" Daisy attempted to defend herself. "I've occasionally tried to deceive an Old English Sheepdog, and I had a Jack Russell terrier once that was awfully gullible..." She trailed off as she realised Melissa was staring at her. "I've been wittering again, haven't I?" she asked in a small voice.

"We only met a matter of a few hours ago." Fred attempted to save the situation with the truth. "Miss Chayne and I were knocked into the boating lake by a dog and she kindly helped me get cleaned up."

"You expect me to believe that?" Melissa withered him with a scornful gaze. She half turned as she heard a commotion behind her.

Professor Masters had succeeded in extricating his not inconsiderable bulk from the white-ribbon-bedecked Rolls that Melissa should have been riding in, and which had arrived at the church a matter of seconds behind her. The big man was charging towards them, bellowing obscenities and waving a pink note not dissimilar to the one Melissa had crammed forcibly into Fred's breast pocket.

Fred recognised all the signs of one of the Headmaster's homicidal rages and surmised that he would most likely bear the brunt of any attack. He contemplated fainting and playing dead. He had heard stories of people attacked by bears avoiding further injury by pretending to have dropped dead, and he was reasonably confident the Headmaster would also be deceived by the tactic.

Melissa also looked around frantically for an escape route. Rather than answer any of her father's awkward questions, she realised actions spoke louder than words. She swung a hefty right hook at Fred's chin that stretched him out on the ground. Giving Daisy an unnerving growl to make her jump apprehensively out of the way, the Wagnerian redhead bolted for her car.

The wedding guests were emerging from the church to investigate the ruckus. Melissa's voice under normal circumstances could be described as strident, but in the last couple of minutes had been approaching air-raid siren proportions. In a matter of moments, the churchyard was filled by what seemed like hundreds of people, Fred's father and mother at the head of the crowd. Daisy took the opportunity in the confusion to drag Fred by the ankles back to the car.

Professor Masters stood in the midst of the multitude, bellowing like an enraged rhinoceros as he saw first Melissa's BMW fish-tailing spectacularly as it screeched through the gates of the churchyard, narrowly missing the bridal Rolls. Then the little black Mini with the semi-naked blonde in it sped off in the opposite direction moments later. He was more interested in snuffing out Fred's worthless life. "Where is he? Where is that imbecile?" he thundered.

Fred's Mum appeared at his elbow. "Who are you calling an imbecile?" she enquired suspiciously.

"Your son, Madam," replied Professor Masters

acidly. "The groom. By some foul chicanery, he has caused my darling daughter to run out on what should be the happiest day of her life!"

Fred's Mum stood her ground in the monsoon of spittle. Her eyes narrowed dangerously as the irate educator continued his rant.

"I thank my lucky stars that she has seen sense, and recognised she was marrying an entire genus of species beneath her. That does not excuse your hellspawn offspring from the anguish he has caused her. When I find him, I shall..."

Exactly what he was going to do to Fred when he found him, he never actually got around to articulating as Fred's Mum stretched him out in the churchyard with a solid swat from her handbag.

-oOo-

Fred regained consciousness somewhere between the church and wherever-it-was Daisy was taking him. Tenderly probing what he suspected was a broken jaw, he looked around suspiciously. "The last thing I remember was being outside the church," he ventured.

"That's right, Fred," confirmed Daisy chirpily, slalom-ing the Mini between a furniture van and a milk-float. She blew a kiss in the rear-view mirror to the milkman she had narrowly missed demolishing and watched him freeze in mid-curse.

Fred was reviewing the morning's events to himself. "Melissa turned up. Wasn't very happy. Then..." It all came flooding back - the kiss, the car door, the bathrobe...

Suddenly he remembered why his jaw hurt. "Melissa!" he exclaimed. "She hit me!" He swore he could feel the imprint of her knuckles in his chin. Julian Ballcock's punch had been a love pat in comparison, although admittedly Melissa had a three-stone advantage over Julian. Including Britannia and Boadicea's tag-team assault, that was four times in one day he had been on the receiving end of a smack in the chops, and the last time he recalled fisticuffs featuring in his daily routine had been shortly after his tenth birthday and Fenwick the school bully had wanted his bike, so he had hit him with it...

"Great right hook that girl's got," Daisy nodded. "Has she ever considered boxing for England?"

"I don't think so," began Fred. Then he realised what he was saying. "Of course not!" His jaw throbbed. "Too many rules." Suddenly everything had changed. He was sure he should be devastated. He was sure he should be something other than numb.

He knew his chin was far from numb. He took the envelope Melissa had thrust into his breast pocket and carefully opened it, just in case it exploded. The paper had that powdery old-ladies'-scent smell about it and looked as if it might have come from a child's stationery set. A single sheet, covered in Melissa's distinctly masculine scrawl. He stared at the paper, taking in the contents which were basically a vitriolic tirade against all things Fred. Her father had been right, and there was a golf pro at the local links where her father was Club secretary who did things for her that Fred never could.

Not without a forklift, Fred thought uncharitably to himself. He screwed up the letter and tossed it out of the window.

-oOo-

Fred looked confused as Daisy pulled on the handbrake and he finally took in his surroundings. Daisy had flung the Mini into the narrow parking slot outside his flat, between the skip outside his neighbour's and the BMW owned by the Iranian gentleman in the first-floor flat. His flat was on the ground floor of a converted two-storey terraced house on the far side of the park to his parents' place, and would be fit for human habitation once it had been pulled down and something better built in its place. As it was highly unlikely that either would happen, the house would stay in its current cheery state of dilapidation for the foreseeable future. Unfortunately, it was the best he could do on his meagre salary and came with some serious strings attached.

"I got your address from your wallet," Daisy chirped. "Are you going to invite me in?"

Fred followed Daisy up the path to the front door and fumbled with the key. "Uh, ground floor, first door," he mumbled as Daisy sauntered past him into the house. He followed the dazzling blonde into the singularly untidy living room cum bedroom cum study of his pokey little flat. He hoped she would not notice the clutter of washing-up in the kitchenette, or the untidy pile that the duvet made on his bed. He skirted round the bed, which took up a considerable amount of the already sparse floor space. "It's no palace, but it's home."

"It's a tip!" exclaimed Daisy with typical candour.

"Coffee?" Fred shambled through into the cramped kitchenette that led off the main body of the bed-sit. The

67

last forty-eight hours he had been camped out at his parents' house preparing for the wedding and he had done less shopping than Old Mother Hubbard. A fresh series of paroxysmal sneezes had him leaning on the refrigerator for support.

Daisy placed a wonderfully cooling, slim hand on his fevered brow and made tisk-tisk noises. She shooed him out of the kitchenette and back into the living room. "Relax, Fred, I'm looking after you now." In spite of his protesting noises, she propelled him towards the bed. "Get into bed."

Fred blinked. "Pardon?"

"Get into bed. We don't want you getting poorly," Daisy waved him towards his roughly-straightened pit.

Obediently, Fred did as he was told. He made a swift side trip into the bathroom to change out of his suit. He quickly shrugged into his bathrobe. It was a little on the worse-for-wear side, a forlorn shade of blue and doubled as a dressing gown and hand towel but it was a better fit than the one Sir Roland had loaned him. His customary nightwear was not the sort of thing to appear in front of a female house-guest in. Returning to the bed-sitting room, he tweaked the bedclothes in an attempt to reduce the unkempt impression, and propped himself up against the pillows.

As he tugged the sheets into a semblance of straightness, he noticed the little red message light on his answering machine blinking angrily. Before he could press the button to listen to the message, the phone trilled loudly, making him jump. The noise half-concealed a watery *whoosh* and a squeak from the kitchen which he made a mental note to investigate after dealing with the phone call.

Cautiously lifting the receiver as if expecting it to explode at any moment, he put it to his ear. "Hullo?"

He was surprised to find Charlie Newton on the other end of the line. He frowned at the agitated chipmunk-noises coming from the receiver. "Charlie? What do you mean 'What the hell am I doing there?'? I live here." His eyes narrowed. "Yes, I've got my passport, and the air tickets. Under normal circumstances I'd be off on my honeymoon." Fred scowled. "I know I'm not on my honeymoon. I didn't get married today, remember?"

Daisy peered round the edge of the kitchen door, water dripping from the ends of her long, blonde hair. Fred pointed at the receiver, covering the mouthpiece. "Best man. Slightly excitable. What's that Charlie? He wants to what?" The colour drained from his face. He replaced the receiver with the absent minded look of someone who had received something akin to a death threat over the phone.

"Who was that?" asked Daisy perkily.

"Charlie Newton, my best man," replied Fred. "He just called to warn me to get out of the country. The Headmaster wants to use me for a re-enaction of a Viking execution ritual."

Daisy made sympathetic noises. Fred promptly stopped worrying about himself as Daisy casually emerged from the kitchen carrying what she had been wearing when she went in. "I tried washing out a couple of cups to make a cup of hot chocolate," she observed ruefully. "Your mains pressure's a lot higher than round my flat. The backwash soaked me." She draped the towelling robe over the chair by the gas fire to dry. She noticed Fred had gone very quiet and wide-eyed again, like he had at the boating lake. "If me strutting about in my birthday suit bothers

69

you," she ventured, slipping off her high-heels to shake water out of them again, "Would you happen to have something I could wear?"

CHAPTER SEVEN:

In Which Fred Gets A Threatening Phone Call

And Then Gets Threatened In Person.

In the great cosmic plan of things, human beings tend to fall into two general categories – those who really should wear clothes and those obviously intended by Nature not to have her handiwork hidden from public gaze. Not that it is as simple as a question of aesthetics or not scaring the horses. Some people have perfect bodies and yet uncovered are a less than inspiring sight, while others may be pear-shaped but somehow look perfectly proper even when wearing nothing more than an embarrassed smile. Daisy just happened to be one of those people Nature must have said to herself: *"Yes, this one only needs the one suit – the birthday variety."* If anything, Nature seemed to have gone on to decide that Daisy not only looked more suitable in the buff, but that circumstances should endeavour at all times to render her into that state of grace.

"Something to wear?" Fred, mesmerised by the vision before him, looked startled then galvanised himself into action. He hopped out of bed and snatched up his bright red, school sweatshirt; the one reserved for the occasions when he was shanghaied by Mr Wustock the games master to help out; and passed it to her.

Daisy wriggled fetchingly into the garment and offered him a bright, if slightly self-conscious smile. On her slim form, the sweatshirt hung like a tent. The hem was only within the bounds of maidenly modesty. "I'm afraid the kitchen's in a bit of a mess as well," she confessed, shrugging fetchingly and almost sliding out of the neck of the sweatshirt.

Fred was sufficiently distracted by this manoeuvre to accidentally sit down on the answering machine. The device gave an indignant beep and suddenly the voice of the dreaded Melissa barked out of the speaker. *"Frederick Herbert Longfield!!"* the machine shrieked like a banshee.

Daisy took a step back in alarm. The machine proceeded to launch into a venomous tirade that comprehensively questioned Fred's intelligence, virility, mental competence and legitimacy in the space of thirty seconds. At least a couple of threats made on his life were thrown in for good measure before a final, chilling "Goodbye," and the receiver was crashed down.

They both stared at the answering machine in mute horror as if expecting it to explode for an encore. Daisy took a breath and broke the silence. "In spite of everything that's happened this morning, do you think you'll be able to patch things up with your bride-to-be?"

"*Ex* bride-to-be." Fred shook his head. He pointed at the answering machine, which by rights should still have been sizzling. "I'm pretty certain a reconciliation isn't on the cards, judging from the language just used." He shrugged ruefully. "If I'd been here rather than spending the night at Mum and Dad's, I'd have taken the call and we'd have all been saved a lot of trouble." He looked thoughtful. "But then, I wouldn't have gone to the park and I wouldn't have met you, so something good came out of it."

"She left breaking off the engagement to the last possible moment, didn't she?" Daisy raised an eyebrow.

"Once her father had accepted the idea, there was no telling him otherwise. If the wedding had been called off, there would have been blood shed. Mine." Fred sat down on the edge of the bed. "It started off as a couple of fairly cordial dates and suddenly we were looking at engagement rings. I suppose it might have been all done in the first flush of romance, but I honestly don't recall much romance. Her father was dead set against the marriage from the word go. So were my parents. But then the entire fiasco just sort of got out of hand." Daisy offered a sympathetic expression. Fred shrugged. "I think I've had a narrow escape."

Daisy perched next to him on the edge of the bed. "So... you're a teacher." She tried to change the subject. "You mentioned something along those lines back at the Manor."

"Some people might disagree with the description, but in essence it's right," confirmed Fred. "Chemistry, with a little relief Physics thrown in."

Daisy nodded. "I can imagine it would be."

Fred was still in a bit of a daze following his recent adventures, and this comment threw him completely. "Pardon?"

"A relief. Teaching a bunch of ankle-biters Chemistry, I can imagine teaching them Physics for a change is a relief." Daisy explained her thinking, but it did little to clarify the situation to Fred.

"That's not what I meant," he said slowly.

Daisy nudged him playfully with her shoulder. "I know. I was winding you up," she chortled. "I went to finishing school in France. We were taught by nuns. The Headmistress looked just like Boris Karloff except for the moustache."

Fred looked puzzled. "Boris Karloff didn't have a moustache?"

"Sister Concepta was the one with the moustache."

Fred looked dubious until Daisy reached into her cluttered handbag and produced the proof, a crumpled colour photograph of a group of her friends on a school trip to what looked like the red light district of Hamburg with the good Sister. Daisy smiled to herself as Fred stared at the photo in disbelief. "She's the spitting image of him. Except for the moustache and the bolt-through-the-neck."

"Sister Concepta didn't have a bolt through her neck?" Daisy nestled up to Fred, sending his blood pressure through the ceiling. She craned her neck curiously as a movement outside the window caught her eye. Three middle-aged gentlemen were walking up the path to the front door. Or more precisely two middle-aged gentlemen were being swept along in the wake of the third. One was small and timid-looking, carrying a doctor's black bag. The second was tall, thin and gimlet-eyed. The one in the lead was built like a retired, all-in wrestler. About six foot tall and approximately the same in width, he moved with a silent menace redolent of a western gunslinger about to turn Gary Cooper into a colander. He wore a dark, three-piece suit immaculately tailored to fit his threatening frame. As he got nearer to the door, she was able to sort out his features, which were crumpled into a beetroot-coloured frown. Piggy, little steely-blue-surrounded-by-red eyes blazed like twin lasers from under a severely knotted brow. He was bearded, a bushy salt-and-pepper growth of some abundance. "Fred," she ventured hesitantly. "Would you

74

happen to know a large, rather threatening-looking gentleman with a beard?"

Fred had settled back into his what was fast becoming his new pastime of Daisy-watching. "Mmm?"

"'Cause there's a fellow who fits that description standing at the front door with an expression on his face that would curdle milk," continued Daisy.

The doorbell rang.

Daisy tucked her legs out of harm's way as Fred, somehow suddenly aware of danger as if scenting a predator, leapt across the room to the window. He peered out into the street and felt an icy, sinking sensation in his lower abdomen. "Oh my sainted aunt!" he gurgled in sheer terror. "It's him."

"Who's him?" Daisy was puzzled.

"The Headmaster. My Boss. My girlfriend's father. My prospective father-in-law. The man who will probably serve a life sentence for my murder."

Daisy looked mildly perturbed. "What's he doing here?"

"I think he might be here to kill me, or at the very least maim me." Fred had acquired the hunted look of a fugitive. Then his gaze fell on Daisy, and just how much of her person was visible. It would have been bad enough if she had still been wearing just her bathrobe, but standing there in barely his sweatshirt... "What's the old bastard going to think if he finds you here dressed like that?" he squeaked. Daisy looked down at herself and had to concede that as far as circumstantial evidence was concerned, the odds were stacked against Fred.

The doorbell rang again, a little more aggressively, and Fred made a valiant attempt at the proverbial out-of-skin jump. "*I'm dead meat*!!!" he squeaked.

"Calm down, Fred, you're having kittens before my very eyes!" Daisy hopped lithely off the bed. Fred watched spellbound as she strolled over to the wardrobe next to the bathroom door and opened it. "I think I may have the beginnings of a plan." She reached up to take a garment down from the rail. The item she had taken down was the white coat that Fred wore around the school laboratory. Unhurriedly, she shrugged into the white coat, buttoning it up. She gathered her hair up into a business-like bun, securing it with a handful of pins from her voluminous handbag, and adjusted the fit of the way-too-large-for-her white coat with a couple of expertly positioned safety pins. She bent over to pull on her high-heels and Fred gave a gurgle of alarm.

"Whatever you do, don't bend over!" he squeaked. "You can see *everything*!"

Daisy straightened up. "If you were a gentleman, you would have averted your gaze," she sniffed mildly. She advanced on him with a purposeful look.

Fred stared at her dumbfounded. "What are you doing?"

Daisy took his glasses off. "I'm going to pretend to be your doctor." She put on his glasses to complete her disguise. She peered myopically through the lenses. "Where have you gone?" She peered over the top of the spectacles to reorient herself. "Get back into bed."

Fred shot under the covers and pulled them up over his head in the hope that the Headmaster would think he was not there. He jumped as Daisy tapped him on top of the head. "It's no use hiding, Fred. I'm sure he'll spot you."

Fred surfaced and watched as Daisy made a last inventory of her appearance in the mirror before strolling unconcernedly over to the door to open it. Fred's gaze fell on Daisy's robe, which was draped over the back of a chair by the fire. He vaulted out of bed, grabbed the damp item of clothing and dived back into bed as Daisy opened the door. He grimaced as he discovered the towelling robe was soggier than Daisy had intimated.

"Who the devil are...??" demanded the voice of the Headmaster. Icicles made their presence felt all the way down Fred's back.

"Shush." Daisy silenced him. "Mr Longfield is resting. I'm his personal physician and I'm here making a house call." She moved back into the room followed by the Headmaster and the short, timid looking little man in his late fifties. Behind them, the gimlet-eyed gentleman seemed to glide into the room. Fred tried to sink deeper into the bed and did his best to look mortally ill.

The Headmaster was not interested in observing the niceties of bedside-manner. "Longfield, you repellent, dog-kissing excuse for a human being!" he thundered venomously. "I have no idea what vile perversions you perpetrated that made my daughter run away from her wedding. And if I ever find out, I will hunt you down and gut you like a fish!"

The gimlet-eyed gentleman gave a soft cough like a sheep clearing its throat.

The Headmaster ground his teeth audibly. "This gentleman is my legal advisor, Mr Sheister. Against my better judgement he has convinced me that homicide would not be the most satisfactory course of action at this moment." He looked up at Sheister and bared his teeth alarmingly. "Although I reserve the right to reconsider his advice." He leaned in close to Fred and dropped his voice to an ominous, volcano-like rumble. "If I were able to fire you on the spot, I would do so without a second's hesitation, and I would enjoy the experience immensely. Unfortunately, even if I were to use the proper channels, you would no doubt cower behind the protection of your Union. I refuse to give you that satisfaction. I will, however, take the greatest delight in accepting your formal resignation from the teaching profession on the grounds of ill health. Physical or mental makes no difference to me. To this end, I have brought Doctor Wilson with me. He will examine you, certify you unfit for work, and you will tender your resignation forthwith. If you refuse to resign, Doctor Wilson will be able to sign your death certificate. Mr Sheister will confirm that an act of self-defence on my part was indirectly involved in your dismemberment."

Fred winced. The Doctor moved around the side of the bed to examine him. Daisy bent over to plump up Fred's pillows, and the good Doctor, given an excellent view of what Fred had warned Daisy about accidentally disclosing, dropped his bag with a loud crash. "P... pardon me," he stuttered. "W... with your permission, Doctor?" he asked Daisy, indicating the patient.

"Knock yourself out, Doctor," replied Daisy, graciously. "Mr Longfield is suffering from an acute case of post-prandial upper abdominal distension. Brought on by severe stress and a large fry-up." Daisy was trying to be helpful, but Fred had the sinking feeling she was simply wielding one of the shovels involved in digging his grave.

Doctor Wilson looked at her levelly. "I'm not surprised."

The Doctor's examination was thorough and completed in a matter of moments. Fred rearranged the sheets with as much dignity as he could muster under the circumstances. Everything the good Doctor had touched him with seemed to have been deliberately refrigerated first. Matters had not been helped by Daisy's interest in the subject.

"Well?" rumbled Professor Masters dangerously.

"This man is gravely ill," jabbered the Doctor nervously, who was even more intimidated by the Headmaster than Fred. "He needs plenty of bed rest, a light diet and plenty of liquids."

"What's wrong with him, man?" roared the Headmaster.

"Ohhh!" squawked the Doctor, his mind racing for a convincing diagnosis. "In... inflamed cuc... cuc... car... carburettor," he spluttered. Fred moaned and slid beneath the sheets.

The Headmaster turned slowly and gazed down at Fred's shape under the covers. "That'll do nicely. Well, Mr Longfield, I'd love to say it's been a pleasure working with you, but it has not." He poked the lump under the sheets with a ramrod-straight forefinger and was rewarded by a yelp and a flinch. He gripped a handful of the counterpane and snapped it back to uncover Fred. With a flourish, he flipped open the typed letter of resignation Mr Sheister had brought with him. "Sign here," he grated with a sadistic smile, indicating a space at the foot of the letter with the fountain pen from his top pocket.

Fred briefly scanned the letter before signing it, just in case it turned out to be a combined suicide note and bequest for his mortal remains to be used for scientific experimentation. He handed the paper and pen back to the enraged educator and cringed as the sheets were swept back over him as if draping a corpse.

"You may also wish to seek alternative accommodation," the voice of the Headmaster grated ominously. Fred heard the door slam and peeped out nervously from under the covers. The Doctor and the Solicitor had also vanished, doubtless swept out of the door by the great man's wake.

"What an unpleasant man!" exclaimed Daisy, aghast. "I'd hate to meet him in a dark alley." She shuddered, hugging herself, and edged closer to Fred just in case the Headmaster returned.

Fred nodded morosely, accepting his spectacles back from Daisy. "It looks like the dole queue in the morning," he observed, an air of long-suffering in his voice.

Daisy frowned. "Did I hear him right? Did he just run you out of town as well? It wasn't quite 'there's a stagecoach out of town at noon - be on it,' but it was close."

"Not quite," admitted Fred. "He also happens to be my landlord."

Daisy looked horrified. "But you've got rights! Your lease..."

"Things were arranged on the understanding that after the wedding Melissa and I were moving into a larger flat nearer the school." Fred gave a fatalistic shrug. He stared around the flat reflectively. "I can always move back to Mum and Dad's," he sounded optimistic. "On the whole I'll be glad to see the back of this dump, but I don't know how I'll be able to afford a new place."

Daisy drew back apprehensively as Fred was racked by a series of explosive sneezes, followed by a howl of pain as he was sure his nose had fallen off. It felt as if it was only just attached to his face following the assaults by Melissa, Julian, Boadicea and Britannia.

"You're catching a cold," she observed astutely.

"Terminal, I hope," Fred growled.

The touch of self-pity in his voice shocked Daisy and she looked at him sharply. "Now, Fred, just because your girlfriend gives you the elbow on your wedding day doesn't give you the excuse to wallow in depression."

Fred goggled at her. "Yes it does, and I wasn't wallowing!" he protested.

"You were wallowing," confirmed Daisy. "Like a manic-depressive hippopotamus!"

"Well, under the circumstances, I thought I might have some justification!" Fred put a hand to his head, which had started to throb. "I can't think of much else that could have gone wrong today."

"What do you mean, gone wrong, Fred?" Daisy looked surprised. She thought she had managed to salvage the day pretty well. She had got his suit cleaned, she had got him to the church on time; she was sure she could straighten out the misunderstanding with his bride about the bathrobe if she was inclined.

"Let me see," Fred started counting points off on his fingers. "I was walking in the park when you and a dog jumped on me and knocked me into the boating lake..."

"Ollie and I didn't *jump* on you, we were being pursued by a duck," Daisy corrected him.

Fred held up a finger that was not engaged in counting things that had gone wrong. "My *best* suit was covered in mud and ruined."

"Got it cleaned for you," pouted Daisy.

"You dragged me off into the countryside to meet your parents - not that I'm complaining about that - but then your boyfriend turned up and punched me in the face."

"He is not my boyf...." Daisy fell silent as Fred gave her his best schoolmaster's glare.

"Your two looney friends assaulted me when I explained I was on my way to be married."

Daisy went to make an interjection then thought better of it.

"When you ultimately returned me to the church where I was supposed to be married," continued Fred stonily, "I was punched in the face by my bride-to-be and *dumped!!*"

Daisy flinched with each word of the last sentence as if stung to the very core. At the word 'dumped', her bottom lip started to tremble, and Fred could see those big, blue eyes brimming with tears.

At that moment, Fred realised that the last thing in the world he wanted to see was Daisy in tears. Especially if he was the cause of those tears. "Looking at the greater picture, however," he continued almost without pausing, "there have undoubtedly been mitigating circumstances for all of these incidents and certainly the ultimate ramifications of this morning's events will turn out to be beneficial..."

Daisy emitted a series of small, hiccough-style noises and Fred snatched up the box of tissues from the nightstand next to the bed. Daisy helped herself to five or six sheets and blew her nose loudly. "No, you're absolutely right, Fred. I'm always doing this kind of thing - ruining peoples' lives. It's just a talent, I suppose."

"Who says you go around ruining peoples' lives?" Fred was indignant. "Is my life ruined? Of course it isn't." He looked surprised as he realised that was the truth.

"If you're sure..."

"Today has been an unmitigated disaster from the start," Fred confirmed. "The fates conspired against that wedding from the start - my stag night was a disaster. An entertaining disaster, but a disaster nevertheless. The wedding cake burnt down with the caterers' last week, and there's a civil war going on where the honeymoon was booked for. None of that had anything to do with you."

Daisy gave him a wan smile. "I don't think I've ever started a civil war," she said in a small voice. "A smallish riot perhaps..."

"As I recall," Fred ventured, gesturing back over his shoulder, "that little fracas at the church really had nothing to do with you."

"Apart from me falling out of my robe," shrugged Daisy, nearly managing to do it again with the white lab coat. She bit her lip, wishing she hadn't reminded him. "But she hit you!"

"I'm sure I had it coming."

"Any girl who plants a haymaker on her boyfriend without giving him a chance to defend himself isn't good enough for a nice fellow like you."

Fred looked bashful. "Thanks for the compliment," he mumbled. It was funny, but he could remember his mother saying something along the same lines when he returned from the holiday he had taken with Melissa to the Algarve, and they announced their engagement. He had to admit to a peculiar sensation - instead of feeling upset about the day's adventures, he felt relieved, if not pleased at the way it had all turned out. His deliverance from Melissa and her evil-tempered father had been a narrow escape. This admission, although he would only make it to himself, shocked him. "Volatile temper that one, just like her father. Nothing you did contributed to her dumping me." He paused as he realised what he had said, a shocked expression spreading rapidly across his face. "She dumped me." He repeated the phrase, mulling it over and rolling it around his mouth like a boiled sweet. "She dumped me. *She* dumped me. She *dumped* me. I'm not getting married."

"I still feel terrible about it." Daisy's expression

was truly tragic.

"*I'm not getting married!*" repeated Fred, to make
sure he had the concept straight in his head. He took a
deep, cleansing breath of the type the school psychologist
had advised him to take whenever the third form got too
much for him. A peaceful smile suffused his whole being.
He opened his eyes and seized Daisy by the shoulders as if
about to shake her and planted a kiss full on the lips. "I am
not getting married!"

Daisy staggered backwards as he released her.
"Congratulations?" she queried, then taking in the look of
sheer relief on Our Hero's face, she beamed
"Congratulations," and throwing her arms around his neck,
kissed him right back.

CHAPTER EIGHT:

In Which Fred and Daisy Get To Know Each Other

And Fred Makes A Move

As much as Fred would have liked to spend the rest of the day barricaded in his flat, hiding from the world and getting to know his beautiful new friend Daisy; the worry that the Headmaster might return in a hockey mask and wielding a chainsaw made concentrating on the task difficult.

It was with some relief that he received Daisy's suggestion they go round to her flat for tea. The lack of supplies in his kitchen taxed even her ingenuity in the kitchen. Her robe dry enough to wear once more, Daisy had discarded Fred's sweatshirt and labcoat in its favour, causing him to bump painfully into the bathroom door in passing. She had driven them the short distance round the corner and down towards the town centre to her flat.

They pulled up outside a large, stone-fronted, mid-Victorian house. It was a tall façade, three storeys, built on imposing lines. Once, it would have been the town house of some grand, probably landed family. The last few years had seen it and its neighbours converted into a number of flats - although "flats" did these luxurious surroundings an injustice. They were *luxury executive apartments* according to the "for rent" sign bolted to the iron railings by the window of the ground floor flat.

Daisy had already hopped out of the car and was heading up the short flight of steps to the front door. "This is my place," she chirped as Fred hurried after her. "Top floor, flat three." Fred stored away the piece of information as something useful. He passed this way quite frequently *en route* to the shops. Considering what had happened to him in the past eight hours, prudence might suggest he should consider another route. He had no idea who this Prudence might be that kept making suggestions, but then he seldom listened to unsolicited advice.

Daisy let him into the communal hall beyond the front door and checked her letter-box. "Bills, bills, bills," she muttered to herself, thrusting a handful of brown envelopes into the pocket of her robe. She turned to Fred. "Come on." She started up the stairs at a rate of knots.

-oOo-

On the first landing, they were greeted by the muffled barking of a large dog. As Fred started along the landing, the door of the first-floor flat was yanked open and he found himself pinned to the wall by a freshly-laundered Old English Sheepdog. The herbal-shampoo-scented animal had propped itself up on its hind legs, forepaws on his shoulders, wet nose millimetres from his. Not that his nose was wet, but you get the picture.

Daisy was having problems of her own. She had been surrounded by the Ballcock Twins, both attired in white towelling bathrobes so that Fred got the impression he might be seeing double. "Where the hell have you been?" demanded Boadicea. "We got back here ages ago."

"I've been with Fred!" exclaimed Daisy, as if that had been obvious.

Boadicea's eyes narrowed. She grabbed the lapels of Daisy's robe and yanked the garment open.

87

Daisy snatched the material out of Boadicea's hands and covered herself up again. "What are you doing, you psychotic cow?" she squeaked indignantly.

"Checking for fingerprints," replied Boadicea, glaring at Fred. "What have you been doing all this time? We followed you two to the church in case there was some way we could rescue Fred."

"We reckoned you were all right when Crusher chinned him," chortled Britannia. "Then you took off just before the fight broke out. Missed all the fun."

"Fight?" bleated Fred.

"Some old bird in the wedding party sloshed Crusher's Dad with her handbag and a sort-of fight broke out." Boadicea shrugged. "We hung around to see who won, but of course by then you two had disappeared. When we got back here, there was no sign of either of you and we were wondering where you'd got to. Which brings me to the small matter of Ollie here. What on Earth had you done to that poor old dog?"

"We had to hose him down before we could even let him in the house," Britannia commented chattily. "He'd have stunk the place out!"

"Sorry." Daisy looked sheepish enough to be rounded up by Ollie.

"Of course, Ollie thought it was all a tremendous game," complained Boadicea. "Chasing the hose, shaking himself every couple of minutes. Britt and I got soaked to the skin!"

"I ended up having to pin him down while Bouncy

hosed us both down." Britannia sounded aggrieved.

"Then of course, he'd rather take off down the road than be towelled dry like any civilised dog," sniffed Boadicea. "We've only just this minute finished cleaning him up and the flat looks like a tornado's blown through. We had to strip off to give him a bath." She opened her robe to demonstrate.

"A duck went for him down by the boating lake and he knocked both of us in the water," Daisy sounded defensive. "I told you before, and would you mind not flashing Fred?"

"Hmph! Sticking to your story." Britannia frowned at them.

Fred was still pinned to the wall by the Old English Sheepdog. The creature had been regarding him silently and inscrutably for a couple of minutes and had decided to give him an experimental lick. "Erm..." Fred made his first contribution to the conversation.

"Oh, don't mind Ollie," Daisy said reassuringly. "He's hardly a tooth in his head. Even if it was in his nature, he wouldn't bite you."

"But he can still give you a really nasty suck," cautioned Boadicea. "So watch it."

"Scratch his chest and you'll have a friend for life," offered Daisy.

As Fred saw it, he owed the dog quite a debt of gratitude for the day's events and that was the least he could do.

-oOo-

Daisy's flat took up the whole of the top floor of the building, and Fred surmised the rooms might have been servants' quarters in the old house's original state. Above the head of the stairs, an ornate stained glass skylight provided illumination. Daisy took her key out of her pocket and unlocked the door of her flat. "Here we are, *Chez Moi.*" She chirped, ushering Fred inside.

Fred was intrigued. For all the talk of luxury, here was a flat that was almost as pokey as his own. The flat consisted of one long room that ran from the bay window at the front, to the back wall. A bathroom and a small bedroom led off, the bedroom door replaced by a hanging bead curtain. For all its bedsit-ness, the flat was comfortably furnished in what could best be described a Bohemian style. The walls were hung with Persian rugs and framed photos and knicknacks she had picked up in her travels.

The bed, which took pride of place in the bay window because there was no room for it in the cramped bedroom, was a huge, brass monstrosity. Kicking off her high-heels, Daisy threw her keys casually on to the bedside table, and once again without a second's thought for propriety, shrugged out of the towelling robe. The springs of the bed creaked and groaned as she took a short-cut across the satin sheets, flitting through the bead curtain into the bedroom. The bedroom beyond was little more than a glorified box-room-cum-wardrobe. Looking in through the door, Fred could see more clutter and racks of clothing that echoed Daisy's distinctly individual tastes. First and foremost a gentleman, he moved away from the doorway and sat down on the plush leather settee. To the rear of the

90

flat, an L-shaped polished pine counter separated the living room from the small kitchenette.

"With you in a second," Daisy's voice drifted through from the box room. She emerged straightening the hem of a white, silk slip that moulded itself to her figure. The hem was only just within the bounds of decency. Fred had little time to admire her dress-sense as she shot through on the way to the kitchenette. He stood up and hurried after her. "What are you doing?" he asked.

Daisy opened the door of the fridge and looked inside. "I don't know about you, but it's way past my teatime. I thought I'd knock us up a nice little something to tide us over 'til dinner. Call it high tea."

Fred perched on one of the high, wooden stools on the living room side of the wooden kitchenette counter, watching as Daisy bustled round raiding the refrigerator and powering up the café-style capuccino machine at the far end of the counter. Melissa's idea of kitchencraft had been to get him to make coffee, and if a meal was required, then she would drag him off to the most expensive restaurant in town - his treat.

Daisy had retrieved a large, home made Black Forest gateau from the refrigerator and proceeded to cut two generous slices. Licking her fingers clean, she put two mugs under the Espresso spouts of the coffee machine and proceeded to steam-froth a jug of milk. The kitchen was filled with strange whooshes and gurgles and the smell of freshly-brewed strong coffee. She put a large slice of Black Forest gateau down in front of him and a steaming mug of strong, hot, sweet coffee and sat down opposite Fred on the kitchen side of the counter to attack her matching slice with gusto.

Fred gazed at his hostess, still scarcely able to come to terms with how much his existence had changed in the matter of hours since she breezed into his life. He could not take his eyes off her. He was absolutely dazzled by her in a moth-flame kind of way and he would be happy to get his wings singed.

Daisy was warming her cheek with her cup. One of the straps of her slip had slipped from her shoulder and disclosed an amount of cleavage. She hooked the strap back into place with a finger and tossed her hair out of her eyes. "Fred!" she exclaimed shyly. "You're staring at me again!"

Fred blinked and looked surprised. He hadn't realised he had been staring. He thought he had simply been indulging in his new favourite pastime of Daisywatching. He floundered helplessly. "Sorry, does it bother you?"

Daisy bit her lip, wishing she had never mentioned the topic. Fred looked genuinely stricken. "Well, it did a bit," she admitted. "Just a little. Hardly at all, really. Not in the least." The more she thought about it, the less she realised she minded at all.

"I can't help it," Fred said defensively. "When you come into a room, I just have to stare - you fascinate me. You bewitch, mesmerise and bedazzle me. If there's a law against that, then I'm afraid I'm guilty as charged. If you want me to stop looking at you, I will, but I'd hope I could at least admire you out of the corner of my eye."

Daisy went a pretty shade of pink. "Well, perhaps I was being a little hasty..."

-oOo-

The ringing of the doorbell intruded upon Fred's sleep befuddled mind and he opened a bleary eye to peer at his bedside alarm clock. If he had been going into work that morning, he would have been extremely late. As it was, he no longer had a job to be extremely late for, so the matter was not a moot point. On the positive side, there was no need for him to face either his demonic pupils or his even more demonic Headmaster. On the negative side he was going to have to start looking for gainful employment, and on the neutral side he would have to move back into his parents' house. But at that moment, he did not have to stir if he did not have to. He was about to burrow back under the pillows and attempt to resume what had been progressing into a spectacularly filthy dream about a girl called Daisy when the doorbell rang again. He craned his neck to peer out of the window and leapt out of bed.

The subject of his dream was standing on the doorstep. Fred drank in the details of the vision: smartly-tailored pinstripe jacket, blue tee-shirt with Superman emblem and an is-it-a-skirt, is-it-a-belt, is-it-a-pelmet pinstripe micro-mini-skirt. Daisy's dress sense was unique. Not that she had been wearing a lot for most of the twenty-four hours he had known her. He had last seen her when he had said goodnight to her on the step of her apartment house around half-past two the night before and she had been wearing little more than a scrap of silk and a big smile.

Daisy regarded Fred with a sunny smile as he opened the front door. Suddenly self-conscious, "I wasn't sure I'd be welcome after yesterday," she said quietly.

"Welcome?" exclaimed Fred. "I haven't been able to get you out of my mind since yesterday!" He looked uncomfortable, as he had not intended to make his feelings so blatantly clear. "I can't think straight because of you. Since last night when you said goodnight, I've been racking my brains for an excuse to go round and see you."

Daisy perked up at this admission. "I'm glad I could save you any further mental stress." She held up a plastic shopping bag straining with groceries. "I... er... I just dropped by on the way back from the shops. I thought you might need some odds and ends."

"Thanks!" Fred relieved Daisy of her burden and ushered her into the flat. Having deposited the groceries in the kitchenette, he returned to the bed-sitting room to find Daisy in the process of shedding her pinstripe jacket and other items of clothing she deemed superfluous.

"First things first." The dazzling creature held up a finger. She yanked open his dressing gown, nodded satisfactorily to herself, threw her arms around his neck and kissed him passionately. Momentarily thrown off-guard, Fred rallied magnificently and threw himself into returning the embrace.

-oOo-

Some considerable time elapsed before Daisy released him and finally took in her surroundings properly. She gazed around the bed-sit in alarm. Overnight there had been some changes. When Fred had arrived back at the flat from his evening in her company, he had found his landlord, the Headmaster, had visited in his absence. A "Ground Floor Flat – To Rent" sign at the gate, packing cases and cardboard boxes had been waiting for him. He had got the message and had only been too happy to start packing up before sinking into his pit in the wee hours. Under the circumstances, he considered himself lucky that

94

his key had still worked when he got to the flat and that the Headmaster had not been lurking somewhere in the flat, harbouring Fredicidal tendencies.

"The Professor wasn't kidding about wanting you out of here," observed Daisy once Fred had conveyed the preceding plot exposition to her. "So what are you going to do now?"

"I'm moving back in with my folks," Fred shrugged. "When I got back here there were half a dozen messages on the answering machine and they phoned again while I was packing. Mum's happy about the situation and even happier about the wedding being off."

"That makes two of us," Daisy observed under her breath.

"Pardon?"

"Do your folks live nearby?" Daisy covered magnificently.

"Just the other side of Park Road." Fred made a left and a right turn gesture. When he had left the nest, he had not flown far.

Relieved that Fred would continue to be in just-dropped-by range, Daisy rubbed her hands together. "Well, let's get you moved out of here, then. It's lucky I showed up."

"In all kinds of ways," Fred breathed sotto voce.

-oOo-

Fred's worldly goods took depressingly little time to pack away in the crates provided by the Headmaster. Most of the junk he had acquired in his thirty-odd years was still cluttering up his parents' house in spite of his Mum's regular threats to hire a skip.

Daisy helped proceedings along with a steady supply of morale-boosting comestibles, and by late afternoon there was little left to do other than hire a van to get it all round to his parents' house.

The kitchenette was the last area of the flat to be put into mothballs - mainly because Daisy was still using most of the utensils and fixtures. Fred stood in the doorway watching Daisy pouring hot chocolate into two mugs. She had retreated into the kitchenette a good three-quarters of an hour previously muttering something about cakes and there was a mouth-watering smell of fresh baking in the air.

Daisy picked up the cups and shooed Fred ahead of her into the main room of the bedsit. She perched attractively on one of the packing crates and handed him one of the mugs. "Are you expecting a delivery?" She craned her neck and peered out of the front window at the Rentavan Ford Transit that had pulled up at the kerb outside.

Fred followed her gaze. "No?"

Daisy suddenly leapt to her feet in agitation. "It's the Headmaster again!" she squeaked apprehensively. Fred drew his feet up as hot chocolate went everywhere. He was amazed there could be so much liquid in one mug. Daisy bounced around the room, dripping cocoa. "Agh! Ugh! Hot! Hot! Hot!"

Fred snatched up a handful of paper tissues and

started mopping her up. She seemed to be dripping chocolate from every extremity.

"Are you all right?"

Daisy wriggled uncomfortably, grimacing. "No lasting damage done," she observed. "I'm just a bit sticky. My skirt's a bit worse for wear, though. I'll try and sponge it clean."

"Bathroom's in there," offered Fred.

"Been there, done that, had the sweatshirt." Daisy shot, gazelle-like into the small bathroom.

Fred craned his neck into the bay window to check that Daisy's premonition was not accurate. He let out a breath of relief that she had not even been close. He had the door open before his father had chance to prod the doorbell. "Mum!! Dad!! What brings you round here?" he exclaimed delightedly. He took in the expressions of concern sported by both parents. "Er… what's the matter?"

"We came to see how you were," replied his mother. "We got worried. When we phoned last night, all you'd talk about is some girl called Daisy. Your father's been worried sick!"

"We reckoned we'd help you move back home," added Dad. Ever the pragmatist, he had gone out first thing to rent a van for the purpose of shifting Fred's goods and chattels back to the family residence.

"Come in! Come in!" Fred ushered his parents into the flat.

Mum looked around the flat critically. She had never liked the place, and in its current state of disorganisation, it was even less appealing. Dad, however, approved of Fred's getting stuck into the job. "I reckon we can have all of this stuff packed up in the van inside of half-an-hour."

At that moment, Daisy made her customary grand entrance from the bathroom. Given her previous record for remaining fully clothed, it should have been no surprise to Fred that in the process of sponging her skirt clean, she had succeeded in soaking herself to the extent that her entire ensemble was hung on the shower rail dripping dry, and the hand towel he had forgotten to pack with the rest of the bathroom contents was the only thing between her and giving his parents the vapours. Realising she was under observation, or more precisely being stared at, Daisy looked self-conscious and offered her audience a slightly cheesy smile. "Oh, Hullo," she chirped.

"This is Daisy," Fred said absent-mindedly, admiring the view. He pulled himself together. "Daisy, this is my Mum and Dad."

Daisy gave a squeak of delight. "I'm *so* pleased to meet you, Mr and Mrs Longfield," she gushed, clutching the towel to her person with the extremity that was not being used to shake hands with Fred's parents'. "Fred's told me so much about you."

"You're very naked... I mean, you're very pretty," Fred's Mum beamed back with equal intensity. "At the moment, you're Fred's favourite subject." The sole topic of conversation when her son had finally phoned home in the middle of the night had been some wonderful blonde he had met. One who had ploughed him and an innocent Old English sheepdog into the Chayne Park boating lake. They had caught a brief glimpse of this fair-haired disaster area at the church under the circumstances of Fred's deliverance from the clutches of Melissa. From what she could see of Daisy, which was virtually everything, she could understand why she was all he had talked about, and judging from the glazed look on his face, so could Dad.

Dad gazed at his son with new eyes. "Are you two living together?"

Daisy looked startled, shooting a coy look at Fred. "We only met yesterday!" exclaimed Fred.

Prompted by a tap in the shin from Mother, Dad caught the look between his son and the dazzling creature and suddenly realised he and Mother were being serious gooseberries. "We just dropped by to see how you were getting on, Fred. I can see you're doing fine." He started steering Mother towards the door.

"Oh, please don't rush off on my account. I was just about to make elevenses," Daisy offered. "I made cakes. We could have a nice cup of tea and you could embarrass Fred by telling me all his little secrets."

Fred's mother decided she really liked this girl. Disclosing all of Fred's embarrassing little secrets was her favourite pastime.

The subject of all this potential embarrassment had quickly dug something out of the suitcase containing all of his clothes to salvage Daisy's modesty. He swept his best white shirt around her shoulders and steered her into the kitchenette.

"The kettle just needs topping up," chortled Daisy over her shoulder. "I'll just be a minute."

"Can I help, dear?" asked Mum.

"Oh no, that's quite all right. You're guests," smiled Daisy.

The kitchen door closed behind her. Fred's Mum leaned towards her son. "She's very pretty," she said pointedly.

Fred looked embarrassed. He had been on the receiving end of one of Mum's matchmaking drives before. "Mum!" he exclaimed.

"She's a vast improvement on that Melissa," Mum cooed. "Bring her round to tea and we can all get properly acquainted."

Fred's father stared after Daisy, completely captivated, until he was brought back into the conversation by a poke in the ribs from Mum. He leaned forwards to Fred confidentially. "She's a real cracker, that one."

Fred nodded. "I know."

The door of the kitchen opened again and Daisy entered with a tray laden with cucumber sandwiches, scones and pink fondant fancy cakes. "That looks delicious." Fred's Mum regarded the repast approvingly.

"I hope you like the little cakes," smiled Daisy anxiously. "New recipe." She self-consciously poured the tea.

"You cook as well!" Mum was impressed. "You'll make someone a wonderful wife." As she said this, she nudged Fred.

Both Fred and Daisy went bright red at this. Dad looked startled. "Snap!" he exclaimed.

-oOo-

Fred's Mum took the last of Fred's baby pictures out of the wallet she always carried with her and passed it to Daisy. "That one was taken on holiday in Blackpool. For some reason he didn't like riding on the donkeys."

"Awww." Daisy made cute noises and Fred ground his teeth. He and the donkeys had not seen eye to eye over the candy floss he had been eating; but then could any three year old win an argument with one of those fly-ridden braying machines? He was glad Boadicea and Britannia weren't present. They were the sort of girl who would hold pictures like those over his head for the rest of his life.

"Of course, we have hundreds more in the photograph album at home," his Mum mentioned conversationally.

"Really?" Daisy shot Fred a broad grin. "I'd love to see those."

"You'll have to come round to tea."

"Oh, you can count on that," Daisy assured her. She passed the wad of photos back.

-oOo-

Fred's face was getting longer and longer. His mother was giving Daisy the third degree, finding out everything she could about the girl. Daisy seemed quite happy about being vetted, as she was gleaning as much information about him as she was parting with about herself.

One fascinating fact he had discovered about Daisy was that she too had almost been married. It had happened when she studied for her honours degree in Astrology at UCLA. The mix-up had involved a packet of Earl Grey tea, a laundry bag of her underwear, her passport, a fellow student named Dwight and three-quarters of a ton of Oreo cookies. He was not sure how these ingredients had come together, but the outcome had been her deportation directly after receiving her diploma.

With every piece of information that Mum approved of, she telegraphed a look to Fred that seemed to scream out *marry this one* - but he had only known Daisy just over twenty-four hours. Popping the question at this stage in the relationship might be a little premature.

CHAPTER NINE:

In Which Fred Comes Into An Inheritance

And Finds Himself Owning An Old, Dark House.

A week had passed since Fred's unceremonious final departure from the school. *Cashiered* might have been a more accurate term. The Headmaster had taken a sadistic pleasure in breaking his sticks of chalk and ripping the buttons off his lab coat in front of the entire, assembled school. Fred had considered the letter of resignation had been of sufficient indignity, but the Headmaster had insisted. He knew his teaching career, what there was of it, was pretty much finished. He had half-heartedly sent out a few applications for teaching posts, but he knew full well that the Headmaster would have already got there first and blackened his name. He took a philosophical view of the whole business. He was tired of the mindless tedium, the strange and fussy rules and the bullying. There was little difference between being a teacher and a pupil, he had realised. He was free now to do whatever he felt like doing. What surprised him was the sense of relief that thought gave him. He had never wanted to be a teacher. He had always wanted to be a lumberjack. No. Seriously, he had always fancied a post at that very hush-hush Government Research place on Allfall Down. He had applied for jobs there on numerous occasions but had never got anywhere, which led him to suspect the malign hand of the Headmaster might be involved. Perhaps it was time for a change.

Fred had settled into a new routine he was more than happy with. The typical day started with Daisy dropping round to mooch what for her was the second breakfast of the morning. Poor Daisy. She still blamed herself for getting him the sack, and had been round every day to see how he was, in spite of his protestations that he was glad to be out of the job. Not that he did not look forwards to her visits. He felt as if a tornado had passed through afterwards, but it was a situation he had high hopes of becoming permanent.

Her suggestions as to his new career had been imaginative, to say the least. Each evening she had turned up with an armful of papers so that they could scan the jobs column together. Taxi Driver, Private Eye and Plumber's Mate had all been rejected, as had Civil Servant, Bartender and Solicitor's clerk and the advertisement for a "Stout Person Required To Dress As A Bumble Bee And Hand Out Publicity Material" at the local amusement arcade.

That morning, the pair were concentrating on a pile of toast and marmalade before Daisy's departure for work. Although there were compensations such as cooked meals having returned to the nest, Fred was finding living at home with his parents an exercise in style-cramping. His relationship with Daisy was still in the cannot-keep-their-hands-off-each-other phase, and for much of the time that was difficult in the presence of his parents. If he and Daisy wanted some hands-on-each-other time, they were forced to retreat to her flat, where they were equally restricted by the threat of the Ballcock Sisters popping up to break things up, or more alarmingly join in.

Dad returned from the front door carrying the morning's mail. He sorted through the pile quickly. "Junk, junk, junk, junk. Bill, junk, Radio Times. Fred." He paused and held out an official looking envelope to his son.

Fred licked marmalade off his fingers and took the missive. He borrowed Daisy's unused knife and slit the flap of the envelope. The letter inside was printed on an expensive bond, with a solicitor's heading. He quickly scanned through the contents.

"Bad news?" Mum craned her neck in the process of pouring Daisy another cup of tea.

"It's about Great Uncle Plum," Fred offered absent-mindedly, still in the process of analysing the contents. "It's from his solicitor's. If I drop by the offices, I may learn something to my advantage."

"That sounds promising," commented Dad. "Isn't that solicitor-speak for 'You've come into some money'?"

"Who's Great Uncle Plum?" piped up Daisy.

"He was Dad's Uncle," replied Fred. "Eldest brother of Grandad Longfield. Pelham Grenville Longfield."

"Ninety-five on his last birthday," Fred's Dad nodded. "If you looked up the term 'mad scientist' in the dictionary, there would be a picture of Uncle Plum next to it, bless him. And he was proud of it. He wasn't the easiest person in the world to get along with, so the family left him to his own devices. He'd always encouraged me when he was younger, and when Fred came along, he became the old boy's favourite Great-nephew."

"Not that that meant we were any more welcome to visit," grumbled Fred's Mum.

"When he thought I was old enough, he gave me his Meccano set," reminisced Fred.

"Meccano set?" echoed Daisy with a distinct *big*

deal! air.

"He'd been collecting it since he was five. Three-quarters of a ton of metal sheet, angles, nuts, bolts, gears, pulleys... You name it, it turned up neatly packed in boxes in a Transit van he sent round," continued Fred.

"We had to stack it in the garage, the loft, the spare room and the cupboard under the stairs," added Fred's Mum in slightly aggrieved tones.

Daisy still had her head cocked on one side, reading the letter from the solicitor over Fred's shoulder. "I'll drop you off in town on the way to work, if you like," she suggested.

"I'll make an appointment with Mr Crosby." Fred picked up the phone.

-oOo-

Fred sat in Mr Crosby's office on the ground floor of the law firm of Crosby, Drumble and Axemurder, Solicitors; looking very uncomfortable in spite of Daisy's presence in the adjacent chair for moral support. Mr Crosby was sitting behind a large mahogany desk that looked as if it might have once belonged to Ebenezer Scrooge, barely visible over the top. Hunched up in the ancient leather chair like a gargoyle on the corner of a cathedral spire, he was peering myopically at Uncle Plum's will. He was muttering to himself, an alien drone that was beginning to send Daisy to sleep. Every so often he would make them both jump by jerking upright as if waking suddenly. About the eighth time he did this, he fixed Fred with a bright, beady gaze. "Good news, Frederick, my boy," he quavered.

"Good news?" said Fred.

"What is?" asked Mr Crosby.

"The will," said Fred, getting confused.

"What will?" asked Mr Crosby, already confused. He looked down at the will on the desk in front of him and remembered. "Ah yes..." he said. He put on a pair of pince-nez and began to read. "'I, Pelham Grenville Longfield, being of ... blah blah blah ... leave the bulk of my estate to my favourite great-nephew Frederick Longfield. Favourite because he had the courtesy to stay away from me as much as humanly possible, and because he is the only member of my miserable family with sufficient intelligence to know what to do with my life's works. The residue of my estate I leave ...'" Mr Crosby looked up at Fred. "Well, just sums amounting to a few thousands of pounds to his servants and one or two other relatives, including your father."

Mr Crosby picked up another sheet of paper. "The estate consists of your Great-Uncle's house at Grisley End and its contents, and the income from some eighty-six international patents."

Daisy gripped Fred's hand in excitement.

"Unfortunately," Mr Crosby injected a tone of caution, "your Great-Uncle's liquid assets have been practically wiped out by taxes owed, outstanding bills and the other bequests made."

Daisy squeezed Fred's hand for reassurance.

"I'm also sorry to say the property at Grisley End is in serious need of remedial building work and redecoration before it could possibly be placed on the market." Mr

107

Crosby took off his pince-nez. "Not without considerable investment."

Daisy patted Fred's hand in consolation.

"On the bright side, the royalties earned by Professor Longfield's international patents are paid into his bank account in the first and third quarters of the year," Mr Crosby continued. "While only a nominal amount remains from the first quarter, the September balance should be in the region of..." He checked his paperwork again. "Approximately one-and-three quarter million pounds."

Daisy gave a squeak and accidentally dug her fingernails into Fred's palm.

Fred opened his mouth to say something, but nothing came out.

Mr Crosby took a bunch of keys out of the envelope that had contained the will and handed them across the desk to Fred. "These are the keys to the house," he said. "Once again, my heartfelt condolences." He rose rheumatically from the chair and offered his hand to Fred.

Fred shook Mr Crosby's hand, his own already shaking adequately. He stood up with the unsteady air of someone recently smacked in the gob.

-oOo-

"Here we are!" Fred made the turn, passing through a rusty gateway that someone had spray-painted with the name "Castle Frankenstein". They had been negotiating the country lanes beyond Nether Fondling for what seemed like hours, making turn after turn. Daisy had picked up the keys Fred had been given at the solicitor's, and she was twirling the ring on the end of her finger idly.

The drive wound tortuously up the hill the old house was perched upon, the gravel drive shrouded much of the time in a murky tunnel of overhanging trees. The first sight of the house was made on finally emerging from the trees, looming over them menacingly like something out of an old horror movie. If it wasn't already creepy enough in itself, behind it squatted the ruins of a medieval watch tower of the variety latterly used by mad scientists for the purposes of reanimating corpses.

Fred pulled up on the gravel forecourt at the top of the drive, close to the stone portico that sheltered the entrance. They had started out late and it was getting dark. The house and its surrounding sinister forest made the evening even gloomier and he wondered how they might negotiate the dark country lanes on the way home.

The house was ancient and untended, in serious need of renovation. Ivy grew unchecked all over the front and what was left untouched by the ivy looked as though it might fall down at the first opportunity. The windows were dark, covered by heavy drapes, and the house had an eerie, desolate air. As darkness was falling, the house seemed to get creepier by the minute. Fred realised he had a tune playing over and over in his head. He identified it as the title music from the TV show *"The Addams Family"*.

Fred stepped out of the car and gazed up at the imposing façade. "It's... erm... creepier than I remember," he said in a small voice. "I've visited with Dad on a few occasions, but it's been years since I was here last, and I think if anything, the place has got spookier."

"Spookier?" Daisy gazed up at the house with the expression of a dazzling blonde in a haunted house story

109

about to enter the aforementioned haunted house. "I'm not very good at spooky," she admitted. "And I reckon your average spook would find this place too spooky."

Fred was of that breed of scientist who viewed the supernatural with healthy scepticism. "The sooner we get these papers together, the sooner we can be out of here."

Daisy nodded. She was sure she had seen a house just like it in a number of old horror movies starring Peter Cushing and Christopher Lee. If they found the ghost of Vincent Price in residence, she would not have been remotely surprised.

Fred sorted through the set of keys for the front door key as they approached the stone arched portico of the property. The entrance to the house was made through double, oak doors half as tall again as a man. Fred looked for the lock, frowning to himself when he could not find one.

"Try the doorbell," suggested Daisy. She pressed the doorbell for him. Nothing happened. She looked at Fred, who simply shrugged. He knocked on the door. They looked at each other nervously as the doors swung open seemingly of their own volition, a deep, rusty creaking emanating from the hinges. They peered into the dark interior of the house and stepped cautiously over the threshold. "Hello?" Fred called into the darkness.

"Good Evening, Sir," said a sepulchral voice at his shoulder.

Later that day, Fred was able to marvel at the sideways kangaroo leap he had made. At that moment, however, he was busy having what felt like a coronary. *I do believe in spooks. I do believe in spooks. I do I do I do I do believe in spooks...* Daisy self-consciously climbed down out of his arms and tugged her short skirt straight.

"You'll have to excuse the lack of illumination." The owner of the voice produced a lighter and proceeded to light the candles in a candelabra on the hall table. "The mains electricity is on the blink." As the candles were lit, the figure in front of them was revealed in more and more detail. An ill-fitting tailcoat stretched across broad but hunched shoulders. The sleeves of both the tailcoat and the white shirt beneath were too short, exposing hairy forearms and slender, spider-like fingers. The skull-like rear aspect of the head was surrounded by a halo of backlit wisps of white hair. Picking up the candelabra, the figure turned and in spite of himself, Fred drew back apprehensively. Daisy peeked nervously out from behind him.

From the front there was little improvement. The tailcoat was spattered with splashes of wax from the house's primary source of illumination and heavily mildewed. The face that leered unnervingly up at them would not have looked out of place on the parapet of the cathedral of Notre Dame. A hooked nose, grizzled chin; deep-set, piercingly blue eyes and a cavalier attitude to dental hygiene. The head was carried at an odd angle.

"Master Frederick?" enquired the cadaverous figure that stood before them.

"That's right." Fred pulled himself together with an effort – at least fifty percent of the atoms in his body had been running at full tilt back down the driveway. "This is Ms. Chayne. She'll be helping me sort out Great Uncle Plum's papers."

The figure bobbed perfunctorily. "I am Rummidge, the late Professor Longfield's personal valet and butler." He looked up at Fred and Daisy expectantly. "Do you wish to look around the house, Sir?" Rummidge bobbed again. Daisy was too polite to say anything, but she was certain that the creaking noise was coming from the butler every time he bowed, rather than the front doors behind them. She gripped Fred's arm nervously in case he wandered too far away.

"The late master partially rewired the house to aid the power requirements for his experiments," Rummidge growled apologetically. "Ever since, we have experienced a little trouble with the fuses. Fortunately, they only seem to fail five or six times a day nowadays. This way." Behind them, with a creak like a dungeon door closing, the front door swung closed cutting off the last vestiges of natural daylight.

Fred and Daisy followed the butler nervously as the flickering light of the bobbing candelabra ahead of them picked out details of the main hall. Nightmarish shadows that danced through the cavernous space and up the grand staircase that led away into the gloom. A boar's head mounted on a plaque, a portrait of a sad-looking woman in Regency costume. A suit of armour shrouded in the life's work of generations of spiders. The walls were covered in vast oak panels of the type that usually slides aside to reveal a dark, dank passage and lurking nutcase with an axe. The light from the candles fell across a doorway. A set of double doors with polished brass handles.

"We could always come back in the morning," suggested Daisy in querulous tones.

"Pardon, Miss?" Rummidge turned, tilting his head stiffly. "You'll have to excuse me. I have trouble turning my head."

"Oh, you poor thing." Daisy made sympathetic noises. She had suffered from a terribly stiff neck after falling asleep at the Manor in a draught. "Have you tried an ointment like *Fiery Jack*?"

"Alas, Miss, my neck would require more than *Fiery Jack* to put it to rights." Rummidge reached a set of double doors at the end of the passage and opened them with a flourish. The room beyond was completely dark. "You see, I had the misfortune to break it."

"Oh my goodness," gasped Daisy. "You poor thing."

"I fell through a trapdoor, Miss." Rummidge ushered them through the doorway.

"Oh, that's simply awful." Daisy made sympathetic noises. Before she could stop herself, she heard herself ask: "How did that happen?"

"They were hanging me, Miss," said Rummidge with relish. He offered her a smile which would terrify small children and animals.

CHAPTER TEN:

Fred and Daisy Explore the Old House

And Fred Makes A Scientific Discovery

"The Library." Rummidge held his candelabra aloft like the Statue of Liberty illumining the New World. The room beyond smelled well-thumbed. It was pervaded by the musty, damp and dusty odour of ancient tomes, of yellowing paper falling victim to marauding bookworms. The walls were lined from floor to ceiling with hundreds, if not thousands of weighty volumes. A spiral staircase of polished oak in the corner of the cavernous room gave access to a mezzanine level which ran round the three internal walls. Beneath the mezzanine, a set of steps could be moved along a rail to retrieve texts that were out of reach. The shelves and the books were thick with dust, as were the two reading tables, the large Chesterfield settee by the fireplace and the two matching armchairs that flanked it. The reading tables, the chairs and settee and much of the floor were littered with large, ancient volumes that the old man had taken down for reference but had never returned to their rightful places. Where there were gaps on the shelves, neighbouring books had collapsed sideways so that whole rows of books leaned to one side or the other like tumbled dominoes. One or two particularly impressive tomes lay open on one of the reading tables. Fred craned his neck to read the text of the uppermost work. The immaculate script was in Latin, but he could make out enough to realise that it was a work on alchemy, of sufficient rarity that the curators of many libraries would have sold close members of their families into slavery to have such a book on their shelves. He moved around the room carefully, trying to keep dust and cobwebs off his jacket.

Rummidge leered evilly at them. "Will that be all, Sir?" he asked. Daisy regarded the butler with wide eyes. "Excuse me, Miss." Rummidge blew out the candles again.

Fred hastily relit the candles and looked around. The butler had vanished. "This place gets creepier by the minute," Daisy shuddered. "He gives me the heebie-Jeevesies."

As they turned to leave, something caught Fred's eye. "Good God!" he exclaimed in horror.

"What is it?" Daisy peeped round him apprehensively. She followed his gaze and found what had caused his outburst. Against one wall of the dining room was a monstrous clock. Hideous hardly described it. It filled the room with a steady tick that sounded like water dripping in a crypt. It was a carefully carved model of the façade of the Cathedral de Notre Dame in Paris, complete with gargoyles. The face of the clock displayed not only the time, but the date, sign of the zodiac, depth of water at high tide, the phase of the moon and a myriad other useless functions. Suddenly it gave a loud whirring noise as it prepared to strike the hour. The doors at the foot of the cathedral opened and a tiny, carved figure of a hunchback dropped into sight on the end of a tiny rope. As the hunchback reached the bottom of its descent, the clock chimed, a deep, sonorous death knell. The hunchback was hauled swiftly out of sight, then it dropped again with the next chime as if it were pulling the bell rope. Fred watched the proceedings with amazement and leaned against the wall. He vanished from sight as the panel in the wall opened and he fell through.

Daisy cautiously descended the stone steps and illuminating his fallen form with her candle, gazed down solicitously at Fred. "Are you all right?"

"Just about." Fred slowly and painfully picked himself up from the bottom step, rubbing his head and making a quick inventory of how many suspected broken bones he had acquired in his descent.

Daisy held up the candlestick to shed a little light on the scene. "Where are we?" she asked. The passage they were standing in was dark and dank. Generations of spiders had spent lifetimes decorating the place. The walls and ceiling were thick with cobwebs. Somewhere up the passage, they could hear water dripping, a steady splashing noise.

"Coal cellar?" hazarded Fred.

Daisy peered at a door in the passage wall. "*La...*" She wiped a layer of grime away from a small brass plaque with her fingers. "*...boratory.*"

"Pardon?" Fred's expression was that of a startled owl.

"That's what it says on the door," shrugged Daisy.

"This must be where Great Uncle Plum did all his inventing," ventured Fred. He looked embarrassed as Daisy gave him a stating-the-obvious look. "Shall we go in?" Scientific curiosity had overcome his initial nervousness. This was one room he wanted to investigate.

"I'm not sure I like it down here," Daisy opined

nervously. "It's spooky."

"No spookier than upstairs." Fred pushed the door open. Daisy gripped his arm nervously as the door hinges creaked loudly. Fred peered into the darkness. "Can you see anything?"

"Not a lot," Daisy peered into the shadows. "Except for the big, nasty-looking switch on the wall."

"Switch it on," suggested Fred.

"Do I have to?" asked Daisy. "It looks like it might be attached to a chair." She grasped the handle of the switch and pulled it down with an impressive spray of blue sparks. A single, bare, 60 watt light bulb came on in the middle of the room.

The room was decorated in early Mad Scientist. Strange electrical contraptions lined the walls while a large bench in the centre of the room supported the jumble of glassware of a complex chemical experiment. Daisy watched Fred indulgently as he wandered round the laboratory with a nostalgic smile on his face. "Do you think Doctor Frankenstein is missing any of his laboratory equipment?" she asked. She walked around the large bench in the centre of the room, examining the complex plumbing of the old man's last-and-greatest experiment. A pile of dusty, dog-eared papers covered in a wandering, spidery script caught her eye. "What's this?" she asked.

Fred looked up. "What's what?" he asked. Daisy held up the top sheet for him to see. He narrowed his eyes, peering at the hieroglyphics. "They must be Uncle's notes."

"Do you want to have a look?" Daisy picked up the

sheaf of notes and hopped back in alarm as she uncovered something hairy. *"Wah-hah!!"*

Fred craned his neck, peering at the object. "Oh, that's just Chester, Uncle's toupee."

"He named his toupee?" Daisy prodded the object with an apprehensive finger. Centre parting. Uncompromisingly ginger. Once she was satisfied it was not a demonic familiar or zombie guinea-pig, she climbed down again from the laboratory stool she had mounted.

"He rarely actually wore it," Fred commented. "Nobody in the family is a redhead, but I think he just took a liking to it in the shop. He'd put it on his bedroom dressing table with a saucer of milk."

"I don't like this place," muttered Daisy.

"I don't know," Fred shrugged cheerfully. "It's rather cosy really." The laboratory brought back memories of long afternoons in the science lab at the school, when he and Charlie would endeavour to blow the place to smithereens as part of the never-ending quest to expand the frontiers of human knowledge. He sat down on a stool and swept some of the debris covering the table on to the floor to clear a space to put down the sheaf of notes. He fell silent as he started to read the notes and Daisy looked around the room for some fresh distraction.

A beaker stood on one of the side benches, with a rack of test tubes beside it. She leant over to examine the test tubes closer. They were full of prettily coloured chemicals, and on a whim, she poured the particularly fetching turquoise solution in the third test tube into the beaker. Another test tube contained a red suspension and she cocked her head on one side, wondering what the two colours would look like mixed together. She shrugged and poured the red stuff into the beaker. She was startled to see the contents turn a bright, canary yellow and start to expand up the sides of the beaker. A squeak escaped her lips as the garishly coloured foam flowed over the top of the beaker and crept across the bench top like a fungus. She retreated apprehensively until her back was pressed against the benches by the wall.

A chuckle from Fred distracted her. Keeping a nervous eye on the sinister ooze that was starting to drip over the edge of the bench on to the floor, she sidled over to Fred for protection. "What's tickling you?" she asked.

"It's rather sad, really," replied Fred. "There's a formula here for turning just about any other element into gold."

Daisy's eyebrows shot up.

"I would never have thought Uncle Plum was the type to try alchemy," continued Fred. "He must have been really mixed up towards the end." He sighed sadly. "It's funny though. His inventions always tended to be a little on the eccentric side, but there was a time he was considered one of the leading authorities in his field." He cast a wistful gaze around the laboratory.

Daisy held out a laboratory smock, an indulgent look on her face.

"What?"

"You know you want to." Daisy cajoled.

Fred draped his jacket over a lab stool and pulled on the white coat with the air of a super hero revealing his emblem. He regarded the bottles of chemicals he had gathered from the shelves of the adjoining storeroom and the items of laboratory glassware that would complete the complex distillation and catalysation experiment described in the notes. Much of the epic construction had already been completed by the old scientist before his passing, and the remaining components boxed away in the storeroom in anticipation. The task was not going to be quite as daunting as he had first thought. He rubbed his hands together eagerly, ready to set to work. "Let's give it a go, then."

Daisy perched on a neighbouring stool and watched as Fred started to work with the air of a mad scientist about to split the atom or reanimate a corpse.

-oOo-

Re-constructing the apparatus described in Uncle Plum's notes took Fred back to his childhood and epic fabrications in Meccano. His father and Great Uncle were keen Meccanoists, and wet weekends at the Longfield residence had frequently been occupied building scale replicas of cranes, bridges and one memorable time Blackpool Tower, complete with working lifts. The experiment was the most complex assemblage Fred had ever put together in his career as a chemistry teacher and took up nearly half of the cavernous dungeon-basement of the old house. Literal miles of glass tubing, burettes, retorts and reaction vessels snaked around the room in a process that involved a hundred or more chemical reactions, distillations, fermentations and catalysations. Ultimately this led to a centrifugal twelve-stage master process that would theoretically turn lead or any other substance into gold.

The old man's chicken-scrawl handwriting was difficult to decipher, and Fred only hoped he would not blow them all up by misreading them. Carefully, he poured the hundred-and-third noxious substance he had mixed that morning - a green, mucilaginous jollop - into the uppermost reservoir of the apparatus. The smelly, yellow, oily stuff he had mixed first thing had come to the boil and had already percolated down through the apparatus. It was about to start dripping into the red stuff that Daisy had commented she would like a pair of shorts in that exact shade. He turned the tap to let the yellow stuff start mixing with the red stuff and sat back, looking around the laboratory thoughtfully. At the other side of the table, Daisy was sitting on a stool, watching him with wide-eyed intensity, munching an apple she had acquired from the kitchen. Noticing his pensive expression she asked, "What's the matter, Fred?"

"I need something to try out the formula on," he replied.

"Don't look at me," Daisy cautioned.

"You wouldn't fit in the reaction vessel." Fred had already thought of that.

"What kind of something are you after?" Daisy craned her neck with a thoughtful expression.

"It needs to be small enough to fit in here." Fred tapped the side of the beaker.

Daisy considered donating her apple to science, but then decided her need was greater. Her eyes alighted on Uncle Plum's discarded toupee. "How about this?" She picked it up gingerly between finger and thumb.

Fred gazed at the object somewhat nonplussed. "I... um... I suppose so." He took it from her with the forceps and dropped it into the first of the twelve reaction beakers, the one full of boiling, distilled water that the red and green mixtures would shortly start dripping into. It bubbled as it sank. He attached the heavy, high-tension leads to the electrodes that stuck out of the vessel like antennae. He sat back, rubbing the back of his neck. "We're all ready to go. Where are you going?"

Daisy paused guiltily on the way to the door of the laboratory. "Making myself scarce?" she replied.

"I need you on the big switch." Fred indicated the scary-looking power switch on the main electrical control panel, a large, dangerous-looking metal box covered in a mystifying array of dials and switches. He watched Daisy's reluctant progress across the laboratory and when she arrived at the panel, pulled on a pair of heavy gloves and a welder's-style visor. "Ready on the power?"

Daisy donned a pair of heavy, insulated gloves of her own. "Ready," she responded.

"We'll start at 40,000 volts." Fred turned on the tiny taps of the red and green mixtures, the two halves of the first catalyst. The chemicals started to drip into the first reaction beaker and the water turned an alarming shade of puce. Fred started the next chemical reaction in the process and signalled to Daisy. "*Power on!*"

Daisy set the rheostat on the panel to the required voltage, took a deep breath and threw the switch on. Fred took a step back in alarm as the apparatus on the bench gave a shudder and sparks flew out from the electrode connections. He watched as electricity arced across the reaction beaker. A shower of sparks from the ceiling.

"Power off!"

Daisy snapped off the power and Fred darted forward with the forceps. He plucked the now-smoking toupee out of the first reaction vessel and dropped it into the second where it made the burgundy-coloured potion froth and smoke alarmingly. Then into the third reaction vessel, another one with heavy high-tension leads attached. *"Power on!"*

Daisy obediently applied the current, flinching at a series of alarming pops from the experiment. She watched Fred with a mounting feeling of pride as he darted backwards and forwards between the experiment and safe cover, shouting for the power to be either switched on or off.

"Daze! Take it all the way up to full power!" Fred had to shout over the crackle of electricity.

"No, not full power!" cried Daisy.

Fred turned to look at her. "Why ever not?"

Daisy shrugged sheepishly, a nervous smile twitching her mouth. "I don't know," she admitted. "I thought you're supposed to say something like that at a time like this."

Fred gave her a sideways sort of look. "Full power," he reiterated. Daisy turned up the voltage. Smoke began to pour from the final reaction vessel. "Careful," shouted Fred. "Take the voltage up slowly, or you'll blow us all up!"

"Blow us all up??" yelped Daisy apprehensively.

Fred was peering into the fierce glow from the twelfth reaction vessel, narrowing his eyes against the glare. *"Cut the power!"* he shouted. When the power was not immediately snapped off, he looked across to the control panel, where Daisy was supposed to be standing. Hinging back his visor, he could see that Daisy had vanished. He dived across the room and yanked down the big switch on the front of the apparatus and the readings on the dials sank to zero. The bright, flickering lights and the loud crackling noise subsided. Fred hinged down his protective facemask again to peer cautiously at the steaming beaker at the far end of the complex experiment on the table. His eyes widened at what he saw and he snatched up his trusty pair of forceps. With trembling, gloved fingers, he detached the electrodes from the beaker and reached into the still bubbling fluid with the forceps. He lifted Uncle Plum's matted toupee out of the fluid and allowed the excess fluid to drain back into the beaker before dunking the toupee into a beaker of clean, distilled water to rinse it. The metallic glint from the filaments of the wig was unmistakable.

Daisy peeped round the door of the laboratory nervously. "What happened?" Daisy approached the experiment as if she expected it to explode noisily at any moment.

"It certainly looks like gold," Fred pondered thoughtfully, peering at the wire-wool-like object between the jaws of the forceps.

Daisy peered round him at Uncle Plum's now blond wig. "If it has turned to gold, then one thing is for certain," Daisy took the forceps from Fred and stared at the object.

"What's that?" asked Fred.

"This thing is definitely a hairloom now."

This observation received the stony silence it richly deserved. "I'll have to make a few tests first, just to make sure," cautioned Fred. "But offhand, it looks to me as if Great Uncle Plum's formula really does work!"

Daisy gazed at the golden wig. "You'll be richer than the dreams of that Rice woman, Ava!"

Fred sat down on one of the lab stools, looking as if the rug and the floor under it had been pulled from under him. "I need a drink."

-oOo-

CHAPTER ELEVEN:

In Which Fred Comes To His Conclusions and

Daisy Makes A Toast

The hideous Gothic clock in the Library read eleven o'clock when they emerged from the secret panel. Fred regarded Daisy sheepishly. "I... er... I hadn't realised how late it was," he apologised. "We'd better be making tracks."

Rummidge appeared at his side, making them both jump again. "Am I to understand that you do not wish to stay for the night, Sir?"

"Well, we weren't going to." Daisy's expression made it obvious that had been the last thing on her mind.

"I can assure you that it would be wiser to stay for the night, Miss." Rummidge intoned. "The roads hereabout have no lighting and can be more than a little treacherous after dark unless one is familiar with them. I can have the guest rooms ready in a trice, Sir." This last was an aside to Fred. Without waiting for a reply, the butler melted into the shadows as the lights flickered once more. Fred had the distinct impression that the butler had left the room without passing through any door.

Daisy was troubled. She ruminated on the problem briefly and put a finger on exactly what was amiss. "I'm starving." She looked at her watch. "It's way past my suppertime." She turned to ring for Rummidge and nearly jumped out of her skin again when she found herself face to face with the ancient retainer. He was covered in more cobwebs than normal and seemed as startled as her. "Oh! Ah! Mr Rummidge!" Daisy squeaked.

"Yes, Miss?"

"Would there be any chance of some supper, Mr Rummidge?" Daisy regarded the sinister figure hopefully, although neither she or Fred were enthusiastic at the thought of eating anything prepared the butler's fair hands.

"Alas, Miss, the cupboards are bare." Rummidge was apologetic. "The housekeeper resigned from her duties a few weeks before the Professor's passing in a disagreement over remuneration. At a pinch, my culinary expertise is limited to beans on toast."

"That's quite all right, Mr Rummidge," smiled Daisy. "It's lucky we stopped off on the way over to do some of my shopping." One of the reasons for their late arrival had been her insistence on a detour to the hypermarket to replenish her larder. Taking charge of the situation, "Where's the kitchen?" Daisy breezed.

-oOo-

Fred descended the steps from the hidden panel to the laboratory once more, navigating with the aid of the battery torch he had recovered from the glove compartment of the car. Daisy had taken charge of making supper, with the shanghaied assistance of the cadaverous retainer. He had left the experiment in the laboratory deactivated, but he still had to make certain elements completely *safe*, just in case the house blew up in the middle of the night. Quite apart from the fuses having blown in the laboratory once more, circuit-breakers had still to be tripped and the cables attached to the experiment stowed properly to make things secure. Working quickly, he isolated the control panel

127

power supply and started spooling the high-tension leads back from the experiment. He still had to neutralise some of the more dangerous formulae, a chore that back at the school he would have left to his best pal Charlie.

It took Fred the best part of half-an-hour to put the experiment completely to bed, and he shone the torch around the laboratory one last time to make sure he had not forgotten anything. He started violently and swung the torch back as the beam briefly illuminated something at the back of the room. He could have sworn it was a face, but in the split-second whatever he had seen had disappeared. He could feel the hairs at the back of his neck rising. Daisy was quite right, the old house was just *too* spooky.

Fred closed and locked the door of the laboratory and froze at a distant clatter from somewhere deep in the house. He knew the source was almost certainly Daisy, but his nerves were on edge. He ascended the steps back to the library. He tripped the hidden catch at the top of the stairs and the wooden panel swung out of the way with an unsettling creak. He stepped through into the lib—

"Hullo." Fred stopped in his tracks as he discovered he was not standing in the library. The room he had emerged into was cold and dark, and had not been on his earlier exploration of the house with Daisy. He shone the torch around, putting a hand behind himself to push the secret panel open again. Somehow, he must have made a wrong turn on the steps, although he was almost certain the run from the library to the laboratory was a straight line. The panel behind him refused to budge. He put his shoulder to it but resolutely nothing happened, apart from him getting cobwebs on his sleeve.

The room was, like much of the ground floor of the house, long disused. Like the library and the dining room, generations of spiders had busied themselves spinning webs - or possibly a single web of epic proportions - like the things were going out of style. The sparse furnishings consisted of a couple of wing-backed leather armchairs, a chaise-longue and at the far end of the room a grand piano. More creepy-looking portraits hung on the wall and Fred began to feel genuinely unsettled returning the gaze of his long-departed forebears. The beam of the torch fell across a doorway beyond the grand piano and Fred crossed the room to investigate.

As he passed the piano, there was a musical rustling noise that almost had him bolting from the room. Tremulously, he pointed the torch at the piano, disturbing a small brown mouse out for its evening constitutional across the strings. He stared at the mouse, and the mouse stared back at him. Then it darted away across the inner workings of the piano making a noise that would have graced the score of any Alfred Hitchcock movie. The sooner he found Daisy, the happier he would be, thought Fred. He would even settle for just finding Rummidge, and that made him realise just how spooked the house was making him. Leaving the musical rodent to its own devices, he moved through the doorway and was able to reestablish his bearings.

The entrance hall was, at least, familiar territory. He headed over to the doorway of the library and threw the door open, expecting to be greeted by at least one friendly face. The room beyond was dark and deserted, lit only by the crackling fire in the grate, and flaxen-headed inhabitant was conspicuous by her absence. "Okay, not good," Fred muttered to himself. This was not a state of affairs he was happy with. "Everybody's in the kitchen," he reasoned with himself. Now, where *was* the kitchen?

He shone the torch up the dark passageway that led out of the entrance hall at the side of the grand staircase. If the creepy butler loomed out of the darkness, he told himself, he would hit the ground running. Squaring his shoulders, he started into the bowels of the old house.

Within a matter of moments, he wished he had stayed where he was. The powerful beam of the torch had yellowed and was dimming at an alarming rate. He had put fresh batteries in the damn thing only a couple of days ago. He turned the beam on himself and slapped the battery compartment in the hopes of encouraging the torch to rally.

The beam flared full in his face, then went out completely.

Swearing under his breath, Fred took a step forwards. His eyes needed time to acclimatise to the darkness, having been dazzled by the beam of the torch. He missed his footing and fell.

Daisy looked up from the mixing bowl as Fred tumbled through the kitchen door. "...Add three eggs and whisk. Hiya, Fred," she grinned. "Care to give me a hand?"

Completely nonplussed, Fred picked himself up from the distinctly sticky floor. "What are you doing?"

Daisy looked around the kitchen as if it were a silly question. There were splashes of egg, flour and tomato ketchup on the walls. The sink was beginning to overflow, heavily laden as it was with bowls and utensils that needed washing up. The door of one of the cupboards hung at a drunken angle, one hinge broken, and there were black scorch marks on the wall behind the cooker. A bottle of Curaçao stood precariously at the edge of the work surface where Daisy was standing, and as Fred approached, he could see a pool of milk spreading across the floor from the foot of the refrigerator. "We're making the supper," she explained.

Fred rescued the bottle of Curaçao from its suicidal perch and put it on top of the refrigerator. "What happened?" He looked around the room in disbelief. The kitchen bore a striking resemblance to Passchendaele.

"Mr Rummidge has been helping me." Daisy waved a dismissive hand.

"That explains a lot." Fred opened the refrigerator door and an egg rolled out and smashed on his foot.

Daisy put what she had been preparing in the oven and set the controls. "There. It'll be ready in half-an-hour."

"What are you cooking?"

"That's for me to know..." Daisy tapped the side of her nose secretively.

-oOo-

Fred was amazed. Daisy's idea of supper could easily have sustained a small army intent on invasion. The kitchen might have looked as if a bomb had hit it, but the results more than made up for it. Never one to do anything by halves, she had provided them with a three-course repast that more than made up for the evening's missed dinner. An ample sufficiency later and she and Fred returned to the library for a small digestif before bed.

Daisy craned her neck. "You look like you have something on your mind," she observed playfully.

Fred pointed to the sheaf of notes in his hand. "I've gone over the figures, double-checked the formulae, and triple-checked the theory," he ventured. "There's only one conclusion I can come to."

"Do tell!" Daisy perched on the edge of her seat.

"Men of learning have been searching for the Philosopher's Stone since Biblical times," Fred started, building up his moment. "In 1471, Ripley wrote a treatise *The Compound of Alchemie* which described twelve stages of transmutation: Calcination; Dissolution; Separation; Conjunction; Putrefaction; Congelation; Cibation; Sublimation; Fermentation; Exaltation; Multiplication and Projection..." He realised he was losing his audience as Daisy's eyes were glazing over. "Legend has it that Noah used the Stone as illumination aboard the Ark." When it was obvious that little gem failed to impress his one-woman audience, he let out a small breath of defeat. "As far as I can figure it, from any element or substance, Uncle Plum's formula can transmutate every last atom of an object into one hundred percent pure, twenty-four carat gold."

"I could have told you that ages ago," chirped Daisy gleefully.

"Ah, but now it's been scientifically verified," said Fred, not wanting his thunder stolen.

"Well, either way, it's a matter to celebrate," Daisy opined brightly. She pulled the bell rope to summon

Rummidge, who came in immediately as if he had been lurking outside the door.

"You rang, Miss?"

"That was quick." Fred looked startled.

"I jog regularly, Sir," Rummidge replied, deadpan. "Do you require anything, Miss?"

"Oh yes." Daisy remembered why she had called Rummidge. "Drinks all round, Mr Rummidge. The finest champagne in the house!"

"Very good, Miss," Rummidge bobbed, caught up in her enthusiasm. "Is there something to celebrate?"

"Something," acknowledged Fred.

"Very good, Sir," leered the butler. He loped out of the room with the gait of a lowland gorilla in a tailcoat.

Fred and Daisy fell silent as Rummidge returned a matter of moments later with an ice bucket, glasses and a bottle of what Daisy identified as a very fine champagne. "Might I ask what the occasion is that we are celebrating, Miss?" Rummidge set up the glasses and the ice bucket on the small table beside Daisy's chair.

Daisy patted Fred on the back. "Mr Longfield here has made a rather interesting discovery," she said.

"That's nice, Miss. Might I ask what kind of discovery?"

"Ah, that would be telling." Fred tapped his nose secretively.

"Very good, Sir." Rummidge feigned indifference, popping the cork and pouring out the champagne. Once he had filled the glasses, he exited in his customary style when the lights flickered momentarily.

"Here's to your Great Uncle Plum." Daisy raised her glass to Fred's, "and his Midas formula!"

Outside the drawing room door, Rummidge's blank expression dissolved into a confused mix of panic and incredulity. The Midas Formula?? Generations of mad old Longfield scientists had obsessed about turning base elements into gold almost as long as he had worked at Grisley End. Could these idiots have succeeded where previous Professors had failed so spectacularly over the years?

-oOo-

CHAPTER TWELVE:

In Which Fred Spends The Night In Cold Water

And Daisy Goes For A Midnight Snack

Fred followed Daisy up the stairs, following the candle she was holding high to illumine her way. The soft, flickering light of the candle caught her hair and made a honey-gold halo around her head. Their explorations had not extended as far as the upper floors, and Fred was relieved to see that upstairs was distinctly more welcoming than downstairs. Ahead of her, Rummidge led the way, illuminating their path with the light of a large, six-candle candelabra of the variety favoured by Liberace.

A hallway led off the landing at the top of the stairs. "I've taken the liberty of putting you in the 'Green Lady' room, Miss," rumbled Rummidge, opening an anonymous door in the oak panelling of the passageway. The door creaked like the lid of a coffin.

"Green Lady?" squeaked an apprehensive Daisy, blue eyes like saucers.

"A previous occupant of the room, and its resident spectre who just happens to be that colour." Rummidge led the way into the room. He had previously been upstairs to make the bed up and light a fire in the grate, so the fire was casting dancing shadows on the walls, illumining a huge four poster bed. He lit the bedside candle from his candelabra. "The Green Lady's identity has been lost in the mists of time, Miss. She was the wife of just twelve hours of Sir Simon De Longuechamps, the first Earl of Chortlesford. She was found strangled in the morning after their wedding night, and Sir Simon reduced to a gibbering madman who had to be bricked up in a cell down in the dungeons of the original castle." Rummidge lit another candle on the mantelpiece. "They both roam the house in search of each other. Legend has it that whenever they meet, there is a death in the house."

"Dud-death??" squeaked Daisy.

Rummidge glided in and out of the adjoining dressing room, picking up a candy-striped bundle of linen in the process. "Some nightwear, Miss," he growled with some relish, handing her the bundle. "The late master preferred nightshirts to pyjamas. Something about air circulation."

"Thank you," Daisy was verging on going hypersonic in tone. Soon only dogs would be able to hear her.

"The… ah… facilities are at the end of the passage, should you require them, Miss." Rummidge offered Daisy a small bow. "Pleasant dreams, Miss."

"Are you kidding?" Daisy squeaked.

Rummidge ushered Fred out of the room. "This way, Sir." Daisy cast a quick glance around the room, gave a little squeak of alarm and hurried after them.

"This is the 'Headley Sauceman' room, Sir." Rummidge opened the door across the hallway to the Green Lady room and raised an eloquent eyebrow as he noticed Daisy was clasped like a mustard plaster to Fred's arm.

"Headless Horseman?""

"*Headley Sauceman,* Sir. Sauté chef to the Court of King Charles I. The King wouldn't touch a meal that didn't include one of Headley's sauces. Sauceman's devotion to the King was so great that he paid the ultimate price. He was beheaded at Cromwell's order the day after the King. He roams the passages of the East Wing with his head under his arm, in eternal search of his lost peppercorns, moaning at his misfortunes."

"Cosy," nodded Fred.

"If that's all, Sir, I'll bid you a good night." He bowed and handed Fred the candelabra.

"Good night, Mr Rummidge," Daisy responded, but as usual, the spooky-looking retainer had done his habitual disappearing act.

They both fell into a slightly awkward silence. It was broken by the female of the species. "I've had a very interesting day, and a pleasant evening, Fred," smiled Daisy. She gave him a light peck on the cheek. "Thank you."

Fred smiled bashfully. "Shall I see you back to your room?" he offered.

"No rush," Daisy replied, a little quicker than she would have liked to.

"Is something the matter?" asked Fred.

"I have absolutely no desire whatsoever to go back into that room," Daisy stated flatly. "Not no way, not no how."

"Okay," Fred nodded. "We'll stay here. You take the bed. I'll take the settee."

Daisy was touched by Fred's show of old-fashioned chivalry. "Fred," she tutted.

"Don't tell me, *you'll* take the settee and I can take the bed."

"No, I was thinking we'll both take the bed and the settee can sort out its own sleeping arrangements." Daisy replied, throwing her arms around his neck and kissing him passionately. She kicked the door closed with her heel.

-oOo-

Daisy had withdrawn into the adjoining dressing room to change. Rummidge had supplied her with a long, candy-striped nightshirt, explaining the late master's preference for such night-attire over pyjamas. It reached the floor in true Wee Willie Winkie style, a shapeless garment that hung around her slim form like a shroud. She had found a pair of bed socks in one of the drawers in the dressing room, and they were saving her toes from freezing.

In the bedroom, Fred had swiftly changed into a matching outfit. He regarded the bed thoughtfully and tested the springs with his fingers. They creaked and twanged in complaint. Turning back the sheets, he slid between them.

There was an ominous *clunk.*

The bed dropped precipitously and tipped forwards, causing him to fall back against the pillows. The bed shot, as if on rails, through the hatch in the floor that had opened

138

up at the foot.

Fred levered himself up into a sitting position. The bed was in fact on rails, scooting like a mine car into the depths of the house. Down, down, it careered through the fabric of the mansion, into labyrinthine tunnels in the promontory it and the watch tower were built upon. Then ahead he could see the end of the line. Darkness ahead. There was a jolt and he was tumbling through space. He hit icy cold water with a tremendous thump.

Fred clawed his way to the surface, fighting not to drown, and trod water as he broke the surface. Coughing, spluttering, he realised he was in sea water. He could see the opening of the sea cave he had landed in up ahead and moonlit breakers beyond. There was a wooden jetty projecting out into the water to the side of the opening and he struck out for that.

In the Headley Sauceman room, an identical bed to the original had slid soundlessly into its place just in time for Daisy to emerge from the dressing room buttoning the cuffs of her Wee-Willie-Winkie ensemble. "Not exactly the slinkiest of nightwear," she opined, "but it has a certain something." She did a twirl in front of the fireplace, fully aware that the light from the fire would silhouette her against the cotton. Then she noticed the bed was empty. "Fred?" She checked under the bed. "Fred?" She checked the wardrobe. "Fred?"

Daisy peeped out on to the landing furtively. "Fred?" she squeaked tremulously.

No sign of him. Tucking the tatty teddybear she had found sitting on the nightstand under her arm for protection, she crept out on to the landing. Holding up a candle to see where she was, she padded along to the end of the hall and stood at the top of the stairs.

-oOo-

Beyond the jetty was a cobbled stone slope that rose steadily up from the sea cave into the fabric of the ancient watchtower behind the house. Fred followed the slope, feeling his way in the darkness with one hand on the outer curve of the wall. Ahead, he could see light at the top of the slope and as the illumination improved, he quickened his pace.

He emerged into the roofless, moonlit void that was the ruins of the watchtower. It stopped him in his tracks. It was like stepping on to the set of a 1930s Frankenstein sequel. Quite apart from missing a roof, the outer curtain wall of the structure had been breached. A vee-shaped gouge that overlooked the sea and the Grisley Rocks lighthouse. Much of the wooden floor in that part of the building was burnt or smashed away, leaving the labyrinth of sea caves under Grisley Point open to the skies.

The watchtower floor where he had emerged from the slope was the solid rock of the Point itself, and the most substantial part of the remaining structure. The walls were lined with ancient electrical and chemical apparatus. It slowly dawned on Fred that he was looking at an almost industrially scaled-up version of his Uncle's experiment in the laboratory of the house. He ran a hand over one of the huge electrical capacitors. The faded stencilling read *Siemens* and a little lower down *Eigentum Des Deutsches Reich*. He pulled his hand back as if given an electric shock. He remembered that Uncle Plum had bought the

140

house in 1945, from the estate of *his* Great Uncle's son Linus Longfield. What could *he* have been up to with *that lot*?

He spotted a doorway on the house side of the watchtower. He picked his way through the tangle of wreckage littering the interior of the building and prised the door open. He peered into the darkness beyond, wishing he had a candle or a torch.

Daisy smiled to herself, sniffing the leftover egg, bacon and vegetable flan from their substantial supper. The willowy blonde had become distracted in her search for Fred upon finding the kitchen again. She closed the refrigerator door and put the flan dish down on the kitchen table. Cutting herself a generous portion, Daisy paused, hearing the hiss of a bottle of beer being opened. "Fred?" she whispered.

"Pass the salad, please, Miss." Rummidge put a bottle of Guinness down in front of her and reached for a glass from the shelf. He turned back and looked around in surprise finding her disappeared. "Miss?"

Teetering on the brink of panic, Daisy shot up the stairs, taking them three at a time, hoisting her night-shirt to her knees. She hardly noticed when the lights went out, until she reached the top of the stairs. She felt her way forwards, using the wall as her guide. She was desperately trying to remember if her room was the second or third door down.

It was definitely the second.

Or it might have been the third. She was pretty sure it was the second, so she pushed the door open and felt her way blindly to the bed. She breathed a sigh of relief as she curled up under the covers.

The bed tipped up.

Daisy was quite surprisingly sanguine about the whole floor-opening-up-beneath-her thing. She allowed herself an initial startled yip as she fell, but remained quite calm. She only fell for a couple of seconds, and as quickly as her predicament arose, she sliced gracefully feet first into deep, if somewhat chilly water. It was not an unfamiliar experience for her, falling into deep water being a tediously regular occurrence. She had been a star high-diver at school and plummeting into the wet stuff had become second nature. She scored herself a 5.5 as she surfaced and found her bearings.

An ancient bulkhead light attached to the rock wall illuminated the foot of a spiral staircase that emerged from the waters. Daisy clambered out of the water and wrung out the hem of her nightshirt, then more gently her own long blonde hair. She started up the stone steps. "Fred?" she called, but her own echo was the only response.

-oOo-

Daisy pushed open a door at the head of the stone staircase and was hit by a wash of hot, humid air. There was a heavy canopy of leaves overhead, but she couldn't be outside. She heard a noise ahead of her and moved forwards nervously. "Fred? Is that you?" she called querulously.

"It's only me, Miss." Rummidge appeared in front of her like something out of a bad horror movie and made her jump out of her skin for the umpteenth time. He switched on the light and Daisy discovered she was standing in the huge, glass conservatory at the rear of the house. "I've managed to temporarily fix the fuse box, Miss." The lights flickered for a moment. "Although I don't know how long the repairs will last." At least now she knew why it had been so hot. Steam rose from cast-iron radiators around the walls of the glass-house, lending a sultry, wet-earth smell to the air. Broad-leafed, tropical plants vied for space, climbing high towards the roof. The only thing missing was the sound of cicadas and monkeys. Looking around, she half-expected to run into some long-lost relative of Doctor Livingstone. The bushes parted in front of her and she relaxed as Fred emerged.

"Fred!" she squeaked happily and threw herself into his arms with a damp *squelch*. "You're all wet," she observed, although she was not about to let him go any time soon.

"So are you," Fred pointed out, in an identical frame of mind. "The bed upstairs?"

Daisy nodded. "Got in, curled up and *whoosh!*"

"Splash!" agreed Fred.

Rummidge had disappeared again. "This way?" Fred gestured towards a doorway a few feet away from the one Daisy had come through.

Daisy shrugged. "Why not?" She clasped herself to Fred's arm as they moved back into the main body of the house.

Neither Fred or Daisy trusted the bed in the Headley Sauceman room after their experiences and they had decamped to the Green Lady room in the hopes that the bed in there had fewer nasty surprises. Having comprehensively tested the bed and the floor around it for secret panels, and having changed into dry nightwear from the adjoining dressing room, they cautiously took to the bed.

They had already got a candle, and Daisy had found a small Bible in the night stand. Their only problem had been finding a bell in a strange house at two in the morning. Thus armed, they fell into a fitful sleep.

Down in the laboratory, Great Uncle Plum's toupee suddenly vanished with a soft 'pop' and a shower of pixie dust.

CHAPTER THIRTEEN:

Fred and Daisy Survive The Night

And Then See Rummidge In A Different Light

Fred was woken by a shaft of bright sunlight slicing through a gap in the bedroom curtains. Daisy was curled up at his side, using his chest as a pillow. She stirred as he did and opened a big, blue eye. "We're still alive, then," she observed astutely.

"Apparently." Fred squinted in the shaft of sunlight.

Daisy levered herself up on to her elbows and the bed gave a strange *twang* and sort of quivered. She looked apprehensively back over her shoulder. "I'm not sure I'm in the mood for a morning dip," she observed.

"Me neither." Fred slid to the edge of the bed. "Out of bed on three?" he suggested.

"Uh - huh." Daisy concurred, sliding to the opposite edge of the mattress. *"A-one, A-two, A-three!"* They both hopped out of the bed. There was a *clunk* and it folded up into the wall like a giant-sized mousetrap. "Do you think all the beds in this place are booby-trapped?" she mused.

Fred pulled the bedroom curtains, stirring up a cloud of dust motes that swirled in the bright shaft of sunlight. With the introduction of daylight, the room had lost its malign air. But not completely. In keeping with what appeared to be all the rooms in the house, at least one wall was panelled with wood. The panelling, and Fred suspected a hidden passageway, ran along the wall behind the head of the bed in the Green Lady room, and had accommodated it when it folded up into the wall. While he had been pulling the curtains, the bed had returned to its usual place within its four posts and connecting framework. He probed the panel experimentally and found a narrow gap through which he could feel a breeze and smell salt water. Another route down into the sea, he thought to himself. He was going to be kept busy nailing up the house's nasty little surprises.

Thankfully, the former occupant of the room had not made an appearance during the night, so they had managed to snatch a few hours uninterrupted sleep after the night's adventures. Daisy was first to avail herself of the adjoining dressing room to get dressed again. She left the door ajar so that they could carry on their conversation.

"Should we head for home, or investigate the place further?" Fred gave her the option of running for it.

"Given the choice, I'd be sprinting down the drive, screaming my head off," replied Daisy. "Even if we did come here in my car."

"Explore the place it is," nodded Fred briskly.

"Do we *really* have to look round?" Daisy asked.

"We'll only have to come back and look round another time," replied Fred.

"We?" Daisy raised her eyebrows.

"You don't think I'm coming back here on my own, do you?" Fred asked reasonably.

Daisy emerged from the dressing room, looking her customary million dollars in the clothes she had arrived at the old house in. She perched on the dressing table while Fred took his turn dressing. He emerged, straightening his tie.

Daisy hopped to her feet and gestured *after you*. "Lead on, Fred."

Fred took the lead with the air of a man who would rather bring up the rear. They moved out on to the landing. Daylight hours were little comfort in the house, which took its dinginess very seriously. The drapes on all the windows could have easily dated back to the War and were of blackout weight. They started down the passage, pulling curtains as they went to introduce a little light into the house.

They descended the main staircase to the entrance hall. All dark mahogany panelling and forbidding-looking family portraits. Fred stood in the middle of the hall and looked around thoughtfully. "Pick a door," he suggested.

"Let's start in there," suggested Daisy apprehensively, indicating a doorway to the left of the main staircase.

Fred looked at her nervously. He would probably open the doors and come face to face with his namesake, the gentleman in the striped jersey and the claw glove - Mrs Kruger's little boy.

"Go on." Daisy was keeping a sensible distance.

Fred found his mouth had gone dry. He knew

where all the water in his body had gone. It had mysteriously appeared on the palms of his hands. He wiped his hands on his jacket and gripped the handles of the doors. He peered through into the room beyond. "Ah!"

"What is it?" Daisy had closed her eyes in case it was something she would rather not see.

"Dining room," ventured Fred. The room beyond was long and narrow, and an equally long and narrow dining table ran down the middle of the room, with places for at least twenty people. The table had been set for some formal occasion in the dim and distant past and never cleared. Place settings complete with silver cutlery and fine crystalware, dried floral centrepieces which Fred realised had been fresh when originally placed on the table, and ornate silver candelabra were providing a rich and challenging environment for the resident spiders - or perhaps a single hyperactive spider. The entire spread was festooned with dusty cobwebs. The only thing missing was Miss Havisham and her wedding dress.

On the walls were further imposing portraits of the late Professor's ancestors. A collection of alarmingly strange-looking people, and Daisy cringed inwardly as she realised there were family connections with Fred.

"I believe Queen Victoria was entertained here once," Fred observed.

"How many other times did she come here?" asked Daisy brightly.

"Uncle didn't do much entertaining."

"That I can believe," muttered Daisy. "This place is a barrel of laughs." Heavy, velvet curtains hung at the windows lining the long wall. Daisy moved over to the curtains and went to draw them in the hope of shedding some light on the subject. They refused to budge. She tried again, a little harder.

Fred whirled at a soft *whoomph* and a muffled exclamation. The curtains had simply collapsed on top of her, enveloping her. Dust rose into the air in clouds as she struggled to free herself of the enveloping mass, squeaking and coughing. Holding his breath to avoid inhaling the dust, Fred hefted the weighty material aside and Daisy surfaced, looking a little worse for wear, wafting her hand in front of her face and coughing. "Are you all right?" Fred brushed grey dust from Daisy's cheeks.

Daisy sneezed explosively. "I think this place is going to need an awful lot of spring cleaning," was her considered opinion. She stepped over the remains of the curtains as Fred helped her up.

-oOo-

Raymond "Knuckles" McCallister and his Brains Trust were exactly the kind of individuals you would imagine with sobriquets of that nature, and sported a wondrous variety of bruises and contusions as credentials. Admittedly these battle-wounds had been acquired while attempting to strong-arm Miss Esme at the Tea Shoppe in Chortlesford over the price of three cream teas. They hadn't been aware her older sister Fanny was visiting and both ladies were rolling-pin ninjas.

Bearing a striking resemblance to Neanderthal Man in spite of a well-worn red cardigan and carpet slippers, Knuckles was in his late forties and hid a distinct follicular disadvantage under an ill-fitting toupee. His relationship with the Warmhamptonshire Constabulary was strictly professional. While the county enjoyed a quite surprisingly low crime rate - the national press tended to use the adjective "sleepy" when describing the area - it still had its miscreants and Knuckles McCallister was the nearest thing to a crime boss or Godfather in that neck of the woods.

He was in his garage honing his working skills to perfection. The Baxendale and Sweetly R643 was one of the most resilient safes known to the criminal fraternity, and cracking the beast was Knuckles' latest project. His intelligence grapevine indicated there was one such safe, containing share certificates and bonds to the tune of £500,000 at Ballcock Hall. Or so the bloke in the pub had said. He turned off the oxyacetylene torch and hinged back his facemask visor to peer at the door of the safe. The locking assembly was almost cut through. He checked his watch. Twenty-five minutes, thirty-three seconds. He would have to halve that time to get in and out of the hall without alerting the security patrol that made a half-hourly circuit of the grounds. He dropped the facemask back into position and turned on the gas to relight the cutting torch. There was a knock at the garage door. "What is it?" he roared, deafening himself. "I'm busy!"

The voice of his right hand thug Llewellyn drifted through the locked door. "It's only me, Boss," he called. "There's a bloke here who wants to talk business with you."

"Tell him to come back tomorrow," Knuckles shouted back. "I'm busy!"

"He says it's worth a lot of money."

Knuckles pulled off his facemask and placed it and the oxyacetylene torch carefully on the floor. He opened the garage door. "Why didn't you say that in the first place?" He closed the garage door behind him, leaving the unlit torch to quietly hiss explosive gases into the floor drain. "Who is it wants to talk business with me?" Knuckles pulled on his jacket.

"I do." Rummidge appeared at his elbow. Like many others before him, Knuckles started violently.

"Who the hell are you?" Knuckles demanded shakily.

Rummidge bowed perfunctorily. "I am the late Professor Pelham Longfield's manservant Rummidge, Sir."

Knuckles looked blank.

"You know him, Boss," Llewellyn prompted. "That potty old scientist who owns that big, creepy old house behind the golf course. The local kids call it Castle Frankenstein."

"I'm not surprised." Knuckles nodded, eyeing Rummidge.

"The old gentleman passed on recently," Rummidge pressed on. "His executors have taken over the house and they've made a rather interesting discovery concerning the late master's experiments."

"What kind of discovery?" asked Knuckles dubiously.

Rummidge looked around furtively and beckoned for Knuckles to listen closely. Knuckles leaned forwards to hear. "A formula for turning other elements into gold," Rummidge confided.

"Oh yes?" Knuckles straightened and turned to Llewellyn. "You and Bert take this gentleman away and beat him up for wasting my time."

"Wait a moment," said Rummidge hastily. "If you don't believe me, then would you kindly account for this?" He produced an apple, one of the many items which Fred had used to verify the working of the formula, from his pocket. Daisy's teeth-marks were visible in the polished surface, as she had attempted to appropriate the fruit for herself once more, but Fred had insisted he needed it for the experiment.

"Stone the crows!" muttered Knuckles. He took the apple from the grizzled individual and weighed it critically in his hand. It looked like gold... It felt like gold... By golly it was gold! The whole thing sounded far-fetched, but the object in his hand was definitely not the handiwork of some crazed goldsmith. He peered at Rummidge suspiciously. "What's your angle, then?"

"My angle, Sir?" quavered Rummidge.

"What do you want to get out of this deal?" Knuckles enquired shrewdly.

"Well, Mr McCallister." Rummidge stared at the floor. "I simply thought that in gratitude for my bringing this information to your attention, you might conveniently forget the gambling debts that I owe you."

"Gambling debts? How much?" Knuckles asked cautiously. Gambling debts were the principal source of revenue for his enterprises and he hated to write off so much as a penny if he could help it.

"Two hundred and twenty three pounds, thirty one

pence." Rummidge revealed the figure as if it were the deficit of the Bank of England. He rolled his eyes alarmingly.

Knuckles came to a decision immediately and beamed. "Certainly, my friend," he patted Rummidge on the back magnanimously. "Consider them forgotten. Your slate is wiped clean." He wiped his hand surreptitiously on his cardigan.

"That's most gracious of you, Sir." Rummidge bowed low.

Knuckles' mind was racing at the possibilities - providing the creepy old manservant's story panned out. If it didn't, then Llewellyn's skills at concrete mixing would be called for. If it did, there was the distinct possibility that people would mention the name Raymond McCallister in the same way they talked about Bill Gates, the Sultan of Brunei or Jed Clampett. He turned to Llewellyn at his most ebullient. "Llewellyn, see this gentleman out. We have some business to attend to." He rubbed his hands together eagerly.

"Yes, Boss." Llewellyn gripped Rummidge's collar. "Do you still want us to beat him up, Boss?" he enquired.

"Certainly not," Knuckles reproached. "We're not hoodlums. Mr... um... Rummidge here is a valuable friend to our enterprises. Without him, we'd have never found out such an interesting piece of information."

"Okay, Boss." Llewellyn frogmarched Rummidge away to the gate, and having ejected him, returned to Knuckles.

Knuckles was changing into his sports jacket. "What now, Boss?"

"You're going to drive me round to this scientist's place. We're going to discuss a little business," replied Knuckles.

"How, Boss?" Llewellyn looked at him blankly. "The old boy's dead."

Knuckles gazed at Llewellyn with a jaundiced expression. "I know that," he said patiently. "I meant have a word with his executors."

"Oh, gotcha, Boss," Llewellyn tapped his temple.

"We'll want Bert along with us," growled Knuckles. "Where is he?"

"He's in the kitchen, Boss. Making a cheese souffle for lunch."

Knuckles had to decide what was more important - one of Bert's cheese souffle's or checking out this gold formula business. He came to a decision. "Well, go and get him. Bring the car round the front." Llewellyn started away. "Hold on," shouted Knuckles. "You'll need the car keys." He took the keys out of his pocket and threw them to Llewellyn. Llewellyn grabbed for the keys, missed and watched them sail down the grid into the drain at his feet.

"Oops, butterfingers." Llewellyn bent down and levered open the grid to retrieve the keys. He reached a hand down and groped around vaguely for the keys.

Knuckles pushed him out of the way. "Don't bother," he snapped. "Just get Bert and meet me round the front of the house."

"Okay, Boss." Llewellyn tugged his forelock and wandered off towards the house. Knuckles sighed and peered into the open drain, but it was too dark to see anything. He rummaged in his pockets and found a box of matches. Just the thing. He took a match out of the box, struck it and leaned into the opening.

Unfortunately, he was unaware that the oxyacetylene cutter he had left in the garage had been leaking explosive gases into the drain all the time he had been talking.

Llewellyn jumped as the house was shaken by a tremendous blast. He rushed over to the window to see flames gushing out of the garage. The safe that Knuckles had been working on thudded into the soft turf of the immaculately kept lawn, digging a rectangular hole. He looked over to see where Knuckles was.

"Boss?" he called. "Are you all right...? Boss?"

-oOo-

Having completed their exploration of the premises, Fred and Daisy had returned to the Kitchen in search of sustenance. The old family retainer was conspicuous by his absence, much to their mutual relief. Raiding the walk-in chiller in the Kitchen, they gathered the makings of that most important meal of the day and the dietary needs of lorry-drivers, builders and willowy blondes called Daisy. An epic fry-up.

Working together like a well-oiled machine, they juggled eggs, bacon, mushrooms, stewed tomatoes and fried bread on the cooking range. Daisy had toyed with the

155

idea of a kipper as well, but changed her mind after she ran out of frying pans. Fred was constantly amazed by her appetite, which could best be described as horse-like. What was even more astonishing was the way she never put on weight no matter what she ate, while he ballooned if he simply looked at a cream cake. His figure was nothing to write home about at the best of times, which made putting on any extra tonnage less than desirable. She was slim and svelte, yet all he could usually manage for breakfast was cereals, or toast and marmalade.

Fred brewed his tea the way he liked his women — hot and sweet — and before long, they were seated at the kitchen dining table.

It started with a slice of toast. Daisy offered Fred a bite of her toast. He reciprocated with a forkful of fried mushrooms. A rasher of bacon shared in the manner of *Lady and the Tramp* ended in a full-on, passionate, if greasy kiss. She cupped his face in her hands and kissed him the way she had at the boating lake.

Fred was still reeling from the experience when the girl of his dreams frowned and rubbed his cheek with her fingers. "Ooh, it's like kissing a loo brush!" she exclaimed, her fingernails rasping through the growth he had inadvertently cultivated upon his chin.

Fred rubbed his chin self-consciously. If he wanted her to do that more often, he had better scrape off the bristles pronto. "Sorry, I'll go and have a shave."

-oOo-

Fred hurried down the stairs to answer the doorbell, which turned out to be a gong of the variety used to introduce British movies back in the day. He had located a razor in the bathroom down the hall from their nighttime accommodation, and luxuriated in a glorious wet shave. His noble physiognomy thus rendered to the finish of an infant's fundament, he was sure he would pass muster with Daisy.

He opened the door to find his parents on the step. "Mum! Dad! What are you doing here?"

"Usual story, Son," shrugged his father genially. "Any time your Mother loses track of you, she panics."

"You can talk," retorted Fred's mother. "Pacing the front room yesterday evening, wondering where you'd got to."

Fred held his hands up. "I'm sorry I didn't report in. We finished here late and we didn't fancy negotiating the roads in the dark."

"I told you there'd be a reasonable explanation, Mol," observed Dad. "The roads around here are a nightmare after dark."

"You had enough trouble with the roads around here in daylight," retorted Mum.

"Well, come in. Come in." Fred was glad to see his parents whatever the circumstances.

"So what's the story, Son?" Dad stepped into the hall after Mum.

"Great Uncle Plum left me the place in his Will," replied Fred. "The whole estate - the house, the inventions, the patents."

Dad nodded happily. "You always were a favourite of his. Once it's been done up a bit, this place'll be worth a bob or two," he commented. "A real stately home."

"You mean a home in a real state." Mum was completely unimpressed.

"Hullo hullo hullo!" The three of them turned as one to see Daisy skipping down the stairs. Fred's father acquired the same kind of silly smile that was adorning his son's face.

Fred's Mum was the first to recover. "Are you two living together now, then?" she enquired of her son.

"Only overnight, so far," conceded Daisy, treating Fred's parents to a group hug. She caught the look on Fred's face and looked coy. She gathered up Fred's parents in a hug and steered them towards the Drawing Room. "Let's see if we can't rustle up some elevenses."

Before his disappearance, Rummidge had lit the fire in the Drawing Room, and it was roaring lustily in the grate, casting a golden glow on the surrounding Chesterfield armchairs and settee. Daisy took to the role of hostess like the proverbial anatidine waterfowl to H_2O. Fred's Dad took the armchair to the right of the fireplace, while his Mum took to the Chesterfield settee directly in front.

"Tea or coffee?" Daisy enquired.

A moment's telepathic communication between Fred's parents and Mum voiced a preference for tea. Daisy straightened up and flinched as Rummidge made his reappearance at her side in his customary, silent style. He was getting more like an escapee from the Addams Family with every day. Daisy turned to apologise to Fred's parents and was surprised to see neither had jumped out of their skin. "This is Mr Rummidge," Daisy started.

"Oh, we know Reggie very well, Daisy love," smiled Fred's Mum. "How are you, Reggie?"

"Very well, thank you, Molly." Rummidge bowed deeply.

Fred looked as startled as Daisy that his parents knew the sinister retainer, and possibly more so that their resident zombie was called Reginald. His mother noticed the owlish quality her son had taken on and offered an explanation to Daisy conversationally: "We've known Reggie here for absolutely *ages*. He's quite the fixture at the Darby and Joan club. A one with the ladies at the Friday afternoon Tea Dance is Reggie. You should see him dancing the Veleta."

Rummidge rolled his eyes alarmingly and Fred and Daisy exchanged an incredulous look. Rummidge regarded Daisy quizzically. "Was there anything, Miss?" he enquired.

"Oh... um... any chance of a spot of Elevenses, Mr Rummidge?" Daisy asked, still having difficulties with the idea of Rummidge as a ladies' man at the Darby and Joan.

"Very good, Miss." Even in daylight, the man seemed to fade out of focus and disappear rather than exit through the door. For once, Daisy spotted his escape strategy and having excused herself, followed him.

-oOo-

Rummidge had been charmed by Daisy's assistance. While he had brewed a pot of tea and retrieved the milk from the walk-in chiller, Daisy had managed to materialise a large plate of sandwiches and some cupcakes she had made the previous evening. Together, they took the victuals to the Drawing Room and he took his respectful place by the door while Daisy basked in the approval of Fred's parents. He was rapidly warming to the young woman in spite of his initial reservations against the couple.

"So what are your plans for this place?" asked Fred's father, expertly balancing a plate of sandwiches and cupcakes in one hand and a cup and saucer in the other.

"Well, now I don't have a flat in town, I thought I might move in here, and do the place up," replied Fred.

"To sell it on?" asked Fred's Dad.

"Actually I was thinking of living here," Fred shrugged. The news was greeted with incredulous looks from Fred's parents, surprise from Rummidge, and approval from Daisy.

-oOo-

CHAPTER FOURTEEN:

In Which Fred Finds Gainful Employment

And Daisy Almost Falls Out Of The Window

Fred hurried out into the hallway as he heard the front door open. Standing in the doorway was an enormous stack of rolls of wallpaper, supported by a pair of slim hands and a terrific pair of tanned legs that appeared to be in serious danger of collapsing under the weight. He rushed to Daisy's aid and relieved her of the wallpaper. "What's this all in aid of?" he asked, putting the wallpaper on the hall table. He turned back to find that Daisy had gone outside again. He hurried after her and found her unloading more wallpaper and cans of paint from the car.

Daisy handed him two cans of brilliant white emulsion, which he clutched to his chest as she piled a further five rolls of wallpaper on top. "You were talking about doing the place up last night," replied Daisy, breezily. "I thought I'd call your bluff." She finished loading Fred up and sauntered back towards the house, swinging a can of sunshine yellow gloss in her hand. Fred staggered after her with his burden.

"I really meant get somebody in to do it," Fred grunted.

"Maybe," admitted Daisy. "I reckoned if we did it, it'd cost less."

Daisy's logic was faultless as ever but for one little detail. "We?" Fred dumped his burden on the hall table.

"I was hoping you'd help me," Daisy wheedled. Unfortunately for Fred, she knew exactly what kind of pressure to apply and where, to get him to do what she wanted. It was awful her being able to twist him round her little finger like that, thought Fred, but somehow, he did not seem to mind.

He shrugged. "Why not?" So now he was a painter and decorator as well.

"There you go, Miss," beamed Rummidge. "I told you you'd be able to con Master Fred into helping."

Daisy, who did not have a disingenuous bone in her body, gave a squeak of protest and tried to deny any duplicitousness. She grabbed Rummidge and steered him back towards the lounge. "Why don't you start by getting a little light into this place? You could get the blinds drawn while I nip upstairs and get changed."

-oOo-

Daisy strolled back down the stairs half-an-hour later having changed her smart jacket and skirt for a more workman-like outfit of scruffy dungarees and a paint-spattered baseball cap which she had tucked her long, blonde hair under.

She stared round the hall in amazement at the transformation that had taken place. With the front doors wide open and the heavy velvet drapes on the windows drawn, light was flooding into the hall. What had been a forbidding, black void a few days before before had become a spacious, airy and surprisingly inviting entrance to the grand old house. "Well, there doesn't look like a lot for us to do here," opined Daisy optimistically. She ran a finger along the bannister and wrinkled her nose at the sooty deposit that came off on her fingertip. "Apart from a good spring clean." She looked around critically. "Perhaps a lick of paint here and there... Revarnish the front door... Replaster that bit over there..." She allowed herself a depressed groan. "Who am I kidding? This place could do with accidentally burning down or something!" Not wanting to look any more, she shielded her eyes with her hand and went into the lounge in the hopes of better news.

The night before, the lounge had been cosily dimly-lit. With bright sunlight flooding in through the window, it looked... "Eee-yuck!!" Daisy wrinkled her nose. Years of Great Uncle Plum's pipe smoke had coated every surface in the room with a brown, sticky, translucent layer of tar. The wallpaper was a heavy, dark, flowery print that might have been in vogue some time in the Edwardian era.

Rummidge had got everything in the Drawing Room covered up so that it would not get spattered with paint or wallpaper paste. That included himself. He had gone in for coveralls with a hood, facemask and goggles and Wellington boots. He looked more like he was prepared for chemical warfare than a spot of painting and wallpapering, which made Fred wonder if the butler knew something he didn't.

-oOo-

Fred could not be entirely sure how Daisy had talked him into applying for the job at her father's factory. The only thing he was sure of was a sinking feeling in the pit of his stomach as he stood outside the gates of Chayne and Ballcock Sanitary Fixtures Manufacturers.

The previous evening, Daisy had come back to the old house, full of excitement. There was a vacancy at her

163

father's factory for a Personal Assistant. He had the qualifications, and she had cajoled, seduced and nagged him into making an appointment, in spite of his protestations that he had never been a Personal Assistant before, and had no idea what a Personal Assistant did.

Any second thoughts he might have had about the enterprise had given way to third thoughts. His misgivings were way past sore. Chayne and Ballcock Sanitary Fixtures Manufacturers was sited in the middle of nowhere, surrounded by rolling, empty countryside and chilled by a wind that howled down off the Down all year round. The factory itself was unprepossessing, the four storey administration block surrounded by an assortment of low, breeze-block and brick buildings where lavatory pans were cast, glazed and fired, ready to be made a convenience of by the toilet buying public.

The factory sign, blue letters six foot high standing on the parapet of the roof and supported by a rusting metal frame, had been the target for a sniper with an air rifle. The result was that the 'a' and the first 'c' in 'Ballcock' had become casualties, lying out of sight on the roof. The sign thus attracted much curiosity from passers-by, now reading "Chayne and B-ll-ock."

The bus had dropped him off with what seemed like a mile's hike across inhospitable terrain before he reached the gates of the factory. His poor old Ford Fiasco had fallen apart in the road outside the house when he tried to start it a couple of days ago. Crumbled to dust like Dracula on a sunny day seemed a more accurate way of putting it. He would have to sweep up the remains when he got home, he thought bleakly. People were starting to walk the rust into the hall.

164

The office was about thirty feet long and about half as wide. In the long wall facing the door were two large picture windows which looked out on to the carpark and afforded a glorious panorama of the heath beyond. The windows, which were contemporary with the 1930s building of the current factory, consisted of a narrow fixed border of glass and a centre panel which could open, swinging on a vertical pivot which meant that half the window pivoted out while the other pivoted in.

"There he is!!" Daisy had spotted the lone figure huddled against the elements as he scuttled through the factory gates. Standing beside her at the open window of the third-floor office they shared were Boadicea and Britannia Ballcock.

Boadicea followed Daisy's wistful gaze as the distant figure of Fred reported to Mr Hodgkiss, the security guard in the gatehouse. Boadicea turned as the phone on her desk trilled. She picked up the receiver. "Hullo? Gatehouse? A Mr Who to see Sir Roland? No, I think there must be some mistake."

Daisy snatched the receiver out of Boadicea's hand. "Sorry about that, Mr Hodgkiss. Slight case of crossed lines. Mr Longfield has an appointment. Could you send him straight through?"

Boadicea stuck a tongue out at Daisy and she and Britannia sauntered out into the passageway. Daisy glared after the twins and hung up the phone. She turned back to the window and leaned out.

The wind was blowing fine drizzle in Fred's face as he emerged from the gatehouse and trudged towards the four-storey, glass-fronted administration block. He looked around at a loud, fingers-in-mouth whistle of the variety he had never personally mastered. A second whistle gave him a direction and he looked up to see a familiar flash of golden hair at an open window high in the edifice. He raised a hand in greeting to the exuberant welcome.

He pulled his letter of appointment out of his pocket and pushed open the glass doors. The foyer beyond was sparsely populated, a wide open space of potted plants and seats for visitors. At the far end was a reception desk.

A gruff voice behind him enquired, "Excuse me, Sir, would you happen to be a Mr Frederick Longfield?" Startled, Fred turned to face a middle aged man dressed in a neat blue uniform with the letters CB embroidered on the breast pocket and on the band of the cap.

"Yes, that's me," confirmed Fred.

The craggy faced commissionaire beamed. "You are expected, Mr Longfield. If you would care to take the lift to the third floor."

"Er... thank you." Fred allowed himself to be led over to the lift at one side of the concourse, where he joined a group of neatly dressed drafting office types who had emerged from another doorway that led into the rest of the factory. Fred was by no means a scruffy dresser, but then he could not be described as very Savile Row either. He smiled nervously as they all crowded into the lift, which was operated by a pretty, red haired young woman.

"Which floor, Sir?" she enquired.

"Um... third floor, please," replied Fred. The occupants of the lift took a collective sharp intake of breath. Fred distinctly felt his ears pop. There was an uncomfortable silence as the lift rose up past the first floor. On the second floor, all of the neatly dressed young drafting office types got out, giving him suspicious looks in passing. Fred swallowed audibly as the lift doors closed again, leaving just him and the lift operator. To take his mind off things, he attempted to make conversation. "What's this job like?"

The girl looked surprised. People rarely talked to her other than to tell her which floor they wanted. She smiled cheekily. "It has its ups and downs."

Fred gave Daphne the lift girl a little wave as the lift doors closed. He looked around uneasily. The hallway he had been deposited on was bright after the confines of the lift, large picture windows affording an excellent view of the surrounding countryside. Opposite the lift was a small waiting area with chairs, a coffee table and a drinks dispenser.

"Mr Longfield." He had been intercepted by Boadicea and Britannia Ballcock. They were regarding him critically and he half-expected either to say something like "be off with you" and shoo him out of the building with her clipboard. "We're going to be working together," Boadicea hugged herself to his arm, radiating body heat. "Very closely. Our office is just along here, between Sir Roland's and Dad's. You'll like it here, the pay's great, the holidays are long and Sir Roland's a pussycat. But you know that already. He was very impressed with the way you sorted out the Deluxe 500 problem."

"I'm here for an interview," said Fred faintly, interrupting the Amazon's chatter.

"Interview?" Boadicea looked blank. "Nope, I don't recall you having an interview appointment with Sir Roland. He just said to make you feel welcome and show you where our office is."

"You mean I've got the job?"

"Sir Roland reckons we need a Fred Longfield about the place, and you fit the bill. You'll be sharing this office with Daze and the two of us."

Fred did a wonderful impression of a goldfish as he struggled to come to terms with what was going on. For the moment, he did not know whether hysterical laughter or wailing and gnashing of teeth was the order of the day, as Daisy had mentioned nothing of the working arrangements. He had the nasty feeling he had been set up, but somehow he did not mind in the least.

The first thing Fred saw as he walked through the door was a very familiar pair of long legs. The heart-stoppingly short, tight, pinstripe mini-miniskirt those legs emerged from was riding higher and higher as the owner dangled precariously out of one of those windows. Rump uppermost, only the stunning legs were visible, waving as the owner strained to retreat back inside.

Fred and the Ballcock sisters leapt forward and seized Daisy by the ankles before she toppled out of the window. The four tumbled to the floor with Daisy uppermost. "Leaned out too far," she chortled.

Britannia Ballcock stood up and pushed the inward projecting edge of the window to close it.

Daisy realised somebody's head was under the hem of her pinstripe mini-miniskirt. "Fred! You came!!" She clambered off him and helped him to his feet, dusting him down. Then she hugged him.

"Look, Daze," Fred had a doubtful tone in his voice. "I really appreciate the thought, but I don't know if I'm right for this job. I don't know anything about office work, let alone being any kind of secretary."

Daisy led him over to a desk that unlike the other desks in the room was not piled high with paperwork. It had a large, comfortable black leather chair and a computer workstation, the monitor of which displayed a screen-saver image of a squirrel making a pile of nuts under the legend "Chayne and Ballcock Information Network". She pushed Fred into the chair and perched gracefully on the edge of the desk.

"Both Dad and Lord Ballcock have *secretaries*. They look after appointment books, take notes and do all the kind of secretarily things I haven't a clue about," explained Daisy.

"That's just about everything," interjected Boadicea.

"We're *personal assistants*," Daisy went on, ignoring the barb. "While the secretaries do all the officey stuff, we do all the running around on errands and that kind of thing."

She hoisted Fred out of his seat again. "Come on, Fred. I want to show you round the factory."

-oOo-

Fred had never realised before how much work was involved in the manufacture of sanitary ware and bathroom fittings. As they walked through the factory, Daisy kept up a chatty commentary about the factory, the weather and anything else that happened to come into her head. "Of course, Dad reckons we ought to be introducing more high-tech into the business and addressing ecological issues rather than finding ways to build cheaper loos. Lord Ballcock's pressing to keep unit costs down by importing pans from overseas and fitting them up in the factory, but Dad insists we ought to be making a quality product, not just knocking out cut-price bogs. Whoops!"

She had nearly walked into a vat of porcelain slip, and would have tumbled into it, had it not been for the quick reflexes of one of the workers, who just caught her in time. He was handsome, about Fred's age, with spiky black hair that glistened with gel. "You all right, Daze?" He had a double handful of her derriere.

Daisy turned her dazzling smile on her rescuer. "Thanks, Mick. One of these days you're not going to be standing there and I'm going to go for a swim in that stuff."

"Hope I'm around to see it," replied Mick cheekily.

Daisy gave him a reproachful look. Then she remembered Fred. "Oh, Mick. This is Fred. He's Dad's new Personal Assistant."

"So you're Fred." Mick beamed and shook Fred's hand. "We've heard a lot about you."

"Mick's the staff representative," said Daisy. "He and Dad are the best of mates. Together they run the

170

factory model aircraft club." She kissed the young man lightly on the cheek. "Don't forget Dad's trying out the new wing design this weekend. Come by the Manor early, he wants to discuss the design changes."

She led Fred away. "Nice feller that Mick," she commented. "He dated Bluebell before she went to the States. Now he's dating one of the girls in Accounts."

They strolled past long lines of benches where workers were busily preparing lavatory pans for firing. Daisy kept pausing to chat with friends. She appeared to have friends all over the factory, which didn't surprise him. She seemed to have a happy knack of making friends very easily. He wondered how many she had got jobs for.

They stepped out into the open, crossing a concreted yard that separated one building from the next. "That was the casting works," Daisy explained conversationally. "This," she waved a hand expansively, "is the fitting block where we do all the accessorising. That doesn't mean finding matching handbags and shoes." She chortled at her own little joke, leading him into the next area of the factory. More workers were attaching taps, outlets and other fittings to finished washbasins and bidets.

She checked her watch and gave a squeak of alarm as she saw the time. "We should be in the boardroom," she announced. "Dad'll be demonstrating the Sylph, and he'll want us there." She took Fred by the hand. "C'mon Fred, let's make a lasting impression."

CHAPTER FIFTEEN:

In Which Fred Makes A Lasting Impression

And Daisy Gets Wet.

Fred was not sure he wanted to make a lasting impression on anybody, but he allowed himself to be led down the corridor past Sir Roland's office, to the boardroom at the end of the passage. He stared nervously at the padded leather doors of the boardroom, feeling like a guilty schoolboy summoned to the Headmaster's office for a beating. He hesitated momentarily when he put a hand to the door. Although Daisy had given him every impression that the job was his whether he liked it or not, he suspected any future he might have working there would hinge on his performance in front of the board of directors. A bad case of stage-fright prevented him from opening the door. What if he made a fool of himself? If he blew it, where would he stand with Daisy? Boadicea and Britannia, who had joined them on their return from his guided tour, both put a hand in the small of his back and shoved.

The boardroom was bigger and more imposing than Fred's worst nightmare, all polished mahogany and leather, he noted as he tumbled into the room. The board of directors, a dozen or more smartly dressed executives, were sitting at the long table. They had been gazing across the room at the only friendly face that Fred recognised, but now turned as one to stare at him.

"This is the exhibition stand that our marketing people have put together with the help of Research and Development. It'll take pride of place at the Earl's Court Trade Fair later this month." Sir Roland was standing

172

beside his brand new baby. The 'Sylph Home Spa' was a gleaming chrome, black-marble and etched glass wonder about the size of a double wardrobe. No simple shower cubicle, it harked back to the glorious Victorian contraptions of polished, antique brass piping and nozzles that adorned the bathrooms back at the Manor. It did nothing so prosaic or commonplace as squirting the occupant from above. Instead, the 'Sylph' pumped powerful, massaging jets of water from every conceivable angle in a modern interpretation of the Victorian design. The pipes and nozzles were part of the framework of the cubicle itself. A sophisticated control panel on the wall of the cubicle governed the working of the electrical heater, the pump and the valves that permitted the strong, pulsing streams of water to be emitted from the small nozzles placed around the cubicle. Sir Roland pointed out each of the salient points as if equipping some secret agent for a world-saving mission. He looked up and his face lit up as he noticed Fred, Daisy and Boadicea standing in the doorway.

He bounded across the room to Fred, sweeping an arm round his shoulders, and steered him towards the board of directors. "Gentlemen, I'd like to introduce you to Mr Fred Longfield, my new Personal Assistant," Sir Roland said proudly. "He's the bright young feller who sorted out the Deluxe 500 problem."

"Another Personal Assistant?" A small, but very important-looking, well-dressed, grey-haired man in his late fifties who was seated at the head of the table was the speaker. He eyed Daisy with scarcely concealed disdain. "That can only be an improvement," he added under his breath. Daisy overheard this and her eyes flashed dangerously.

"Fred, this is my partner, Lord Ballcock."

Fred extended a trembling hand to shake Lord Ballcock's. "P... pleased to meet you, your Lordship."

"Hmph," grunted Lord Ballcock, ignoring the hand completely. He stabbed a be-ringed finger in the direction of the demonstration stand. "You were explaining the workings of the..." He checked the sheaf of notes in front of him, "Sylph Home Spa."

"Oh yes," chortled Sir Roland. "Come on, Fred," he beamed enthusiastically. He led Fred over to the contraption. Two hosepipes snaked away across the floor to the adjoining executive washroom. "The idea is to have a fully functioning model of the Sylph with all of the design improvements incorporated into it shown by cutaway parts." Sir Roland went into his sales pitch again.

Lord Ballcock stood up from his plush, leather armchair and strolled over to the Sylph, walking round the stand and perusing the object, unimpressed. "Tell me, Roly. What exactly are the benefits of this admittedly ingenious device, over the traditional power-shower head? I know we can see the thing in action, but I can't really appreciate what's so earth-shattering about it."

"We could do with someone actually trying it out."

All heads turned to stare at Daisy, who had volunteered this piece of wisdom.

"Go on, Daze. It'll be just like that Miss Wet Teeshirt contest on Skiathos," chortled Boadicea mischievously.

"I hope not!" Daisy sounded as if she hoped

Boadicea might have forgotten the episode.

"Of course, you did have an unfair advantage."

Daisy stared down at her toes in embarrassment. "Well, somebody should have told me I was supposed to wear more than *just* the wet teeshirt. We *were* on holiday, and that fellow serving at the bar kept plying me with Pernod-and-Orange." She made an expansive what-the-hell-can-I-do-anyway gesture. "In any case, I haven't a towel with me."

"You were dancing naked on the bar until you passed out," sniffed Boadicea, unwilling to let the topic drop.

"So were you," countered Daisy. "And you weren't even *in* the wet teeshirt contest!"

"That nice girl from the tour company and I had to carry you up to her room, and we had to barricade the door against that rugby team you befriended."

"*You* invited them all back to *our* room!" retorted Daisy. "I seem to recall you making an offer to snog everybody in the bar."

Boadicea's perma-tan acquired a distinctly rosy hue. She had forgotten about that. Fortunately, her father had missed the exchange. She made one last attempt to goad Daisy. "Go on, Daze, I *dare* you."

Daisy was rescued by Sir Roland making theatrical coughing noises to get everybody's attention again. "The pattern of water flow and direction in the 'Sylph' cubicle is designed to stimulate the skin of the user," he continued. "A standard power-shower head merely sprays one from

175

above. The 'Sylph' isn't just a shower unit in any case. It's much more than that."

"Then you're not putting this device forward as a new shower unit," ventured Lord Ballcock.

"It's a *home spa*." Sir Roland emphasised the words by prodding them on the design that was taped to an easel beside the 'Sylph'. "All the benefits of a Jacuzzi or a hot tub in a refreshing shower, with only a fraction of the heating costs and volume of water used."

"Ah." Lord Ballcock made comprehending noises and nodded. He opened the door of the cubicle and the flow of water was instantaneously stemmed.

"Auto shut off of the water supply when the door is opened," observed Sir Roland gleefully.

"Nice." Lord Ballcock looked approving. Possibly against his better judgement, he stepped over the threshold of the device and donned half-frame spectacles to inspect the touch-sensitive control panel on the back wall. He peered suspiciously at one of the nozzles on the wall.

The door swung closed.

Lord Ballcock gave a stentorian bellow as he was squirted in the face by the nozzle he was examining. Suddenly the peer was deluged by swirling jets of hot water, spraying him from every angle, and saturating him to the skin. The toothpaste dispenser ejaculated a spearmint-flavoured gout down the front of his jacket, and not to be outdone, the conditioner dispenser dumped its load dead-centre on the top of his head with the accuracy of a passing seagull. He hopped up and down, swearing bitterly as he tried to open the cubicle door again.

Fred darted forwards and grasped the handle of the cubicle door. He tugged. The door refused to budge as Lord Ballcock's weight was being applied to the other side.

"I'm drowning, you idiot!" gurgled Lord Ballcock.

Fred squared his shoulders and yanked the door open. It was like opening a door on a fishing trawler, mid-Atlantic with a force eight gale blowing — but for the fact the water was hot. He was inundated by spray, blobs of toothpaste and shampoo and conditioner before Lord Ballcock shoulder-charged him aside. Water poured out over the expensive carpet, a pool spreading across the floor as the spray continued to gush forth.

Sir Roland made tisk-tisk noises. "That cut-out is going to be a problem," he observed to nobody in particular.

The front of his suit saturated, Fred struggled forwards to try to get to the control panel. Unfortunately, once he had recovered his wits sufficiently, Lord Ballcock had had exactly the same idea. They collided in the doorway of the cubicle and struggled for a moment. "Out of the way, you moron!" Lord Ballcock pushed Fred out of the way with the intention of stopping the flow himself. Water jetted up the front of his Savile Row suit again.

Matters were not helped by a young man who leapt forwards from the onlookers with a cry of "I'll help you, Sir!" He tripped over the carpet and butted Lord Ballcock full in the middle of the back and sent him flying into the cubicle. Lord Ballcock made further drowning noises. The young man grabbed the peer by the ankles and dragged him out to safety then proceeded to administer the kiss of life.

Lord Ballcock swung a meaty fist at the young man,

but obviously this kind of scenario had taken place on numerous previous occasions and the young man's reflexes meant the blow failed to connect. Only when the junior partner started to flail like an upturned beetle trying to get up did his eager assistant dart forwards again. Lord Ballcock slapped the young man's hands away irritably as he was hauled to his feet. "Leave me alone, Hegarty, or by God I'll do you a mischief." He scraped his soaking grey hair back from his eyes and glared balefully at Fred.

"I'll give it the once over once we've got it back in the workshop," suggested Sir Roland.

"You said your young friend here is some kind of expert in plumbing and mechanics," growled Lord Ballcock. "Why not let him have a look?"

Fred blanched. He had never said he was an expert. Nobody could describe him as an expert. Enthusiastic dabbler, maybe. "Ah... right." He went over to the Sylph and vaguely looked around it to find out where to start. Although the door was safely closed again, water was still gushing out of the unit over the expensive carpet, which was also now dotted with small dirty-fido piles of toothpaste.

Daisy joined him. "Don't worry, Fred," she whispered encouragingly. "I'll give you a hand." She gave his arm a reassuring squeeze.

Fred regarded the device with the air of a bomb disposal expert. "Right, then," he muttered to himself, and arming himself with a screwdriver and adjustable spanner from Sir Roland's toolkit, he went round the side of the Sylph.

Daisy stared at the hurricane-in-a-box, her lips

pursed thoughtfully. An enormous water stain was spreading across the boardroom carpet, and something drastic would have to be done to save the drafting offices on the floor below from flooding. She came to a decision and shrugged out of her jacket. As a man, the board of directors craned their necks in fascination as she swiftly kicked off her shoes and wriggled out of her mini-mini skirt. Down to just her silk slip, "I'm going in," she announced.

Boadicea and Britannia were standing by the door, watching developments with scarcely disguised amusement, waiting to see what Daisy would do to vanquish the shower-from-hell. A mischievous smile played across Boadicea's lips as she and her sister moved to flank Daisy.

Daisy was as usual blissfully unaware of any duplicity. The first she knew anything might be wrong was a blast of warm spray in the face as Britannia gave the door of the Sylph a shove to open it. Then Boadicea's hand was in the small of her back and she had been given a powerful shove along with the exhortation, "Go on, Daze, I know you can fix it!"

The door of the cubicle closed on her and she was engulfed in a maelstrom of hot, soapy water. She was being sprayed from every conceivable and embarrassing angle, pummelled by massaging jets that plastered her slip to her skin one moment and threatened to wash it from her person the next. The onlooking company directors watched mesmerised as Daisy struggled to escape the torrent.

Fred, stationed at the rear of the contraption, was unaware of what Daisy was up to. He had removed the service panel and was probing the workings with a screwdriver. He jumped back as water squirted out of one

179

of the connections he had been examining. He could hears shouts of alarm and saw a deluge of water gushing out of the door of the cubicle, spraying Daisy's executive audience. "Hells bells!" he muttered to himself. He leapt to his feet and raced round to the front of the demonstration stand. Daisy appeared to be trying to strangle the main shower head with her bare hands as it lashed free of its moorings like an enraged cobra.

"Fred! Help!!" she squealed.

· Fred reached into the cubicle and hauled her to safety. Daisy tumbled into his arms like a half-drowned Afghan-hound.

In the executive washroom, having tired of the sport of Daisy-drenching, Boadicea had been making some running repairs to her makeup. Satisfied with the result, she nodded at her reflection, then turned off the taps where the piping from the 'Sylph' was connected. The racket coming from the boardroom suddenly subsided as if turned off along with the water supply.

Fred forlornly watched as a couple of Sir Roland's Research and Development team mopped up the pool of water that was ruining the boardroom carpet. Lord Ballcock was being ineffectually dabbed dry by the young man who had nearly drowned him, using handfuls of toilet paper. His suit was covered in bits of soggy paper, gobs of toothpaste and streaks of hair conditioner. "Hegarty, you idiot. Leave me alone!" he slapped the young man's hands away and glared at Fred.

Sir Roland was the only completely dry person left in the room. Chuckling and wiping a tear of mirth from his eye, he patted Fred on the shoulder. "Never mind, Frederick, old boy. No harm done."

"No harm done?" squawked Lord Ballcock. "We'll have to redecorate the boardroom and the drafting office downstairs! My suit's ruined! What do you mean, no harm done?"

Fred groaned inwardly. He had made the perfect start to his new job - making an enemy of one of the bosses.

"Fred's a great-nephew of Plum Longfield, Sid," Sir Roland observed offhandedly.

This quietly-imparted morsel of information had a quite astounding effect on the enraged peer. The beetroot hue suffusing his features faded as his bushy, salt-and-pepper eyebrows hiked upwards like twin hairy caterpillars facing off. He smiled alarmingly. "Quite, no harm done," he released in a huge rush of breath. At his side, the young Californian looked thoroughly confused.

No more than Our Hero, thought Fred to himself.

Daisy, Boadicea and Britannia were standing over by the door again, and Boadicea had a suspiciously butter-wouldn't-melt sort of expression on her face. Daisy was wringing out her long, blonde hair as if it were a dish rag. In most circumstances she looked stunning; dripping wet, she looked sensational.

"Er... come along, Fred. I've something to show you." Sir Roland led Fred away from Lord Ballcock before any major blood vessels burst. "I don't think Daze has given you much idea about what this job entails, has she?"

"The vaguest intimation, Sir," replied Fred.

"Well, it's pretty straightforward." Sir Roland offered Fred a fatherly smile. "I need someone to run around on errands, personal bits of business. That sort of thing. That's where Daisy comes in. Confidentially though, Fred, our Daisy could do with someone to keep an interested eye on her to keep her out of trouble. That's why I like her working for me. Oh, she's very bright and very capable, but she's also very capable at getting herself into all kinds of trouble." Fred nodded. He could believe that easily. "At any rate, you seem a decent sort of chap. Smart, on the ball and all that sort of thing, and Daisy likes you. That's why I want you working for me."

"I'm flattered, Sir Roland."

"You'll take the job, then?" Sir Roland pumped Fred's hand enthusiastically. He gave Daisy the thumbs-up behind Fred's back. "Daze tells me you're temporarily without transport."

"That's right," Fred confirmed. He was contemplating giving the remains of his car a proper Christian burial.

"Well, no need to worry. The job comes complete with a company car." Sir Roland guided Fred over to the window and pointed down at the gleaming new Mercedes standing in the car park. Fred goggled. He appeared to have hit the jackpot with his new job. But as he looked across the room at Daisy, he could not help wondering if he would be earning every penny of it...

CHAPTER SIXTEEN:

In Which Lord Ballcock Makes Plans Against A Union

And Possibly Underestimates Julian

If Daisy had one fault, thought Fred, it was a tendency to mislay things. Important documents, items of office equipment, her handbag, shoes, articles of clothing of a quite fascinating variety, had a habit of being forgotten when her mind was otherwise occupied. He had been sent down to the car park to retrieve her handbag from under the front seat of his car, otherwise she would not be able to raid the vending machine on the landing outside for her mid-morning cup of hot chocolate.

"Mr Longfield?"

Fred looked round. Heading towards him across the car park was the squat, powerful figure of Lord Ballcock. Trailing in his wake was the young man who had nearly drowned the Great Man in the boardroom. Hegarty was a tall, curly-haired young man of Californian extraction, who according to Daisy had been head-hunted from a major corporation in the States. From first impressions, it had been clear that they might have hunted his head, but not its contents.

Lord Ballcock was a different proposition entirely. Dapper, every inch the successful businessman, it was well known how this life-peer had dragged himself up from being a simple, jobbing plumber in the mid-sixties to running one of the largest plumbing concerns in Europe. A certain amount of shady dealing a few years ago had enabled him to buy up a thirty-five percent share of Chayne Sanitary Ware, and the result was the uncomfortable state of affairs that was Chayne and Ballcock Sanitary Fixtures Manufacturers.

"Mr Longfield." Lord Ballcock regarded Fred with beady little eyes. "I fear we may have got off on the wrong foot." He offered Fred a crocodile smile, extending a suntanned hand to shake Fred's. Fred had the ugly feeling he might not get his hand back, but could not afford to slight one of his employers. He took the proffered hand and shook it, receiving a limp squeeze in return. "May I call you Fred?"

Do I have any option? wondered Fred. "Please do."

Lord Ballcock reached up to put a comradely arm around Fred's shoulders. "Fred, do you know the full potential of the sanitary ceramics market? People are using our products every day of their lives, at home and at work. Sixty million people, visiting the loo at least three times a day. Nineteen million households in this country, each with at least one toilet. Not forgetting baths, basins, bidets, showers, water tanks, hot water cylinders, pipes and taps. Anything to do with plumbing falls within our sphere of interest. And there's only a handful of companies involved in making these products. The potential for our company - and a smart fellow like you within that company - are limitless."

This was leading somewhere, and Fred was not sure he wanted to find out where.

"This company could be going places, and so could you, my friend." Lord Ballcock reached into his jacket and withdrew a large, silver cigar case. He opened it and Fred could hear the strains of Handel's Water Music. Selecting one of the Havana cigars, he returned the case to his pocket irrespective of whether Fred was a smoker or not. He rolled the cigar between his fingers, marshalling his thoughts. Hegarty darted forwards, lighter at the ready. He squeezed the piezo-ignition and was rewarded with a jet of flame and a cry of pain and alarm from Lord Ballcock. "Those were my eyebrows, you idiot!" the peer thundered, throwing the cigar to the ground petulantly. It would be difficult to satisfactorily smoke a cigar from the middle.

Fred looked on with polite interest as Hegarty hovered around his employer, dabbing at the blotches of soot on his face with a handkerchief. Hegarty held the handkerchief to Lord Ballcock's mouth. "Spit." Lord Ballcock irritably slapped Hegarty's hands away.

"Frederick, my boy," Lord Ballcock was at his most expansive. "As long as Sir Roland Chayne is the senior partner in the company, we will continue to trail behind other manufacturers such as the Thunderbox Corporation, Spanner Bros. and Bogges, Carseigh and Privais. What I need is someone I can trust at his right hand who can help me further the interests of the company."

"I am employed by Sir Roland, Sir," Fred knew where his loyalties lay.

"Don't forget I employ you too, Fred." Lord Ballcock wagged a finger at him. "And don't forget that in a reorganised Ballcock Sanitary - sorry - *Chayne* and Ballcock Sanitary Fixtures Manufacturers, there would be a well-paid position for a bright lad like you." This observation was accompanied by a conspiratorial wink.

Fred felt as if he had been cornered by a large, carnivorous creature, and it was licking its chops in anticipation.

-oOo-

"Daisy! Nice outfit!"

Daisy cringed. That voice had set her nerves on edge every time she had heard it. Forcing herself not to scowl, she turned to face the company's top sales representative. Julian Ballcock had almost always made Daisy's skin crawl. When his Uncle had first introduced him to the firm, she had admired his arrogant good looks, but then he had started to romance her, doubtless part of his Uncle's plan to oust her father from the company. Now she felt only disgust that she had ever let him near her, and sickened that he had managed to get so close. She dropped the bundle of papers she was carrying as Julian gave her one of those slick smiles that had once, very briefly, turned her legs to jelly before she had got to know what he was really like.

"What do you want, Julian?" she growled, in no mood for any of his funny business. "I'm busy." She took the opportunity, as he had not been expecting quite such an unfriendly greeting, to brush him aside. He nipped smartly round her and blocked her way again.

"Imagine the scene. Candlelight, champagne. A dozen oysters. How does that sound?"

"Wonderful." Daisy's eyes lit up.

Julian looked as if he had won the lottery. "You really mean that?"

"Mmm," Daisy nodded affirmatively. "Fred would just love it."

"Fred?" Julian looked at her blankly. "What's Fred got to do with it?"

"I was wondering what Fred and I could have for supper tonight. I wanted to make it something special." Daisy grinned. "Thanks for the idea."

"But... but..." Julian did a stunning impression of an outboard motor. "I meant *we'd* be having the oysters and champagne."

"Oh, I don't think so, Julian." Daisy shook her head, tut-tutting. "You know the old saying - *Two's Company, Three's the number before four.*"

"Eh?"

"Problem, Daze?" Daisy felt a rush of relief as Fred loomed up behind her. He had spotted Julian cornering Daisy and in true White Knight style had come to her rescue.

Daisy beamed at Julian. "You remember Fred?"

Julian regarded Fred with the sort of expression most people reserve for slugs and little-messages-left-behind-by-puppies. "Oh yes," he sneered. "One of your hard-luck stories." His eyes narrowed. "You were in Daisy's room. Being a little over-familiar, as I recall. Didn't I have to give you a good thrashing?"

A good thrashing??? Fred presented his best poker face to Julian, but inside his mind was boggling loudly. He raised an eyebrow as if trying to remember something. "I seem to recall a light slap," he ventured slowly. He locked eyes with the young Mr Ballcock. Years of staring down stroppy fifth-formers had stood him in good stead and only a few moments passed before Julian faltered, blinking.

Daisy watched the silent display in mild amazement. "Now now, boys, play nice," she chided. "Shake hands and make friends."

Julian made magnanimous noises and thrust an immaculately manicured hand forwards. Fred accepted the gesture warily. A thin smile played across Julian's lips and he dug his fingertips in, squeezing Fred's hand with all the force he could muster. Fred did not blink, but returned the pressure. After slightly less than a minute, Julian's complexion had gone from its normal tan-in-a-bottle orange to a quite spectacular shade of beetroot. He released Fred's hand, straightened his jacket with as much dignity as he could muster and swept away back along the passage to Lord Ballcock's suite of offices.

"Firm handshake," commented Fred. He allowed Daisy to lead him back towards their shared office.

-oOo-

Lord Ballcock was not a happy man. The compactly-built peer sat behind his polished oak desk, puffing on a Havana cigar and watching his nephew wearing a rut in the office Axminster. Julian Ballcock was pacing across the office, backwards and forwards like a caged tiger in a state of some agitation.

"...I mean, the man is completely unsuitable for a position of such responsibility. He has no clerical qualifications whatsoever. He has been known to indulge in common brawling, Uncle," Julian babbled. "What sort of character is that to bring into the firm?"

Lord Ballcock snorted derisively. As he had his

cigar in his mouth at the time, this had the effect of causing a smallish explosion of blue smoke around his head. He took the cigar out of his mouth and stabbed it in Julian's direction. "I know you're completely spineless, Julian, but I refuse to fight your battles for you. Boadicea and Britannia have told me everything about this Fred Longfield feller. They've told me all about your encounter with the gentleman at the Manor." Julian stopped pacing and looked shamefaced. "I know Fred Longfield is unsuitable for the job, but Roland's given him it. It's a *fait accompli*. Live with it."

"But Uncle," protested Julian. "If Daisy gets romantic about this schoolteacher, where does that leave me?"

"Lonely, my dear Julian," replied Lord Ballcock. "You made a complete hash of your relationship with Bluebell Chayne, and now you've alienated her sister. If Buttercup wasn't already married, you could always go for the hat-trick..."

Julian let out a desolate breath, then noticed his uncle was sitting up with an expression that bordered on the evangelical. "Uncle?"

"I own thirty-five percent of Chayne and Ballcock Sanitary Fixtures Manufacturers, correct?" Lord Ballcock started scribbling on his desk blotter with his fountain pen.

"Uh..." Figures were not Julian's strong point.

"That blasted workforce syndicate owns fourteen percent of the company, and the controlling fifty-one percent interest is Roland Chayne's, right?" Receiving no answer from Julian, he nodded. "Right." Punching the desk calculator with stubby fingers, he continued. "In the unhappy event anything should happen to Roland, his shares in the company pass in equal measure to his daughters Buttercup, Bluebell and Daisy. This means that each of those ladies will receive a seventeen percent share in the company."

Julian sat down in the guest chair in front of his uncle's huge desk. "Uncle, you're not considering bumping off Sir Roland?" He looked horrified.

"Of course not, you idiot boy!" spat Lord Ballcock. "I can always look on the bright side, but I was thinking more along the lines of when Roland decides to retire. He's always said he would divide his interest in the company equally between his daughters. *Seventeen percent each.* Don't you get it?"

Julian nodded happily, then admitted defeat and changed the nod to a sorrowful shake of his 19th Century poet's locks.

"I have thirty-five percent of the shares. Let's say Daisy, *or someone married to her* has control of seventeen percent of the shares. Thirty-five plus seventeen?"

"Oh!" Julian looked amazed. "That's a lot of shares."

Lord Ballcock deflated visibly as he realised the penny had yet to drop. "That would be fifty-two percent of the shares, or *controlling interest* in the company."

"Ah." Julian mulled over the concept, then suddenly sat up. "You would be the senior partner!"

Lord Ballcock rolled his eyes. "I could almost hear the splash," he muttered to himself.

"But what about Auntie Hat?" Julian looked shocked.

"What about your Aunt Harriet?" Lord Ballcock looked confused. His wife, Lady Ballcock, happily distanced herself from the business and usually left him to his Machiavellian devices.

"If you're going to marry Daisy and get all her shares in the company, what happens to Auntie Hat?" Julian looked stricken. "You're not going to get a divorce, are you?"

"Of course not, you dimwit," snapped Lord Ballcock. "If *you* were married to Daisy, *you* would be able to control her shares and with my share in the company, *we* would have controlling interest."

A second splash as the penny dropped. Julian nodded. "Provided I intended to vote with you in the running of the company," he ventured.

Lord Ballcock regarded his nephew in alarm, uncertain if he had underestimated the boy. He stood up and moved around the desk to join his nephew. "Julian, my boy," he beamed expansively. "I've changed my mind. I think it's terrible a smart, charming young feller as yourself should have such trouble romancing a pretty girl. It's been my fondest dream to see you walk down the aisle with Daisy, and I'm going to do everything in my power to make sure it happens." He steered Julian towards the door. "Now, don't give Fred Longfield a moment's thought. I have an idea that's one fine romance that's going to falter before too long."

Julian beamed.

CHAPTER SEVENTEEN:

In Which Daisy Accepts A Lift

And Fred Receives A Visitor

Saturday morning had dawned bright and warm, and Fred found himself cornered on a park bench by the boating lake by hordes of excitedly quacking ducks as they congregated appreciatively around him and his bag of pieces of bread. He had decided to spend the day with Daisy, and to that end had come down to the park to intercept her on her morning jog. Jogging was something he seldom did in the normal course of events, so he was turned out in a sloppy pullover and jeans rather than the Lycra-based, fashionable raiment favoured by most joggers in the park.

He had been sitting on the park bench for about quarter of an hour, waiting for her to come steaming into sight. The ducks on the boating lake had been keeping him company, nipping at the legs of his jeans until he tossed them a few more handfuls of bread from the bag he had brought with him.

He sat up as he saw a familiar flash of golden hair and Daisy hove into view like a prizefighter in training, a towel about her shoulders, bounding along on the toes of canvas running shoes worn without socks. Her hair was scraped back into a ponytail and secured by a multi-coloured scrunchie, and she was wearing a grey, cropped sports top that barely managed to contain her exuberance. A pair of white, boxer-style shorts completed the ensemble. He grinned to himself. She was one of a kind.

-oOo-

Daisy was not having the best of morning jogs. She
was three-quarters of the way round her regular, occasional
circuit of the park. She had let her training programme of
taking a weekly jog around the park to work off Sunday
lunch slip since she met Fred, and was paying for her
laziness. Puffing like a steam locomotive, she had decided
to-hell-with-fitness, she was going everywhere by car in
future when one drew alongside her. There was no
through- road in the park, and cars were prohibited beyond
the gates, so she was not in the least bit surprised to see
Julian Ballcock at the wheel of the Porsche. The repulsive
toad seemed not to consider himself bound by the rules of
ordinary mortals. "'Morning, Princess," he chortled.

"'Morning yourself," replied Daisy sullenly. She
felt Julian's eyes travel down her body, mentally
undressing her with such intensity that she looked down at
herself, half-expecting to discover her shorts down round
her ankles. She glared at him. "What do you want?"

"I'm just passing the time of day, Daisy darling,"
replied Julian lightly.

"Well, I wish you'd go and pass it somewhere else."

Julian looked reproachfully at her. "Is that any way
to speak to someone who's bought you a box of
chocolates?" he asked. He reached over the back of the
seat and hauled a five-pound box of chocolates out from
under his coat on the back seat. He gave the box a gentle
shake to prove it was full of sweets.

Daisy looked startled, then suspicious. Julian was
not the type to suddenly present her with a box of
chocolates. Unless he had laced them with something to

knock her out. Her imagination started working overtime. It would be like the bit in Snow White with the old bag and the apple. She would fall into a deep sleep, but instead of a handsome prince waking her up with a kiss, she would regain consciousness forty-eight hours later in the honeymoon suite of a Las Vegas motel, with him in the process of taking off the electric-blue, shiny, polyester tuxedo he had worn at the wedding ceremony. She shuddered.

As if reading her mind, Julian grinned at her. "It's all right, Daze, I haven't tampered with them. You can see the box is still in the original plastic wrapper. If you don't believe me, unwrap them, pick one at random and I'll eat it, okay? Can't say fairer than that."

Daisy looked at him dubiously and peeled the wrapping from the box. Selecting a soft centre - she hated praline, suspecting as it was brown and smelled of nuts, was secretly squirrel poo - she leaned across and popped it into Julian's mouth.

"See?" he said indistinctly. "No ill effects. I promise you those chocolates are untouched by human hands. And I haven't touched them either." He flashed the sort of winning smile that had once made her weak at the knees. "Anyway, you can't fool around with hard centres, and the soft centres show up where the hypodermic needle went in..." He trailed off as he realised he had said too much.

"Somehow, Julian, I wouldn't put that kind of thing past you." Daisy popped a hazelnut cluster into her mouth.

Julian patted the passenger seat. "Hop in and I'll run you home," he offered.

Daisy looked even more taken aback. Being helpful was so completely out of character for Julian. If she got into the car, she knew her virtue might be in mortal danger. On the other hand, she had inherited a tremendous right hook from her mother that Julian had become acquainted with on a number of occasions. Her legs were aching and she still had half-a-mile of her jog left to do. The kid-leather passenger seat of the Porsche looked terribly inviting. "No funny business?"

"No funny business," confirmed Julian, holding up his right hand and crossing his heart in a hope-to-die manner.

As he was not struck down instantaneously by a bolt from the heavens, Daisy made up her mind. She opened the car door and slid into the passenger seat, the huge box of chocolates balanced on her lap. She fastened her seatbelt and settled back with a gratified sigh as Julian accelerated smoothly away down the path.

Fred leapt to his feet in consternation. He had just seen Daisy accept a huge box of chocolates from Julian Ballcock and hop into his Porsche! He stared after the car in confusion, the bag of bread scattering at his feet and precipitating an unruly waterfowl free-for-all. Daisy cosying up to Julian?? After everything she had said about the repulsive toad??? He gazed down at the rugby-scrum of ducks mobbing his ankles to get at the bread. "The whole world's gone quackers!" he exclaimed.

The ducks knew a lousy joke when they heard one, and ignored him.

-oOo-

For the first time in the years that she had known
Julian Ballcock, he had been as good as his word. He had
driven Daisy straight back to her flat and dropped her off
unmolested. Daisy watched the Porsche accelerate away
up the Park road and against her better judgement gave him
a friendly farewell wave. She started across the paved front
yard of the flats, the box of chocolates under her arm. She
looked up at a frantic squawk of "Daze!!" in the distance.
Boadicea and Britannia were hurrying up the street towards
her, shocked expressions on both aristocratic faces. Daisy
waited for them to catch up with her before unlocking the
front door.

"That was Julian!" Britannia sounded scandalised.
"You just got out of cousin Julian's car! With a big box of
chocolates!" Her face was a picture and Daisy could not
help smiling. "What's going on?" Boadicea demanded.
"You're not letting that repulsive toad near you again?"

"Good heavens, no!" Daisy was shocked either of
them could even think that. "Once was enough. Once was
too much. Ugh. Ahgh. *Eww!*" She shuddered eloquently.
"No, normally I wouldn't let Julian near me without the
protection of a gun, but he offered me a lift and caught me
at a low ebb. I shouldn't have stayed up so late last night."

"And of course, you'd never turn down a free box
of chocolates," smiled Boadicea.

"You know me too well." Daisy threw the front
door open. "Fancy a coffee and a Montelimar?"

-oOo-

Fred's day had been thrown into disarray by the
events in the park. If he was competing with Julian for
Daisy's affections, then he would have his work cut out for
him as the slimy so-and-so had much greater resources with
which to pitch his woo. Fred paused, his train of thought in
danger of derailing. Daisy had made it abundantly clear
that she regarded Julian 'like something nasty you might
find lurking under a rock,' but then again Julian had once
exerted some strange kind of attraction over Daisy. He
could not risk even the remote possibility that the slimy
interloper might yet be able to snatch Daisy out of his
reach.

Fred stood in the first-floor bathroom, applying
cologne-scented shaving foam to his physiognomy so that
Daisy would not be able to complain about bristles when he
kissed her. Fred had no idea why, but his face seemed to
be designed to prevent him achieving the baby's-bottom
finish touted by the shaver adverts. Most work days, he
found a quick once-over with his trusty electric razor
sufficed. That evening, however, he wanted to make a
good impression, and was having a traditional wet shave.
The bathroom was as steamy and close as the Amazon
jungle, and the air was heavy with the smell of male
grooming products. He had applied a Father Christmas
beard of white foam to his face, and was wielding his trusty
Gillette with surgical precision. There was just over half-
an-hour to go before Daisy was expected for dinner, and he
was busy getting ready. He had showered, sprayed himself
with virtually everything on the bathroom shelf, and his
next move was to get dressed. In the bath, propped up with
the stems in two inches of water was a bouquet of flowers
from the florist's. He had seen the size of the box of
chocolates that Julian had given her, and had made no
attempt to compete on that front. He hoped he would not
need to take out a mortgage to cover his credit card bill that

month. Hanging up on the back of the bathroom door was his best suit, ready for him to change into. Down in the kitchen his and Rummidge's culinary skills had been challenged like Hercules by his seven tasks, and a roast was on a low heat in the oven.

-oOo-

Lord Ballcock's Rolls cruised silently past the gatepost of Grisley End, formerly vandalised with the motif "Castle Frankenstein". It glided up the drive like a shark shadowing a bathing beach. It was late evening and the sun was dipping low over the ruined watchtower to the rear of the old house. The shadows of the trees flickered strobe-like against the windows of the slow-moving vehicle. In the rear of the car, Lord Ballcock and his darling twin daughters Boadicea and Britannia were sitting, sipping champagne. Both stunning brunettes were advocates of power-dressing, in spite of whatever mainstream fashion dictated. Long, bare, copper-tanned legs crossed demurely, Boadicea was listening intently to her father.

"Now, Boadicea, m'dear." Lord Ballcock patted his daughter's knee. He indicated the windows of Grisley End ahead of them. "That's young Fred Longfield's place."

Boadicea regarded the façade of the old house with similar emotions to Daisy. In the gathering darkness, she had seldom seen anything quite as creepy, with the possible exception of cousin Julian's passion-pad in town. She wrinkled her nose. "It's a bit of a dump, isn't it?" Most of the men in her life lived in more opulent surroundings.

"Apparently, he's inherited from his Great Uncle," Lord Ballcock curled a derisory lip. "Daisy's always had a thing for lame ducks and hard-luck stories, and young Fred's no exception. What old Roland was thinking about

198

when he employed that idiot, I'll never know. He has no experience in the sanitary fixtures business, or in simple office work. I was checking his personnel file a couple of days ago, and according to that, his last job was as a chemistry teacher at a secondary school."

"He's got a degree in Engineering," offered Britannia brightly.

Lord Ballcock waved a hand airily. "Daisy finds him mysteriously attractive and that troubles me."

Boadicea looked at her father blankly. "Why should Daisy Chayne's love life bother you, Dad?"

"I'm thinking of young Julian." Lord Ballcock did his best to look emotional, but only succeeded in making Boadicea realise what people meant when they talked about 'crocodile tears'. "He's always had a soft spot for Daisy. Carried a torch for her, you might say. He's been a broken man since this Longfield fellow came on the scene."

"Poor Julian," sniffed Britannia sympathetically.

"What, *our* Julian?" Boadicea was less gullible than her sister. "Warmhamptonshire's-answer-to-Warren-Beatty Julian? Bitter ex-girlfriend-in-every-department Julian? After his last performance, I doubt if Daisy would give him the time of day."

"I try not to involve myself in Julian's romantic exploits." Lord Ballcock held up a finger to prevent Boadicea expanding on the theme. "At my time of life, I value my sleep uninterrupted by nightmares." He pointed at the front windows of the house. "The problem is our Mr Longfield is getting too close to Daisy for comfort. If my plans for the company are to come to anything, I need to drive a wedge between those two, so that young Julian can get a look in. I know he's expecting Daisy round for dinner this evening, and I don't want him to keep that date."

Both sisters looked shocked. "Dad!"

"Is there a problem?"

"Daisy's our oldest friend," protested Boadicea. "I know we play tricks on her and that kind of thing, but she's still a chum."

"And you've never....?"

"Well, occasionally we've liberated boyfriends of hers," admitted Boadicea. "But only when she's more or less finished with them. She's really serious about this one."

"That's what I'm afraid of," grunted Lord Ballcock. "All I want you to do is *delay* him a while."

"Really, Father!" Boadicea feigned a shocked look. "What do you expect me to do?"

"Just be your usual, sweet self," smirked Lord Ballcock, tickling his daughter under the chin. "String him along a little. All I need to make my plan work is to plant a seed of suspicion in Daisy's mind. If she turns up for her date and finds young Longfield with somebody else's lipstick on his collar, he may lose his appeal."

"What would it do to your plan if *I* fell for Fred?" deadpanned Boadicea mischievously. Lord Ballcock started making the sort of noises you might expect a strangulated hernia to make. She thumped him soundly between the shoulder blades. "I was kidding, Dad.

Honest."

Boadicea and Britannia stepped from the car. An owl hooted and both sisters were over to the entrance of the dark house in a split-second.

"Woooo-ooo" Britannia was shining a torch under her chin.

"Not funny, Britt, not funny at all!" Boadicea had nearly jumped out of her skin. She glared at her sister. Britannia pouted and turned the beam of the torch off. *Get a hold of yourself, Bouncy,* Boadicea told herself. She was panicking over nothing. There were no bogeymen out there to be afraid of. She lifted the cast-iron knocker on the left-hand door and rapped twice. The sound echoed through the house.

Boadicea turned to say something to her sister, but saw that Britannia was sprinting hell-for-leather back to their father's Rolls. No sooner was her chicken-hearted sibling in the vehicle, but it was speeding off down the drive again. *"Bugger!"* she said to herself. Her blood ran cold as behind her, the door opened with a creak like coffin nails being extracted.

The hallway beyond the grand frontage was completely dark. Swallowing her nerves, Boadicea stood querulously on the threshold and peered into the void. "Hullo?" She moved further into the hall against her better judgement. "Fred?"

The door creaked behind her like a prop out of a cheap horror film. Boadicea spun round and froze as she watched it close with a tremendous crash that echoed through the building along with the squeak of alarm she gave as she found herself in total darkness.

"Hullo, is there anybody out there in the dark?" she quavered unhappily, her voice barely audible. She felt as if somebody had given her a transfusion of ice-water.

"Good evening, Miss." Rummidge offered her his most charming smile as he flicked his lighter and applied the flame to the candelabra in his hairy fist.

Fred raced down the stairs into the hall. "What was that scream?" he demanded, his nerves already on edge.

"The young lady appears to have fainted, Sir." Rummidge had propped Boadicea up on the ottoman opposite the door and was patting her hand solicitously. "I think she might need a drop of brandy." He undid the top couple of buttons of her blouse for her.

"Would you oblige?" Fred asked.

"Very good, Sir." Rummidge bowed perfunctorily and sloped off to the Study after handing the candelabra to Fred.

Boadicea came to with a jolt. She looked around wildly, but calmed down the moment she recognised Fred. She grasped Fred by the lapels of his dressing gown. "Mer... mer... monster!" she squeaked. "I saw a monster!"

Fred removed Boadicea's hands from his person and smiled reassuringly. "You're all right now, Bouncy. We're here." He patted Boadicea's hand. "There are no monsters here." He spoke as if he were reassuring a four-year-old woken from a nightmare.

"Oh yes there are," exclaimed Boadicea as at that moment, Rummidge arrived with the brandy. "There's one." She pointed at the Butler with a quivering finger.

Rummidge looked alarmed and cranked his head round to check behind himself. He tilted his head with an alarming creaking noise. "Miss?"

"That's only Mr Rummidge," Fred smiled. "He's the butler." He took the glass of brandy from Rummidge and handed it to Boadicea. Boadicea sniffed the glass suspiciously, and once she had satisfied herself that it did not contain some evil Jekyll and Hyde formula, she drained it. She watched Rummidge retreating suspiciously. "I don't like that fellow," she muttered. "He's creepy."

That seemed to be the popular consensus.

-oOo-

CHAPTER EIGHTEEN:

In Which Boadicea Attempts To Seduce Fred

And Daisy Gets Some Help With The Decorating.

"Can I get you a coffee? Tea?"

"Coffee. Black. No sugar." Boadicea perched elegantly on the Chesterfield in front of the Drawing Room fire.

In a state of some confusion, Fred retreated to the kitchen. Boadicea's presence filled him with alarm. If he was honest with himself, although she was a friend of Daisy's, the girl scared the wits out of him almost as much as her father. He gathered together the makings of the coffee, as Rummidge was keeping a low profile in the Butler's pantry. He put two spoons of grounds into the cafetière and switched on the electric kettle. What was Boadicea Ballcock doing round at the house? More importantly, how could he politely get rid of her before Daisy turned up for their date? He took a couple of mugs from the mug tree on top of the fridge and put them in front of the cafetière. He took the sugar down from the shelf and put two spoonfuls in his cup. The kettle was boiling and he rolled his eyes as he found he had filled the sugar bowl with boiling water.

He tipped the sugary slurry down the sink and refilled the kettle. "Won't be a moment," he called down the passage to his guest.

"Take your time, Freddie, dahling," Boadicea called back.

Fred quivered visibly. She was calling him 'dahling' now. He paced up and down the kitchen - not a terribly long way to travel, although his old flat would have fitted inside with room to spare. He was reluctant to venture back into the Drawing Room without some form of protection. He darted forwards with a breath of relief as the kettle came to the boil again and he was able to brew the coffee. He filled the cups, wrinkling his nose wondering how Boadicea could drink it black and unsweetened, and carried them through into the living room. He stopped in his tracks, staring at the figure on the settee.

Boadicea had unfastened a number of buttons and was giving every impression of being about to tumble out of her clothing. She looked up unabashed as Fred re-entered the room. "I hope you don't mind," she cooed. "I thought I'd make myself comfortable."

The cups in Fred's hands rattled against each other. What Bouncy had in mind for him was more than obvious. He did not need any diagrams drawing. He watched her in alarm as she sauntered over to the door of the Drawing Room. Boadicea smiled enigmatically. "We don't want to be disturbed, do we, Fred?" she breathed huskily. She locked the door and with a wicked expression, tucked the key into the right cup of her brassiere for safe keeping.

"Wh... what are you doing? Why are you locking the door?" Fred's voice had shot up a couple of octaves. Boadicea advanced on him, radiating body heat as he backed away from her.

-oOo-

Daisy checked her watch and pulled the door of her flat closed, locking it with her key. She was going to be late for her dinner date with Fred if she didn't get a wiggle on. She started down the stairs, hoisting her handbag up on to her shoulder.

As she reached the first-floor landing, she saw Britannia outside the flat she shared with her sister. Britannia was having one of those rare Bouncy-free moments when her sister went off on some sinister commission of her own. Of the two sisters, Britannia was the more reasonable and Daisy frequently suspected that she joined in Boadicea's schemes simply for a quiet life. Left to her own devices, Britannia was as disingenuous as her sister was devious. As she passed the young woman on the landing, she noticed Britannia was watching her with a distinctly woeful expression.

"Something the matter, Britt?" she asked brightly.

If at all possible, Britannia looked even more troubled. "I shouldn't say," she replied in a small voice, "but I think the whole thing stinks!"

Daisy looked surprised. "What does?"

Britannia looked around to make sure nobody who might report back to her father was in earshot. "Bouncy's after Fred." She gave a little squeak and quickly went back to unlocking the door of her flat.

"Bouncy's after Fred?" Daisy blinked. "What do you mean, *after* Fred?"

"She has designs on him." Britannia spoke to the door, *sotto voce*.

"Oh, come on, Britt," chortled Daisy in disbelief. "We both know Bouncy's taste in men. She's only interested in six-figure salaries, washboard abs and English as a second language. There's no way she'd be interested in Fred."

Britannia looked up at Daisy sadly. "Dad's put her up to it. He's plotting to drive the two of you apart."

"And his Machiavellian plan is for Bouncy to seduce Fred?"

Britannia nodded.

"So that's why Julian's been making romantic overtures again," Daisy growled. "I had a feeling something was going on..." Her jaw set.

"What are you going to do?" asked Britannia.

"I'm going to take Bouncy's advice," replied Daisy. "I'm going to play Bouncy's game and beat her at it. She can try and steal Fred, but she's going to have a battle on her hands. I'm going to seduce Fred like no man has been seduced before."

"Well, you'd better get a move on," replied Britannia. "She's over at Fred's place *right now.*"

-oOo-

Fred's back collided with the wall and suddenly Boadicea was pressed up against him, enveloping him in a cloud of her expensive perfume. "We're going to be the best of friends," she sighed softly.

Fred stared into her eyes, hardly daring to move. "Bare-bare-but I've already got a bare-best friend!" he stuttered.

Boadicea raised an eyebrow. "What, Daisy?" she purred dismissively. "You need a *real* woman."

"Daisy happens to be all woman." Fred leapt to her defence.

"Let's go and do something quite disgustingly biological." Boadicea licked her lips and released the pressure of her body from him. She pointed upstairs. "I should imagine the beds in this place are something special, Freddie dahling," she purred. A squeak of fright escaped Fred's lips as he felt her scarlet claws on the cord of his dressing gown.

Boadicea smiled lewdly, finding that under the robe he was wearing very little. "Why, Fred!" she chortled admiringly. "I'm beginning to see what Daisy sees in you."

"This isn't right, Boadicea, and you know it," Fred tried not to compound his problems by looking at the severely underdressed brunette. "I know you're here to sabotage things between me and Daisy. Your father's put you up to this, hasn't he?"

"Of course not, Freddie dahling!" purred Boadicea. "I've always been attracted to you, you stud muffin."

"Come off it, Boadicea," exclaimed Fred. "We both know I could never be described as a stud muffin. Now let's not let this get any more embarrassing for both of us than it already is. Give me the key to that door, and I'll call you a taxi."

"You'll have to make me a better offer than that."

There was a time to be a gentleman, and there was a time not to be a gentleman. This was most definitely a *not*.

Fred advanced on Boadicea, a look of steely resolve in his eyes. Boadicea did not like the look and took an apprehensive step backwards.

"Now, Freddie dahling," Boadicea's resolve had vanished in an instant. Suddenly, she had her gravest doubts about her plan. Fred Longfield might have given the impression of being about as threatening as a teddy-bear, but confronted with him now, looking as... well... *determined* as he did, she was definitely having second thoughts. "Be gentle with me!" she squeaked as Fred lunged forwards and grabbed her around the waist. The look in his eyes was hard to describe. Was it lust, or was it because he had taken off his glasses? Resigning herself to her fate, she had to admit that whatever happened it would be interesting.

"Give me the key!" demanded Our Hero.

"What?" Boadicea looked outraged. She had offered herself on a plate to this four-eyed cretin and all he wanted was the door key? His hands were all over her, and she was slapping them away indignantly. "Stop that! Get off!" She wriggled in his grip, pulling him off balance, and they landed on the Chesterfield, Fred on top, knocking the wind out of her and pinning her to the upholstery.

"Where is it?" demanded Fred.

Boadicea gave him an old-fashioned look. "If you have to ask, you must be inexperienced!"

Fred glared at her. "Give!"

"Never!" squawked Boadicea defiantly.

"Don't make me do something you'll regret,

Bouncy," growled Fred. The steely look in his eye should have told the sultry brunette he meant what he said.

"You wouldn't dare!" gasped Boadicea.

-oOo-

Daisy's Mini pulled up on the gravel forecourt of the old house with a spray of stone chips. She sprang from the vehicle, leaving Britannia who had been riding shotgun, to extract herself. The Ballcock Sister peeled her fingers from the dashboard, where they had been stuck since Daisy had overtaken the double-decker bus on the Chayne Halt bypass. She hurried after the willowy blonde.

Rummidge opened the front door. "Miss Daisy," he beamed unnervingly. He was quite relieved to see her, finding the presence of the young Ballcock woman slightly unsettling. He had found her father similarly far from conducive to the peace of the household on his visits in the past.

Daisy had got used to the ancient retainer in spite of herself. She turned to Britannia, wishing she had thought to prepare the girl for the shock. "This is Mr Rummidge, the Butler."

"Miss," Rummidge bobbed perfunctorily in greeting.

Daisy was surprised to see Britannia was completely unfazed. No screaming, no fainting, no throwing-up. Britannia allowed the Butler to take her coat and hang it by the front door.

"Where's Mr Longfield?" asked Daisy, getting to the point.

"He's in the Drawing Room, Miss Chayne," replied the Butler, indicating the double doors of that room. "With the other Miss Ballcock."

Daisy pushed up the sleeves of her jacket. "He is, is he?" Her jaw set in a most unDaisylike manner.

Britannia's mischievous streak came out in full force and she hurried over to the doors of the Drawing Room ahead of Daisy. She tried the handles. "The door's locked!" exclaimed Britannia in scandalised tones.

"Excuse me, Miss." Rummidge politely disengaged the brunette from the door handles and produced his butler's access all areas keyring. He already had the Drawing Room key selected and in a moment had the doors unlocked. He threw the doors open.

-oOo-

Fred had his forearm wedged down the front of Boadicea's blouse. The key had become displaced from its hiding place in the starboard cup of Boadicea's black Wonderbra and was lost in the turmoil that was her clothing. He was rummaging around for it when he heard an exclamation behind him.

"Fred!" Daisy stood frozen in the doorway.

It was the sort of scenario beloved by writers of farces and romantic comedies - the hero caught in a compromising position with another woman by the heroine. A simple misunderstanding that could so easily be avoided by better communication between the characters, but was inevitably blown up into something that kept hero and heroine apart for virtually the rest of the story. Under normal circumstances, Daisy would flounce away, convinced Fred was guilty of two-timing her and it would be page two hundred and fifty before the misunderstanding could be rectified.

"Daze!" Fred exclaimed. *"HELP!!"*

Daisy launched herself at Boadicea in much the way that a mother tiger must launch herself at a threat to her cubs. She caught the brunette broadside on and the two women tumbled over the back of the Chesterfield, screeching and slapping at each other.

The two women rolled across the carpet, biting, slapping and swearing. What Daisy lacked in technique, she made up for in sheer aggression, and Boadicea was almost completely on the defensive. A table went flying and Fred, Britannia and Rummidge had to jump out of the way as the two women tumbled past in a flurry of arms and legs.

Watching with an apprehensive look on his face, Fred turned to Britannia. "Shouldn't we do something?"

Britannia shook her head. "I wouldn't advise it," she chortled. "Daisy wouldn't thank you, and Bouncy might actually do you an injury." She just wanted to see who was going to win.

Rummidge stood on a chair as they crashed back in his direction. The coffee table in front of the fire was upended. Suddenly there was a lull in hostilities as Daisy executed a sneaky martial arts move and seized Boadicea in a hammer lock. "You thought you could seduce Fred?" she spat venomously.

"Britt!" squeaked Boadicea. *"Help!!"*

"Oh no, Sister dear," replied Britannia, folding her arms and perching on the arm of the Chesterfield for a grandstand seat. "You got yourself in this mess, you can get yourself out of it." And with her neutrality declared, she remained resolutely an observer.

"But we've got to stop them before somebody gets hurt!" Fred hurried over to the two combatants. "Ladies, please!" he attempted valiantly to separate them. Before she could stop herself, Daisy had hit him from the left and Boadicea hit him from the right.

He flopped to the floor like Brian London being sloshed by Muhammad Ali at Earl's Court. Daisy gave a squeak of alarm and crouched down beside his sprawled figure, her fight with Boadicea forgotten. She cradled his head in her hands. "Fred? Are you all right?"

Britannia looked down at Fred in amusement. "I told you not to do anything, didn't I?" she chuckled.

"She's got the key!!" Dazed, Fred was still in the nightmare situation of being locked in the Drawing Room with Boadicea Ballcock in apex predator mode.

"I'd just grab her by the ankles and shake her upside down until they fell on the floor," suggested Daisy, helpfully grabbing Boadicea by one wrist and one ankle. Fred grasped the matching set and between them, they inverted the brunette and shook her vigorously. The key clattered on the floor and Fred unceremoniously dumped Boadicea while he snatched up his prize.

"Why do you need the key?" asked Britannia astutely. "We've already opened the door."

"Ah." Fred stopped in his tracks, half way to the

widely opened Drawing Room doors. Self-consciously, he put the key in his dressing gown pocket.

Britannia hauled her sister to her feet and handed her the shoe that she had lost in the tussle. Boadicea eyed Daisy warily, making sure she kept her sister between herself and the blonde.

"I'll thank you to keep your thieving paws off Fred in future," Daisy wagged a finger at Boadicea.

"I'm standing right here," said Fred, busily gathering his wits about him. Boadicea's right hook had lost none of its power since the altercation at Chayne Manor and he was wondering just how concussed he was. Daisy's left jab had also put him in a state of some discombobulation and he had made a mental note she was not a girl to anger.

"Same goes for you," Daisy declared, turning to Britannia. The brunette took an apprehensive step backwards and almost collided with Boadicea.

Britannia held her hands up. "Thieving paws off Fred permanently," she responded.

Boadicea had been comprehensively slapped, practically all over by Daisy and was in no hurry for a replay. "Sorry, Daze. Dad put me up to going after Fred. He wants to put a wedge between you two to give Julian a chance."

"Told you so," said Britannia.

"Why does he want to drive a wedge between us?" asked Fred, not unreasonably.

"Dad's still got plans for the company that don't necessarily involve Sir Roland," replied Boadicea. "Sorry, Daze." She had seen the stung look on Our Heroine's face. "He reckons he might have more influence with you in the Ballcock family."

"But I'd *never* marry Julian," bleated Daisy in horror. "I mean, the very thought. *Ee-yuck!!*" The shudder she gave spoke volumes and Fred was enormously comforted by the declaration.

"You realise Dad is going to make our lives a misery for not seducing Fred," observed Britannia astutely.

Boadicea groaned.

Daisy tapped her lips with a finger, a diabolical, positively Machiavellian idea forming. "Why don't you move in here, temporarily?"

Fred could not have looked more startled if he had licked one of the high tension cables in the laboratory downstairs. *"What??"*

"Bouncy and Britt are two of my oldest chums," Daisy smiled.

"Steady on with the 'old'," exclaimed Boadicea.

"We've known each other since infant school," Daisy corrected. "I know now that we've sorted this business out that no further hanky-panky will be forthcoming."

"Agreed," nodded Boadicea.

"We can get the decorating sorted out in double-quick time with Bouncy and Britt helping out."

Boadicea and Britannia looked at each other, wondering what they might have signed up for.

-oOo-

CHAPTER NINETEEN:

In Which Daisy Indulges Her Artistic Tendencies,

And Fred Gets An Offer He Cannot Refuse.

Daisy wandered into the kitchen to find that Fred had already prepared Sunday breakfast. Cereals, tea, toast and marmalade. A single, red rose stood in a fluted champagne glass in her place. She sat down and sniffed the flower's fragrance, a shy smile playing across her lips. Fred was sitting at the head of the breakfast table, sipping a glass of orange juice with a far-away look in his eyes. Rolling up the sleeves of her pyjama-top, which happened to be all she was wearing, she let out a little sigh of self-satisfaction and prodded her bowl of soggies - breakfast cereal done the way she liked it - milk-logged.

Boadicea, in a fit of self-sufficiency, was scorching herself and her sister a quite nauseating fry-up at the cooker. She half-turned as Daisy sat down. "Morning, Daze, fancy a cholesterol special to start the day with?"

Daisy recoiled as the sizzling pan of grease was thrust under her nose. "Perhaps another day." She wished she had not made paella as a midnight snack last night. She returned to her cereals, stirring the soggy mess half-heartedly. Resting her chin on her hand, she surveyed the kitchen, her spirits starting to sink. It was looking more and more likely that they would still be cleaning and decorating the old house at Christmas.

-oOo-

Daisy wielded the screwdriver with a little more enthusiasm than expertise. With a loud "pop" and clatter, the lid of the paint tin shot off, somersaulted once and stuck itself, sticky-side down on the lid of the grand piano. "Bum!" she muttered to herself. Now, where was the roller tray? She looked around vaguely for it, and remembered that she had left it at the top of the stepladder. She picked the tin up, and clutching it to her chest, clambered up the ladder. The tin was cold against the square of bare skin at the top of the dungarees between the braces that held them up. As she reached the top, she hefted the tin to pour the contents into the tray. A look of surprise crossed her face as she discovered that the tin was half-empty. It had been full a moment ago. Then she felt something cold trickling down the fronts of her legs inside her dungarees and filling her pumps. She put the tin down and pulled out the front of her dungarees, peering down inside. "Ick!" she grimaced, wrinkling her nose in disgust. She scooped a handful of paint out of the front of her dungarees and wiped her fingers on the edge of the roller tray. That was one way of refilling it... She picked up the paint roller and stared at the ceiling, wondering where to start.

Boadicea and Britannia strolled into the drawing room, having changed out of their usual sharp work clothes into sloppy teeshirts and jeans. Daisy was perched on top of the stepladder, applying the roller to a difficult piece of plaster moulding, concentrating on getting paint into all the little nooks and crannies. "What do you want us to do first?" Boadicea enquired.

"Mmm?" Daisy's attention was centred specifically on applying an even coat of white emulsion to the rounded backside of one of the plaster cherubs that made up the corner moulding.

"I said, 'What do you want us to do first?'," repeated Boadicea.

"Why don't you get changed so you can help me?" Daisy said absent-mindedly over her shoulder.

Boadicea frowned. If Daisy was not going to pay attention, they might as well go home. She put two fingers in her mouth and emitted a deafening whistle.

Daisy looked at the streak of white emulsion running down the window from where the roller had hit it. The roller itself had shot under the settee, while the roller tray had tumbled from the top of the ladder on to the lid of the grand piano, and paint was trickling thickly into the interior. She turned to glare at Boadicea.

Boadicea was making tisk-tisk noises. "Really, Daze, you ought to be more careful..."

Fred rushed into the drawing room as a high-pitched squeal rent the air. He skidded to a halt in the doorway at the sight of Daisy stuffing a roller loaded with paint up the front of Boadicea's teeshirt.

Boadicea retaliated with a faceful of Artex that plastered Daisy's hair back. Spitting out gobs of the thick, sludgy texturing material, Daisy gave Boadicea a shove. Boadicea staggered backwards and sat down heavily in one of the roller trays. Polyurethane paint went everywhere. She leapt to her feet, paint running down her legs and threw herself at Daisy. Fred leaned against the doorframe, watching the proceedings with a slightly gone-out expression. He ducked as a blob of wallpaper paste shot past his right ear. He made, quite possibly, the worst mistake of his life, racing forwards to break up what was developing into an extremely nasty fight. He realised his mistake a moment later, as with a screech of indignation, the two women set on him with a bucket of Artex.

-oOo-

Daisy, into the third change of clothing of the day, was being uncharacteristically tight-lipped as she rollered the drawing room ceiling. Pointedly ignoring Boadicea, she was perched on the top of the stepladder, her face still burning. It was not being overcome with emulsion, or the indignity of having to change again that embarrassed her, but having to be hosed down in the garden by Fred before she could go upstairs and change. Matters were not helped by Britannia, working on the window frame, still chortling to herself.

Fred rushed out into the hall, hearing the crash of the front doors falling in. He should have put a sign up warning that he had taken off the hinges, he told himself. A large gentleman of quietly threatening demeanour was standing on the step in the company of two other, equally large gentlemen who gave off an alarming air of sheer brutish stupidity. "Hello, can I help you?" asked Fred.

"I certainly hope so." Knuckles shook his hand, cranking Fred's arm as if trying to pump water. "Would this be the residence of the late... um...?" His memory failed him.

"Pelham Grenville Longfield," one of the thugs interjected. A look of surprise crossed Knuckles' face and he turned to look at Llewellyn, who had uncharacteristically provided the information. Llewellyn offered his customary blank smile in return.

"That's right," confirmed Fred warily.

"Excellent," beamed Knuckles. "My name is Raymond McCallister of McCallister Industries and I believe that we can do some business together."

"Business?" Fred looked surprised. "I'm sorry, but if you're selling something, then we're not interested." He went to close the door, or at least prop it back up in the entrance again, but Knuckles held it open with a meaty fist.

"I'm not selling anything," Knuckles growled. "I am in the market to buy something, Mr... ah..."

"Longfield."

"Any relation?" Knuckles asked genially.

"Great nephew," replied Fred with an air of caution.

"Excellent! Shall we continue this discussion inside?" Knuckles pressed, not going to budge an inch.

"Oh, sorry." Fred stood to one side and allowed Knuckles and his two hulking associates to cross the threshold.

"Are you Professor Longfield's executor?"

The Drawing Room door opened and Daisy emerged, dripping white emulsion on to the floor from a roller clutched in her hand. Rivulets of paint ran up her bare arms from painting the ceiling and her face was spattered with droplets that made her look as if she was suffering from some strange skin complaint. "Look at this!" She waved the roller under Fred's nose, then Knuckles'. Knuckles took a step back to avoid getting paint on his best suit. He looked down as he heard a soft splat and saw that a blob of white paint had landed on the toe of his expensive Italian shoes.

"Non-drip this stuff's supposed to be!" Daisy was highly indignant. "There's more on me than on the ceiling! Boadicea looks like Frosty the Snowman!" Fred could not help smiling. Only Daisy could make non-drip paint drip. Daisy suddenly noticed Knuckles properly for the first time. She looked at Fred, expecting him to make the introductions.

"Oh, beg pardon." Fred looked self-conscious. "Daisy, this is Mr McCallister. Mr McCallister, this is Miss Chayne."

"Charmed," smiled Knuckles.

Daisy stuck out her hand to shake Knuckles'. However, that was the hand she had the roller in. Knuckles snatched his hand back. "Oops." Daisy grinned, embarrassed. She turned to Llewellyn. "Would you mind holding this?"

Llewellyn grimaced as, unthinking, he grasped the paint-laden roller and thick, white, polyurethane emulsion squidged between his fingers. "Ee-yuck!"

Knuckles planted a kiss on the back of Daisy's hand. Pausing to spit out a fleck of paint, he got straight to the point, turning back to Fred. "Mr Longfield, I've long been an admirer of your late, great-uncle's work. I don't think it would be an overstatement to describe him as one of the great scientific minds of our century. I'd like to see his work continue in spite of his untimely demise." Fred shot a nervous look at Daisy. "The possible benefit to society of one of your uncle's formulae may be inestimable, Mr Longfield," continued Knuckles.

"A formula?" Fred stared straight back at Knuckles innocently. "Any particular formula? My late Great Uncle had rather a lot of formulas lying around the place."

"Specifically a formula for converting any base element into gold, Mr Longfield. A formula which I am prepared to buy the rights from you for a million pounds."

Fred offered Knuckles a sickly smile. He telegraphed an even more alarmed look to Daisy. "That's very generous, Mister... ah..."

"Knuckles," interjected Bert.

"Mr Knuckles." Fred looked surprised. *"Knuckles?"*

Bert nodded solemnly.

"Is there somewhere we can talk privately - and more comfortably?" asked Knuckles.

Fred indicated the door of the front parlour, on the other side of the entrance hall to the Drawing Room where they were decorating. He grabbed Daisy's hand and pulled her after him. "You don't mind if my legal advisor, Miss Chayne sits in on this, do you?" he asked. This was news to Daisy, as she had only just got used to being a painter and decorator.

"This is a handsome place you've got here, Mr Longfield," lied Knuckles, perusing the entrance hall admiringly. With the pots of paint and the decorating dust-sheets strewn all over, the hall looked like a building site. "Moonlighting as an interior designer, Miss Chayne?"

"Daisy. As in 'oops-a-'." Daisy tried to be disarming.

Knuckles strolled through into the front parlour as if he owned the place and sat down on the settee, flanked by Llewellyn and Bert. He put his briefcase down on the coffee table and smiled at Fred and Daisy. "Please sit down, Mister Fieldmouse. Miss Chayne... Daisy. "

"Thank you." Fred sat down in the armchair opposite Knuckles and his hirsute colleagues. Daisy perched on the arm of the chair, feeling extremely unsettled by Knuckles' presence.

Knuckles opened his briefcase and leafed through the contents. He found what he wanted under the neat pack of tuna fish and watercress sandwiches that the senior Mrs Knuckles, his mother, had packed for him. He pulled out the piece of paper and wiped the butter marks off it. "I am a businessman, Mr Longfield. The commercial value of your great-uncle's process will be virtually without measure. A great many very unscrupulous types will undoubtedly be interested in buying, stealing or otherwise extracting the secret of the process from you, but if you deal with me, everything will be above board. A million pounds for the sole rights to the process and in addition you will get thirty percent of the profits once the process has started making money." He took another piece of paper and a pencil out of his briefcase which was on the coffee table in front of him. He closed the briefcase and put the paper down on the lid. He sucked the pencil meditatively for a moment, marshalling his thoughts. "This is a contract," he said at length. "It would assign to me the sole, worldwide rights to the process that your Great Uncle invented for changing base elements into gold. The price for those rights would be one million pounds sterling. All you need to do is sign the contract on the dotted line and the money is yours." He regarded Fred with an intent gaze and sat back, sucking the pencil pensively.

Bert absent-mindedly produced a cigarette lighter from his pocket, lit it and applied the flame to the end of Knuckles' pencil. Knuckles became aware of the smouldering wood and shook out the burning end of the pencil. He glared murderously at Bert and clicked his fingers for Llewellyn to provide him with another pencil. Llewellyn reached into his pocket and took out a fountain pen. He unscrewed the cap of the pen and handed it to Knuckles. Knuckles, who was still busy glowering at Bert, put the pen nib first into his mouth. He grimaced as he found himself with a mouthful of ink. He stood up, spitting ink into a handkerchief. From behind the handkerchief he mumbled: "I'll... um... leave you with the details to think about for a day or two, Mr Shorthouse. We can... um... thrash out the um... small print over a round of golf at the Club."

"That would be fine by me," shrugged Fred. "Erm... round of golf?"

"Nether Fondling Golf Club," replied Knuckles. It had taken him nearly ten years to become a member of that select body of doctors, solicitors and stockbrokers, and he was proud of the fact he had been sufficiently accepted by the community not to be blackballed by the committee the last time he had applied. Of course, it might have had something to do with Colonel Worsted's unfortunate accident with the roadroller the previous week. "You'll be my guest, of course, Mr Longfield. Would Tuesday morning suit?"

"No problem."

"Around nine, then." The smile that accompanied this was pinched.

"Around nine," Fred confirmed.

He and Daisy watched Knuckles and his cohorts hurry down to their car. "Hurry up and get me home," he heard Knuckles growl. "I think I'm going to be sick." Llewellyn patted his boss reassuringly on the back, leaving white hand prints on his expensive, dark suit.

Bert dived behind the wheel. "Righto, Boss." He gunned the engine.

"Too late." Llewellyn was looking over to the back seat where Knuckles was huddled over.

-oOo-

Daisy turned to Fred, puzzled. "What was all that about?"

"I think I just got an offer I can't refuse," said Fred uncertainly. He was a little more worried about playing his first game of golf. Where was he going to get a set of clubs from?

-oOo-

CHAPTER TWENTY:

In Which Daisy Runs Up A Shocking Electric Bill

And Fred Gathers A Brains' Trust

Fred hurried down the stairs to the laboratory as the lights throughout the house dimmed. The dull electrical hum vibrating the house had tipped him off as to where he could find his favourite blonde. He didn't want to be late for his first Monday in the job at the factory, but when he woke up there had been no sign of Daisy or the Ballcock Sisters. Daisy had left his breakfast keeping warm in the oven and once he had eaten it, he set off in search of her.

He arrived to find Daisy, Boadicea and Britannia manning the experiment. Boadicea, protected by visor and heavy gloves, was extracting a gold hair brush from the final reaction vessel with a pair of forceps. From the great variety of gold objects strewn around the room, it was obvious the Sisters and Daisy had been transmogrifying anything they could lay their hands on. "What the hell are you three doing?" he demanded.

"Trying out the formula," Daisy replied innocently. "You wouldn't believe the things we've managed to transmogrify."

"I think I can." Fred picked up a solid gold fried egg between finger and thumb. "You do realise the electricity bill for all this will be astronomical!"

"Do you think we ought to stop, then?" asked Daisy, more than a note of disappointment in her voice.

"Oh, don't be such a stick in the mud," complained Boadicea, strolling past with an armful of gold bullion. The gold heels of her shoes clicked on the stone floor of the laboratory.

"We don't know if there are any problems with the formula yet!" Fred looked exasperated. He had a feeling Boadicea was behind the transmogrification spree, and until he had got a second, or maybe even a third opinion on the formula he would have preferred to take things cautiously.

"Problems?" Daisy looked alarmed.

"You know - side effects, that kind of thing," complained Fred. "We don't know how the formula affects the material at the atomic level properly."

"It turns stuff into gold," chortled Boadicea.

"But is that all it does?" Fred was being a scientist again. "Does it affect the radioactivity of the material? It's changing atomic bonds and doing all kinds of astonishing things to the building blocks of matter itself. We have to be cautious - this is a bona fide frontier of science stuff. You can't just transmogrify things willy-nilly in case something goes wrong!"

"What could go wrong?" Boadicea was unrepentant.

"I'm talking Los Alamos going wrong. Three Mile Island. Chernobyl kind of wrong!" Fred ran a hand through his hair. He started as there was a loud pop like the cork of a champagne bottle. He turned to see Daisy standing in front of him, an alarmed expression on her face and her short, denim, mini-mini skirt round her ankles.

Daisy stared back at him with big eyes. "Dammit, Fred. If you wanted to tear my clothes off, you only had to ask!"

"I didn't touch your skirt!" exclaimed Fred, protesting his innocence. "It was the buckle!"

Daisy wriggled her skirt back up, a disbelieving expression on her face. She went to fasten the belt and discovered that the buckle had vanished. She looked around on the floor for it. "The buckle's gone."

"Exactly," confirmed Fred. "It just disappeared."

"Don't be silly, Fred. Buckles don't just vanish." Boadicea provided the voice of reason. She picked up a couple of gold candlesticks to store them in the cupboard with the other items. As she did so, the candlesticks vanished with a loud pop and a shower of fine dust. So did her golden Louboutins. She found herself flat on her back, flailing like an upturned beetle. "What the f...?"

"It's the gold!" exclaimed Fred. "The process must weaken the atomic bonds in the object when converting it to gold. When the bonds break down, the gold vanishes. Pop!"

Daisy looked crestfallen. "Does this mean we're not rich any more?"

"Well, not unless we can find a way of stabilising the process," admitted Fred.

"Phew, I'm glad I didn't try the process out on any other bits of clothing," observed Daisy.

"I did," Boadicea winced. "I wish I hadn't."

"You could do with some brilliant minds to run this by," commented Britannia astutely.

"I know just the feller," nodded Daisy cheerfully.

"My Dad!" She and Fred chorused simultaneously. They looked at each other, startled. "Your Dad or my Dad?" Daisy asked.

"How about both?" suggested Fred.

-oOo-

Fred stepped out of the lift on to the top floor landing of the administration block, where the boardroom and the offices of the partners were situated. He was only a couple of hours late for work on a Monday morning, but Daisy had assured him that it would be all right. She had phoned ahead to arrange everything with her father.

"Fred! What's happening?" Fred looked around and his eyes narrowed. It was Hegarty, the weaselly Californian of amiable, if sneaky disposition and limited intelligence. Lord Ballcock's other personal assistant besides Boadicea and Britannia. Fred had learnt from Daisy that anything said within earshot of Hegarty was reported straight back to his boss. Britannia had also intimated that there might once have been a slight something between Daisy and the affable Hegarty. That would explain why Daisy referred to Hegarty as "it". It also meant that as far as Fred was concerned, Hegarty was one of the enemy. "Fred, buddy! *Que pasa?*" Hegarty put a comradely arm around Fred's shoulders.

"You what?"

"Have you seen Bouncy and Britt?" Hegarty asked.

"Lord B hasn't seen them since Saturday night and he's wondering where they've got to."

Fred ducked nimbly out of the embrace. "I haven't seen them all weekend," he lied. "Been doing the decorating with Daisy."

"Oh yeah." Hegarty nodded. He had heard something about it. "The old inventor's place."

"That's right," confirmed Fred. "I just called in to give Sir Roland a progress report."

"Hey, don't let me keep you." Hegarty grinned, holding his hands up. "Catch you later."

"Not if I see you first," Fred muttered to himself, heading into Sir Roland's outer office. As the door closed behind him, Hegarty sprinted up the hall to Lord Ballcock's office and shot through the door.

Mrs Bankhead, Sir Roland's executive secretary, looked up from her computer as Fred stepped through the door. She regarded him in much the same way she might a cleaning memorandum left behind by a puppy. "What do you want?" She did not believe in concealing her animosity towards Sir Roland's Personal Assistant Section. She knew it was merely a ploy to keep his dozy daughter and her friends occupied. In her opinion, the girl would be much better suited to a job on the factory floor, where her talents would be better served, and most importantly, Daisy's friends would not be poaching territory that should be strictly hers. She checked her watch critically. "Aren't you a little late to be waltzing into work? And where's Miss Chayne?"

"Progress report for Sir Roland, Mrs Bankhead." Fred was not up on business protocol, and was going to breeze straight into his employer's office. Mrs Bankhead leapt from her seat like a tiger defending its young and interposed herself between him and the door. "Have you got an appointment?"

"Do I need an appointment?" Fred looked surprised. Sir Roland had told him that any time he needed a word, his door was open.

"Of course you need an appointment!" Mrs Bankhead looked at him as if she thought he was a cretin, which she did anyway. "Sir Roland's time is very important. You can't just go traipsing in there at any time."

"But he told me to..."

"Nonsense," snapped Mrs Bankhead. "Sir Roland Chayne is the senior partner of one of the largest sanitary ware manufacturers in the country. He is a very busy man. I can't let you stroll into his office without an appointment, even if you are his daughter's latest boyfriend."

"Now, just a second." Fred wanted to put the record straight.

Mrs Bankhead looked at Fred levelly. "Young man," she said. "You are wasting my time. Go away."

"But...."

"You can't see Sir Roland without an appointment," said Mrs Bankhead steadfastly.

"But..."

The woman just looked at him challengingly.

"All right." Fred was running out of steam. "Can I make an appointment to see Sir Roland?"

"That's more like it," Mrs Bankhead nodded, sitting down at her desk. "Name?"

"You know my name!"

Mrs Bankhead enjoyed being awkward. "Name." Fred closed his eyes, counted to ten, and gave her all the relevant details.

"Now can I see Sir Roland?" he asked.

"Certainly not." Mrs Bankhead looked shocked. "Your appointment isn't until Thursday the eighth of next month."

"What??" squawked Fred.

Mrs Bankhead regarded him with the air of someone who could very easily put a pencil line through the appointment she had just written down.

Fred turned on the charm as best he could. "I'm terribly sorry," he smarmed. "I'd just hoped it might be slightly sooner."

"How soon?" asked Mrs Bankhead.

Fred shrugged. "Some time in the next ten minutes would have been ideal."

"Oooh, no." Mrs Bankhead enjoyed seeing him squirm. "Sir Roland's diary is fully booked."

"Please," Fred wheedled.

Perhaps something in Fred's tone appealed to Mrs Bankhead's maternal instinct. Or more likely she wanted to draw out his agony. "All right," she begrudged. "I'll have a look. Just wait a moment." She turned to peer at Sir Roland's appointment book.

Fred took advantage of the distraction to slip through the inner office door.

Sir Roland was sitting at his desk, folding important documents into paper darts and flying them around the room. A pretty normal afternoon's work. He looked up as Fred rushed in.

"Sir Roland, I've ... oof!" said Fred. The "oof" was caused by Mrs Bankhead seizing his legs in a flying rugby tackle that brought him down heavily. The secretary got him in an arm lock and looked up at Sir Roland apologetically.

"I'm terribly sorry, Sir Roland," Mrs Bankhead grunted. "He got past me while I wasn't looking. I'll have security eject him immediately."

"That's all right, Mrs B, I asked young Fred to drop round for a chat." Sir Roland helped Fred to his feet. "Nothing to worry about."

"But what about your appointment book, Sir Roland?" Mrs Bankhead was sitting on the floor, staring up at him.

"Fred's got special dispensation, Mrs B." Sir Roland, with the assistance of Fred, hauled the secretary to her feet and escorted her to the door. "Open door. Any time." He offered Mrs Bankhead a kindly smile and closed the door while she was still stuttering "But... but... but..."

"So Daisy's helping you decorate Plum's old place?" Sir Roland enquired amiably. He wasn't bothered what they got up to as long as Fred kept Daisy out of trouble.

"And Boadicea and Britannia are helping," nodded Fred. "They're hiding out from their father at our place."

"Our place?" Sir Roland picked up on the phrase.

"Slip of the tongue, Sir," Fred apologised. "Daisy seems to have made herself at home."

"Nothing to worry about, Fred, dear boy," beamed Sir Roland. "Nothing to worry about." He leaned over towards the intercom on the desk. "How about a nice spot of tea and a couple of fairy cakes?"

Hegarty stood in Lord Ballcock's personal washroom, adjoining his office, a glass beaker pressed to the wall, and his ear pressed to the base of that. The washroom shared a common, stud wall with Sir Roland's office; as, it must be said, Sir Roland's personal washroom did with Lord Ballcock's office. Hegarty was listening intently, a goofy smile on his face. He could hear Fred distinctly.

-oOo-

"...we tried out the formula a couple of times and it really seems to work. At least I've done as many tests on the objects we transmogrified as I could, and they all seem to have been turned into gold of at least sixteen carat purity." Fred shrugged, craning his neck over the edge of Sir Roland's desk. "The problem is that the gold produced is atomically unstable. It seems to last between five and eight hours, then *poof!*"

"Poof?"

"Total disintegration. Turns to dust." Fred replied.

"In my experience," Sir Roland ventured, as though he dealt with formulae for turning lead into gold on a semi-weekly basis, "These kinds of formulae are always more trouble than they're worth. Turning lead into gold, finding a replacement for petrol, finding a way to play the stock market without risk. It always ends in tears." He stood up from his desk and walked round to Fred's side. "I remember once - this was long ago when I was just a young shaver - a friend of mine came up with a formula for making diesel out of vegetable oil. You know, the stuff you cook chips in. He took it to one of the oil companies and tried to sell it to them."

"What happened?"

"They said if they bought it, they'd destroy it. He said he didn't want the formula destroyed, and they told him it was a straight choice. Him or the formula. He took the money and ran."

"I don't blame him, Sir." Fred looked horrified.

"This Knuckles feller sounds like a lot of trouble, too. I'll come back with you and we'll go over the formula together. Mind you, I think the best place for a formula to turn base metal into gold would be up in smoke."

The more Fred thought about it, the more inclined he was to agree. "Would you mind if we picked up my father on the way to Grisley End?" he asked.

"Bert?" Sir Roland startled Fred by identifying his father Herbert. "Of course, the more the merrier. I haven't seen your Dad in ages. It'll be fun to catch up."

As the voices got more and more distant, Hegarty took the glass away from the wall. Excitedly, he scampered back into his employer's office to report and otherwise rat them out.

-oOo-

Daisy flew into her father's arms when she saw him sitting in the Library. "Dad! What brings you round here?"

"Fred," replied the old man impishly.

Daisy looked at him blankly. "Pardon?"

"Fred brought me round here," Sir Roland chortled. "He told me all about this formula of his Uncle Plum's you've found."

"That's right, Dad. It turns things into gold."

"Like the old Alchemists' dream, eh?" chuckled Sir Roland. "Very good."

Daisy came to an abrupt halt and stared at her

father. "Don't you believe us?"

"I believe young Fred turned up at my office this afternoon with some yarn about a formula for turning base metal into gold," chuckled Sir Roland. "Very convincing he was, too. All the right chemical terms, the lot. 'Course I realised immediately it was one of your little japes, so I played along. Where is this fabulous experiment, then?"

"Down in the laboratory." Daisy dragged him towards the hidden panel and the concealed laboratory stairs.

"Oh yes," nodded Sir Roland cheerfully. "Where else?"

Fred's Dad was admiring the technical volumes lining the walls of the library. "So how are you getting on with the decorating, then?"

Daisy shrugged. "There's a terrible amount of work to be done on the house," she admitted. "It's all cosmetic. The structure's pretty sound but it's been neglected for years. We've been working for what seems like ages, but we don't seem to be getting anywhere. We've managed to get the drawing room almost finished, but there's still the parlour, the dining room, the library, the..." She trailed off. "The rest of the house to do."

"In other words you've just got started," nodded Fred's Dad. "What you need is organising," he observed. "Ma's great at this sort of thing," he chortled. "She's always sorting me out."

"I've got something to show you both, Pop," said Fred enigmatically.

-oOo-

Good-naturedly, both Fred and Daisy's fathers followed him down the stone steps to the basement laboratory. Fred swept the door open for them. "The La-*bor*-a-tory." Somehow his father didn't seem terribly surprised. The elder Longfield made a circuit of the laboratory with the air of a minor Royal on an official engagement. Every so often, he would nod and occasionally chuckle as if recognising something familiar.

"I suppose you've been down here quite a bit in the past," observed Fred.

"Once or twice," conceded his father. "Uncle Plum used to rope me into helping him during the summer holidays. He peered into one of the reaction vessels of the experiment. "Trying to build a better mousetrap, Fred?"

Fred had to agree that the contents of the laboratory were only missing a tin bath and a huge lump of cheese.

Sir Roland walked around the laboratory table, a broad grin on his face as he surveyed the apparatus. "This has got to be the biggest practical joke you've ever pulled, Daisy," he chuckled. "It must have taken ages to put this mess together." He shook his head laughing, then looked closer at Daisy and her friends and his expression changed to one of alarm. Boadicca placed a gold hairbrush on the table in front of him and he stared at it in disbelief. "You were serious about that formula, weren't you?" he asked. He supplied the answer himself. "Yes, you were." He gazed anew at the apparatus with the expression of a tapdancer discovering he was rehearsing in the middle of a minefield. He gave a carefully considered appraisal of the

239

hardware. "It's a bit of a lash-up, isn't it?"

"All I know is it works, Dad," Daisy shrugged.

"I'll believe *that* when I see it," replied Sir Roland dubiously.

Fred's Dad wore a grave expression that could only mean he not only believed the story, but knew it to be true. "This house was owned back in the 1930s by Linus Longfield, who would be your... cousin three times removed," said Fred's Dad grimly. "Linus was obsessed with alchemy, and there were rumours in the family that he'd actually succeeded. He died under mysterious circumstances in 1935 - the whole matter was hushed up at the time. Your Great Uncle Plum bought this house from the estate to keep the property in the family and to act as the base for his own experiments. Plum was an engineering genius, Fred. There wasn't anything he couldn't turn his hand to. Then he found Linus's old notes and became obsessed with the idea of turning other elements into gold. That formula has brought nothing but trouble to the Longfield family."

Fred stared at his father. He had been unaware that his father had known so much about the whole business.

"I'm inclined to agree with your father, Fred," concurred Sir Roland.

"That said," Fred's Dad continued, "my scientific curiosity would never forgive me if I didn't give this a go." He looked embarrassed at the admission. He draped his tweed jacket over a lab stool and pulled on a laboratory smock that Fred handed him. He rolled up his sleeves, ready to set to work. "Let's give it a try, then."

-oOo-

Some hours later, the group had reconvened in the Library of the old house. "Young Fred, Bert and I have run the experiment over and over again." Sir Roland rubbed his tired old eyes. "And I concur with him that the experiment does indeed transform other elements into gold through some kind of ion exchange mechanism. Nuclear chemistry was never my strong suit." He sipped his after-dinner coffee, sprawled comfortably in one of the armchairs in the front parlour. Daisy was sitting on the sheepskin rug in front of the fire, listening to him intently. Britannia and Boadicea were perched on the arms of the other Chesterfield armchair, flanking Fred's father, who was not complaining. "Unfortunately, the process is inherently unstable," Fred's Dad took over the narrative. "The action of sunlight breaks down the atomic bonds formed by the reaction, with the result that the object converts back to its original form. This reversion tends to cause the normal atomic bonds to break as well, and the object simply disintegrates."

"At least now we know what happened to my belt buckle," observed Daisy.

Fred entered, stirring a cup of coffee to catch the end of the fathers' summation. "With a bit more work, and possibly by using a more powerful energy source, there's a chance the process could be made irreversible," he offered. "Although that may not necessarily be a good thing," he added at a sharp look from his father.

"That's terrific!" Daisy exclaimed. Then she noticed Sir Roland's expression, which matched that of Fred's Dad. "Isn't it?"

"Think what having a formula to make gold would

entail," said Fred. "If gold was freely available to everybody, it would be worth as little as sand. Of course, if the formula fell into the hands of one unscrupulous person..."

"Knuckles," interjected Boadicea and Britannia in the role of a Greek chorus.

"Exactly," nodded Fred. "If he had the formula, there would be no telling what he could get up to. Gold, money, power, it's all the same thing."

Daisy could see where the argument was heading. "Does that mean we'll have to destroy the formula?" she asked.

Boadicea looked horrified. "Do we have to? Can't we make ourselves a bit of gold first?"

Fred's Dad shook his head. "If we did that, we might never destroy the formula, and then we'd be in the same boat Knuckles would be."

Boadicea could not help wondering if that was a bad thing. "So what are we going to do?"

Daisy provided the answer. "We'll burn Uncle's notes."

"I'll get them," offered Boadicea. She hurried out of the room, and returned a few moments later with the dog-eared sheaf of notes hugged to her chest. "Do we really have to do this?" she asked, a pained expression on her face.

Sir Roland nodded gravely and Boadicea tossed the notes into the grate on top of the glowing coals. The six of them watched the flames licking round the edges of the pages.

Daisy lay on her stomach, watching the dancing flames. She rested her chin on her hands, swinging her legs. "What are we going to tell Knuckles?" she asked. "He's not going to be happy."

-oOo-

CHAPTER TWENTY-ONE:

In Which Fred Addresses His Balls,

And Daisy Plays A Round.

Tuesday morning dawned bright and warm. Knuckles impatiently checked his watch, then looked around the first tee of Nether Fondling golf club in annoyance. "Where is he?" he muttered. "I said nine o'clock."

"Dunno, Boss." He was accompanied, as ever, by Llewellyn and Bert, his left and right hand men. Llewellyn was acting as caddy for his boss, and had deliberately chosen an outfit of a red cardigan and white slacks to match Knuckles - in spite of Bert calling him a crawler when he had first seen him. The two men looked like badly-made strawberry milkshakes, and would have put the fear of God in nobody. Bert was the more sensibly dressed, although he was uncomfortably running a finger round his shirt collar. He was wearing the chauffeur's uniform on strict instructions from Knuckles, who wanted to impress the other club members.

A frown crossed Llewellyn's lumpen face. "By the way, Boss, there's something been troubling me."

"What's that?" Knuckles was not remotely surprised.

"Well, you said to that Longfield bloke that you'd give 'im a million pounds for that formula," Llewellyn ventured. "Where are you going to get a million pounds from?"

"Who said anything about getting a million pounds?" Knuckles shrugged. "I offered him a million pounds for the formula. Can I help it if once he's given me the formula, I forget to give him the money?"

"Won't 'e go to the police, Boss?" Llewellyn sounded cautious.

"Who'd believe him?" Knuckles smiled sardonically, leaning on his niblick and bending it out of true.

"Ooh, that's a rotten trick, Boss," Llewellyn sounded shocked.

"I know," Knuckles took it as a compliment. "All I've got to do is sew things up with that legal advisor of his, and she looks dopier than you."

"Here he comes now, Boss." Bert had been staring back towards the clubhouse.

"At last." Knuckles followed Llewellyn's gaze to see Fred ambling towards them.

At Daisy's insistence, Fred had borrowed his golfing gear from Great Uncle Plum's wardrobe and was dressed in a loud pullover, plus fours and an outsized golfing cap. He was pulling along behind him the Professor's moth-catcn leather golf trolley. Spotting Knuckles and his Brains' Trust on the first tee, he waved a golf club over his head and bellowed a greeting to them at the top of his voice.

Knuckles pretended to have nothing to do with him

until he noticed that trailing behind Fred was Daisy, a vision of loveliness in what appeared to be a cricketing pullover and precious little else. The hem of the garment was just within the bounds of decency, and she was barefoot, carrying her high-heels in one hand. Knuckles extended a hand in greeting to Fred. "Mr Longfield," he smiled courteously, shaking Fred's hand. "Miss Chayne," Knuckles kissed her hand. "*Enchantè*," he purred in his best French.

"Pardon?" Daisy looked blank.

"Er... never mind," Knuckles looked self-conscious. "Have you come to watch, Miss Chayne?"

"No," Daisy's cheery smile lit up the first tee. "I thought Fred might need a caddy, so here I am." She gave an eloquent shrug.

"And a delightful caddy too," Knuckles was busy being ingratiating. He turned to Fred, pausing as he took in Fred's sartorial style properly for the first time. He put a comradely arm around Fred's shoulders. "Have you played golf before, Mr Longfield?" he asked.

Fred shrugged. "'Fraid not."

"Neither have I," Daisy added unnecessarily.

Knuckles nodded. "I thought not."

Fred looked surprised. "Does it show?"

Knuckles smiled genially. "Would you care for me to explain the rudiments of the game to you, Mr Longfield?"

Fred and Daisy looked at each other. The unspoken message that passed between them was clear - What kind of idiots did Knuckles think they were? Fred beamed guilelessly. If Knuckles thought he was an idiot, then that was what he would be. "Would you really, Mr McCallister? That would be awfully kind." Daisy looked shocked, then stifled a grin as Fred gave her a sly wink. "As far as I can follow it," Fred continued innocently, "the point of the game is to make one's way round the course using as few strokes as possible to get the little ball in the little hole."

Knuckles nodded. "That's an oversimplification, but essentially true."

"What swing do you recommend, backhand or forehand smash?"

Daisy gave a squeak and bit her lip to stifle a giggle. She stared at her toes, unable to look at Fred.

Knuckles looked startled. "I think you're confusing golf with tennis, Mr Longfield."

"Silly me, but they're so similar."

Knuckles' eyes glazed over. He composed himself with an effort and took a club out of Fred's trolley and handed it to him. "First you make the tee," he said.

Daisy looked at him, patently baffled. "I thought you wanted to play golf." She did not want to be left out of the fun and games.

"We do. You make the tee with one of these things." Knuckles reached into his pocket and took out a plastic tee. He handed it to her.

Daisy weighed the tee in her hand. "Hmm, what will they think of next?" she mused. "Won't it make it taste funny, though?"

"Taste funny?" echoed Knuckles.

"The tea," said Daisy. Knuckles ground his teeth noisily. "I suppose you keep the kettle and one of those little camping stoves at the bottom of your golf bag," continued Daisy, rambling on to herself. "Where do you keep the milk and sugar, or do you have it with lemon?"

Knuckles snatched the tee out of her hand. "You plant the tee in the ground like this," he stabbed the tee into the turf. "You put the ball on top of it like this," he placed the ball on top of the tee. "Then you tee off."

"Pardon?" Daisy deadpanned.

"Tee off!" roared Knuckles.

Daisy took a step backwards. "All right, there's no need to lose your temper," she said quietly. She took Fred's arm and they started away.

"Where are you going?" screamed Knuckles.

"You told us to..." Fred looked surprised.

"No, come back here!" screeched Knuckles, clutching a hand to his forehead as though he had a raging headache. He gazed at the ground to compose himself. "Tee off means that you drive the ball off the tee," he rumbled slowly.

"Oh." Fred's voice betrayed his enlightenment. He ambled back to the tee and went to take a swing at the ball.

"Wait a moment, you've got to address the ball correctly." Knuckles stopped him.

"Oh, sorry." Fred picked up the ball and patted his pockets. He turned to Knuckles. "Have you got a pen on you?" he deadpanned.

*"Just hit the ****ing thing!"* roared Knuckles.

Fred jumped and dropped the ball. Llewellyn looked at Knuckles with a shocked expression. "Language, Mr Knuckles," Daisy reproached.

"Beg pardon," mumbled Knuckles sheepishly.

"Perhaps you'd better show me what to do," Fred was no longer sure he wanted to play golf.

"Yes, I think I'd better." Knuckles selected a club from his own, gleaming, red PVC golf trolley and took a fresh tee and ball out of his pocket. "These are pro-clubs. Five hundred pounds each. Handmade, precision balanced. You really have to know what you're doing to own a set of these."

Daisy leaned on Fred's shoulder and stuck her face close to his ear. "Show-off," she whispered.

Knuckles cleared away Fred's tee and ball and replaced them with his own. He straightened up and gazed out across the fairway. He gripped the club and stood over the ball in the classic position. He took a swing past the ball, passing it by inches.

"You missed," said Daisy.

Knuckles smiled. "No, I was just taking a practice

swing."

"Huh," Daisy muttered under her breath. "I bet they all say that." Knuckles positioned himself over the ball properly and drew back to take his swing. "Fore!" shouted Daisy.

Knuckles started violently. His golf club slammed into the ground just in front of the ball, tearing up a clod of turf. The impact knocked the club out of Knuckles' hands and jarred his toupee off the top of his head. The ball sailed up into the air, ricocheted off a tree and felled Bert, who was standing by the golf trolley.

"What did you do that for?" demanded Knuckles.

Daisy shrugged and smiled prettily. "I thought you were supposed to when you play golf."

"Only if there's someone on the fairway in danger of being hit," Knuckles squawked exasperatedly.

"Sorry." Daisy stared sheepishly at her toes.

Knuckles positioned himself over a new ball and went to take his swing. "'Scuse me." Daisy had picked up his toupee. Knuckles held up a finger for quiet. "But..." Knuckles gave her a stern look and she lapsed into silence. He repositioned himself carefully and took a perfect shot. The ball sailed off towards the green. He waited for Fred to take his shot and smiled to himself as Fred's ball sailed off into the rough.

Daisy looked at Knuckles' toupee thoughtfully and shrugged. He would be bound to miss it sooner or later, so she would put it where he would be able to find it. She popped it into the ball pocket of Knuckles' golf trolley.

"I..." she started helpfully as Knuckles approached. Knuckles glared at her and took the handle of the golf trolley. He strode away down the fairway.

-oOo-

Fred was wandering around in circles in the rough, looking for his ball. He was swishing at the tall grass with his club in the vain hope that he would locate the ball that way.

On the green, Knuckles watched Fred with a sardonic smile. He would give him a couple of minutes longer, and then he would declare Fred's ball lost and that would be a point to him. In the mean time, he was sure Fred would not mind if he just sank his ball. He tapped the ball with his putter and watched it roll gently to within just a few inches of the hole. He strolled over and tapped the ball into the hole. He had taken three strokes. There was no way a complete novice like Fred could do better. He retrieved his ball from the hole and looked over to where Fred was still hacking at the grass like an Amazonian explorer. There was a thud as Fred's club connected with the ball he was looking for and the ball bounced across the green and into the hole. Knuckles ground his teeth. A hole in two.

Fred wandered over with a surprised look on his face. "Did you see that?" he asked.

Knuckles nodded fatalistically.

"Who's won, then?" asked Fred.

"You've won that hole," said Knuckles.

"Really?" Fred looked startled. "Bless my soul!"

"Now we move on to the next hole," Knuckles growled.

"Right-ho," Fred beamed. "Lead on."

-oOo-

Daisy had been watching the proceedings with interest. Golf was a game she had never paid an awful lot of attention, but as the morning had progressed, she found the concept of wandering around the greens after a hard little ball more and more appealing.

Knuckles had lit a pipe of the most noxious weed to calm his nerves, and was puffing away like a steam locomotive as he lined up his next shot. He looked up with a grunt of displeasure as Daisy stepped into his line of fire.

"I've been thinking, that looks a lot of fun," smiled Daisy ingenuously. "I don't suppose you'd care to show me how to play?"

Knuckles, his pipe gritted between his teeth, had been on the verge of shouting at her, but then a charming smile spread across his face. "Certainly, Miss Chayne. Come and stand here, where I'm standing." Daisy watched as he put down a new tee and ball for her. He guided her into position, adjusting her grip on one of his expensive golf woods. "Left hand up a bit... perfect." He was pressed up behind her, his meaty hands on her forearms, hot breath on the back of her neck.

He began to demonstrate the mechanics of the swing. That seemed pretty straightforward to Daisy. She adjusted her hold on the club-thingy she was supposed to hit the ball with. She had watched the Ryder cup on the telly and occasionally played a round of crazy golf in the park. It did not seem much different. Now, what was it she had to do? Oh yes. Address the ball. She wiggled her hips, getting her stance right.

Knuckles bit through the stem of his pipe.

The golf ball took off like a shell from a howitzer, caromed off a tree with a crack like a rifle shot and rebounded back along its original trajectory. "Whoa!" Daisy gave a squeak of fright and threw herself to the ground. Knuckles was a second too late and a high-pitched whinny escaped his lips as the ball impacted painfully just to the right of his flies.

Daisy, sprawled on the grass, watched in mute astonishment as Knuckles bent the golf-club in two and threw it high into the branches of the tree. She stood up, dusting stray blades of grass from her knees. If that was what was supposed to happen when you played golf, she was not sure it was really the game for her.

Knuckles composed himself with an effort and approached the tee once more with the gait of a severely constipated buffalo. He selected a fresh club from his golf trolley and surveyed the onlookers grimly, daring just one of them to do anything. "New ball," he squeaked to Llewellyn, his voice unusually high.

"Righto, Boss." Llewellyn reached into the pocket of the golf trolley. He pulled out something small and hairy with big, white, bulging eyes. Screaming in horror, he dropped the thing like it might be venomous, hauled out his trusty automatic and emptied the clip into it.

Everybody threw themselves flat.

253

Llewellyn hastily holstered the smoking weapon and peered nervously at the object. He prodded it cautiously with his foot and found he had just shot Knuckles' toupee and a couple of golfballs dead.

Knuckles picked himself up from the ground, spitting out a mouthful of turf. "What the f...?" he began.

Llewellyn picked up the mortally wounded hairpiece sheepishly. "Sorry, Boss."

Knuckles snatched the toupee back and put it on his head, neglecting to notice the four, large, bullet holes in it. Llewellyn ducked as Knuckles swung his golf club at him, and retreated to a safe distance.

-oOo-

Between the tee and the twelfth hole was the duck pond, where many a ball had been lost. Knuckles smiled confidently to himself as Fred lined up his shot across the water on the tee. Fred swung his club and the ball hurtled out over the duck pond and landed perfectly on the other side of the pond on the edge of the green.

Knuckles ground his teeth, thoroughly demoralised. He planted a tee in the ground, set the ball on top of it and addressed the ball, adjusting his stance. The tip of his tongue sticking out of the corner of his mouth, he concentrated furiously on the shot.

Llewellyn leaned against the nearby oak that shaded the tee. It was getting on for lunchtime and his feet were killing him. He looked across to Fred and Daisy and smiled to himself. Daisy was sitting on the grass, watching the proceedings with interest. Unless he was very much mistaken, if he sat down just there, Llewellyn reckoned he would be able to see right up the hem of the blonde's outfit. He slid down the trunk of the tree and chortled to himself. He had been right. He idly picked a dandelion and sniffed it, admiring the view.

Oh hell. Me hay fever.

As Knuckles took the swing, there was an explosive sneeze behind him. He cried out as his club dug into the turf, jarring itself out of his hands. The ball took off at right angles, catching Llewellyn a terrible blow on the temple. He sagged sideways to the sod, possibly concussed.

Daisy stood up, watching in amazement as Knuckles bounded round the tee, wafting his hands in the air to soothe them. The impact had almost broken his wrists. The club lay a few yards away, bent neatly in the middle into a right angle. Bert was propping Llewellyn up, wafting the unconscious heavy's face with his chauffeur's cap.

Knuckles' badly holed toupee had been jarred off by the impact. It lay, out of sight under his golf trolley. Daisy was more interested in the clod of earth excavated by Knuckles' shot. Almost perfectly round, the piece of turf had been shaved off at the roots. In the centre, growing impertinently was a single daisy. Daisy picked up the piece of earth to admire her namesake.

Knuckles' temper had not improved. He saw Daisy holding something that was roughly the right size and shape to be his toupee, and without giving it a second's examination, he swept it out of her hand, and planted it on his head.

Daisy looked taken aback. "But..."

Knuckles put a finger to his mouth. "Ssh!" He regarded the others. "And that goes for all of you!"

Llewellyn had come round, and Bert had helped him to his feet. He stared at Knuckles thunderstruck. "Boss!"

Knuckles shot him a look that shut him up immediately. He remembered what had happened to the Ellenbogen brothers. Glaring at Llewellyn, Knuckles put down a fresh tee and ball and took a practice swing. If he allowed for the breeze from the south and hit it just so, he thought to himself. He drew back his club and took a swing at the ball. The ball soared high into the air and then plummeted towards the middle of the duck pond.

The duck pond had only been part of the golf course since 1941 when it had mysteriously appeared one rainy night in August. It was the result of a stray bomb which had been meant for the greenhouses of the local market garden, which the pilot of the bomber appeared to have mistaken for a munitions factory or something. The bomb had not exploded, merely digging itself a large, neat hole on the golf course which soon filled with water. At the time, people had more pressing things to worry about than mysterious duck ponds, and so the bomb had lain undiscovered ever since, until Knuckles' golfball splashed into the water and hit the detonator.

Knuckles staggered backwards as a spume of green, slimy water rose up from the duck pond in a column. It was followed by a prodigious amount of foul-smelling black mud which burst forth sideways, plastering the onlookers from head to foot.

Fred scraped mud from the lenses of his glasses and peered around himself bemusedly. In front of him, he could just make out a glistening, black, muddy figure picking itself up from the ground. "That was quite a shot, Mr Knuckles."

Knuckles spat out a mouthful of mud and growled at him, white teeth bared alarmingly in a shapeless, greeny-black visage.

Daisy wriggled uncomfortably as a blob of mud slithered slowly down inside the front of her pullover-dress. "I don't like this rotten game," she declared unhappily. "I want to go home!"

-oOo-

The group of muddy people trudged into the golf club house. All of the windows had been shattered by the blast, and the members were staring out at the pall of smoke over the twelfth hole in stunned disbelief. The secretary of the golf club was in the middle of a nervous breakdown, and his demeanour would not improve when he saw the muddy trail that they had left behind them on the club house's expensive fitted Axminster.

Fred smiled nervously at Knuckles, who seemed ready to burst a blood vessel or two. "It's been a thoroughly entertaining morning, Mr Knuckles," he said backing away nervously from the mud-encrusted hoodlum. "I've enjoyed every minute of my visit here, but Daisy and I really must be making tracks. So if you'll excuse us, we'll be going." He took Daisy's arm and started to back her away towards the door.

Knuckles watched them go with stoic indifference. With immense dignity, he turned to the mirror by the bar to try to tidy himself up. He stared at his reflection and in particular the reflection of the clod of turf and its perky daisy perched on top of his head.

"Mister McCallister!" exclaimed the golf club president sternly. "Would you care to explain this mess? *Urrkk*!!" Knuckles' large hands closed around Professor Masters' throat.

CHAPTER TWENTY-TWO:

In Which Fred's Mum And Dad Come Visiting

And Lord Ballcock Nearly Gets Blown To Kingdom Come

Fred was woken bright and early the following morning by sunlight streaming in through the window, the curtains having been yanked open by Daisy. At least she had not played reveille on the bugle from the first floor landing. She blew him a kiss in passing that made his day. Gathering his scattered wits about him, he emerged from his bedroom to see Daisy wander into Boadicea and Britannia's to subject them to much the same treatment. He ambled down the main staircase and picked up the mail and the morning paper. Tucking the mail under his arm, he unfolded the newspaper and discovered that the national headline referred to their adventure at the golf club the previous day. *"Riot At The 19th Hole - Fifteen Arrested"* Fred read the headline to himself, making tut-tutting noises. Beneath the headline, six burly police sergeants were separating Mr Knuckles and... He rotated the newspaper. His former Headmaster and prospective father-in-law, identified by the newspaper as the Golf Club President, Professor Mustard.

He folded the newspaper again and started for the dining room for breakfast when the doorbell rang. Fortunately in his renovations of the entrance hall of Grisley End, he had remounted the front doors on new, brass hinges. He opened the door to find Sir Roland Chayne on the doorstep.

"'Morning, Fred," chortled Sir Roland. Behind Sir

Roland, Howard and Fine of R&D were unloading the Sylph unit on the tail lift of the box van they had arrived in. It was perched on a moving dolly, but still needed lifting to negotiate the loose gravel of the driveway before they got it on to the solid stone of the entrance portico floor. Fred had to take a step back as the two men rolled the Sylph over the threshold.

"Damn thing's taking up too much room in R&D," said Sir Roland, regarding the device with scarcely disguised dislike. "I wondered if you might like to give it a look over and see what you can make of it."

"Certainly, Sir Roland," nodded Fred. "My pleasure." Howard and Fine had parked the Sylph in the middle of the hall and rocked it on its base to extract the dolly they had wheeled it in on. Neither having a speaking role, they acknowledged Sir Roland and Fred and went out to their van.

"Uh…" Fred was nonplussed to see the men drive off down the drive again. He turned to Sir Roland quizzically.

"I'll phone the Manor and Wilkins can come and pick me up," Sir Roland said dismissively. His face lit up at a passionate exclamation of *'Daddy, My Daddy!'* behind him. Daisy was a keen fan of the *Railway Children* movie and the greeting was a long-running family gag. She threw herself into Sir Roland's arms.

"How's the decorating coming along?" asked Sir Roland when Daisy released him from a bear hug.

"One step forward, two steps back," Daisy confided. She steered Sir Roland away for a progress report.

Fred turned to close the front door again and hesitated. A second van was coming up the drive, and Fred was surprised to see his father in the driving seat and his mother in the passenger seat. He trotted out to meet the van as it pulled up outside the entrance portico.

"I wasn't expecting to see you two today," exclaimed Fred. "What brings you round here?"

"We got all of the decorating stuff out of the garage like you asked," replied his mother. "We thought we'd come down and offer a little moral support." They moved into the entrance hall and his Mum craned her neck, looking around at the work-in-progress critically. The freshly-stripped oak panelling was a good two or three shades lighter and more cheerful than it had been. "You're not considering a career in French Polishing, are you?"

"No?" Fred looked puzzled.

"'Cause you'll still be working on this place the day you retire," his Mum sniffed. "Luckily for you, I am here and about to organise you like you have never been organised before."

Fred looked startled. He could easily believe that.

His father walked around the Sylph curiously. "Great Glass Elevator, Teleportation Booth or Time Machine?" he asked mischievously, peering round the corner of the device.

"It's a Home Spa, Dad," replied Fred, casting his mother an exasperated look.

"Of course it is," said his father. He opened the door and peered inside at the control panel.

"Not too close, Dad. It bites," cautioned Fred.

Daisy and Sir Roland returned from the Drawing Room with Boadicea and Britannia Ballcock in tow. The Sisters had finished the ceiling and were going to move on to the woodwork. Daisy was overjoyed to see Fred's parents and greeted them warmly.

"You look like you're ready for business, Molly," chortled Sir Roland, indicating the overalls worn by Fred's mother.

"Oh yes, Sir Roly," nodded Fred's Mum. "Somebody's got to organise this lot." She indicated the younger generation present. "It'll take long enough to get this place into shape as it is."

"Well, if there's anything I can give a hand with," Sir Roland volunteered. He gestured towards the hall panelling. "My maternal grandfather was a French Polisher by trade. Learned everything I know about it from him."

"We'll get back to the woodwork in the Drawing Room," suggested Boadicea.

"Fred and I can finish off our structural check of the building," Fred's Dad volunteered. "Reggie can give us a hand," he added as Rummidge appeared and made Boadicea jump.

"What should I do?" asked Daisy. "Maybe sort out the Conservatory?"

"You do that, Daisy darling," smiled Fred's Mum. "I'll give you a hand."

-oOo-

The sun was angling low in the afternoon sky as Fred carried the last of the wheelback chairs from the kitchen through into the Conservatory at the rear of the house. Even in such a short time, Daisy's green fingers had effected a transformation that was nothing short of miraculous, and the conservatory had become one of the more pleasant parts of the house. At least it was beginning to look less like part of the Amazon rain forest.

Daisy's enchanted touch had also manifested itself in the form of afternoon Tea with cucumber and salmon sandwiches, fondant fancies and as a special treat for Fred's father who had voiced a desire for one - a sherry trifle. It was, she conceded, by way of a reward for being roped into the day's decorating.

Fred's Mum had been the organising force the three friends had needed, and Fred's Dad and Sir Roland had provided the practical expertise. Together they had made more progress in the one day than they had made since they first arrived at the old house.

Fred, his parents, Daisy, Sir Roland and the Ballcock Sisters sat down to the repast in the shade of the date palm and surveyed the grounds through the glass which Daisy had spent the best part of the morning attacking with a bucket of hot soapy water and a squeegee.

Boadicea Ballcock, as ever, was not above a little mischief. She leaned over to Fred's Mum conspiratorially. "Daisy was telling me about Fred, on holiday, when he was little," she primed. Fred's mother beamed, pleased at any excuse to discuss her little boy. Fred buried his head in his hands with a low moan as the four women went into a huddle.

-oOo-

Lord Ballcock stepped down from the blue and white Ford transit van and adjusted the false, toothbrush moustache adhered to his top lip. Peering over the top of a pair of pebble-lensed half-frame spectacles, he checked his disguise in the wing mirror. He could not afford to be recognised by Daisy and her strange friends. Bowler hat, blue dungarees and a donkey jacket meant that he was completely unrecognisable as a peer of the realm and a high-powered businessman. He looked around furtively and crept round to the back of the van to open it.

Hegarty was sitting inside the van, perched on top of a gas boiler, dressed identically to him. He was wearing an absurdly bogus false beard that would have fooled no-one. Lord Ballcock stared at him for a moment, then reached forward and yanked the beard off. The glue took a layer of skin with it. "Ow!"

Lord Ballcock glared at Hegarty and put a finger to his lips. He gestured for him to get out. "Come on," he spat. "Cretin," he muttered under his breath.

The gas company van was parked on the grass verge running alongside the main road outside the grand, old house, a few hundred yards down from the gates. The crumbling, brick wall surrounding the grounds was too high to see over. Lord Ballcock beckoned Hegarty to follow him, and they scuttled across the grassy verge to the foot of the wall.

Hegarty staggered after him, carrying their bag of fitter's tools with him. He dropped the heavy bag, wiggling his fingers to make sure they still worked. He looked surprised as Lord Ballcock let out a howl and started hopping up and down on one foot, clutching the other.

"Right on my corns!" Lord Ballcock complained, leaning against the wall. He whipped off his bowler hat and swatted Hegarty across the back of the head. "Give me a leg-up."

Obediently, Hegarty crouched at the foot of the wall, making a stirrup with his hands. Lord Ballcock planted a foot in the stirrup, and Hegarty boosted him aloft. He stared at the hole in the wall that had appeared, and craned his head through. Lord Ballcock was lying on top of a pile of bricks on the other side of the wall. "Are you all right, Sir?"

Lord Ballcock sat up and gestured for Hegarty to follow him. Hegarty ducked back out of sight and picked up the heavy bag of tools again. He hefted it through the hole in the wall and cringed as there was a bellow of pain from the other side.

-oOo-

Lord Ballcock peeped out of the bushes like a sniper, hinging his spectacles back on his head to see clearly. They were within a few yards of the side of the house, and he could see Daisy and her friends entertaining a couple of old folk in the ricketty conservatory that jutted out from that wing. "Hegarty?" Hegarty appeared at his side, dropping the bag of tools. Lord Ballcock stifled a cry of pain as the heavy bag landed on his toes again. Composing himself, he pointed towards the house. "Find a way in," he hissed.

"Yes, Sir." Hegarty saluted and scuttled out of hiding.

Fred's Dad had been pressed to another fondant fancy by Daisy. He could tell his wife did not approve, but this was a special occasion. He sipped his tea, and was about to comment further on Daisy's baking skills when he caught a movement out of the corner of his eye. He watched the idiot in the bowler hat and the overalls scurrying across the lawn. "Are you having trouble with the gas in this place?" he asked.

"The gas?" Fred looked surprised. "What gas?"

"Cooking and heating gas." Dad looked at his son exasperatedly. Sometimes young Fred could be slow on the uptake. "'Cause there's some bloke from the gas company creeping across your lawn."

Fred and Daisy turned to look and Daisy gripped Fred's arm. "Fred, unless I'm very much mistaken, that's Hegarty!"

"You mean Lord Ballcock's Hegarty?"

"I sincerely hope there aren't any more of them."

Hegarty had strolled up to the front door and was about to ring the doorbell. Lord Ballcock leapt out of hiding and threw an adjustable spanner, or as Hegarty would describe it a monkey wrench, to attract his attention and stop him.

"There's another one." Fred's Mum had seen Lord Ballcock breaking cover and sprinting after Hegarty.

"And that one's Lord Ballcock!" exclaimed Daisy. "What's he doing round here?"

"Dad??" chorused Boadicea and Britannia apprehensively. They had been actively avoiding their father since Saturday when he had set Boadicea an assignment to seduce Fred and steal him away from Daisy.

Lord Ballcock stepped over the unconscious figure of Hegarty and picked up the adjustable spanner from where it had fallen. Slipping it into his pocket, he looked round furtively and hooked his fingers into the back of Hegarty's collar. He dragged the body round the side of the house.

Fred opened the front door and stepped outside, a look of confusion on his face. He was sure he had heard the doorbell *and* seen Lord Ballcock and Hegarty, but now there was no sign of them. Shrugging to himself, he closed the door and returned to the others.

Hegarty sat up, blinking bleary eyes and rubbing the painful lump on the back of his head. He gave a cry of fright as the bowler-hatted figure loomed over him.

Lord Ballcock clamped a hand over Hegarty's mouth, waving the adjustable spanner in his face. "Keep a look- out," he hissed through his teeth. "I'm going to look for a way in." He took his hand away from Hegarty's mouth.

Hegarty nodded vigorously and squatted at the corner of the house, keeping an eye out for trouble. After a few moments, an uncertain expression clouded his open features. What was he keeping a look-out for? "Sir?"

He was answered by a high-pitched scream, a clattering, rumbling noise and a hefty crash. He leapt to his feet. Lord Ballcock had vanished. He ran around in a circle, disoriented, then noticed an open manhole. He could hear distant profanity coming from it. Taking a torch from his belt, he squatted by the opening and shone the beam into the murky depths. "There you are, Sir."

"Ssh!" Lord Ballcock put a sooty finger to sooty lips. He had slid down the coal chute and was sprawled on top of a pile of nutty slack, covered in coal dust. He sat up painfully, unsure where one bruise ended and another began. He took out his torch and shone it around the coal cellar, a slow smile crossing his dusty features. He shone the light up in Hegarty's face. "I think I've found a way in."

"That's great, Sir!" exclaimed Hegarty. He lowered his voice as Lord Ballcock frantically gesticulated for him to shut up. "What do you want me to do?"

"Come down here and join me." Lord Ballcock enunciated the words as if talking to a moron - which he reckoned he was.

"Fine." Hegarty swung his legs into the manhole and eased himself through the opening.

There was a frantic scrabbling noise, a thud and silence. "Hegarty," Lord Ballcock's muffled voice drifted up from the depths. "Would you get your backside out of my face?"

268

Fred ambled back into the conservatory where his parents, Daisy, Britannia and Boadicea were waiting nervously. He shrugged eloquently.

"What would bring Lord Ballcock round here?" asked Daisy, not unreasonably.

Boadicea's eyes narrowed. "Call me an old cynic if you like, but I can't help wondering if a certain somebody hasn't heard a certain something about this place and is trying to find out another certain something to his advantage."

Daisy nodded. After a painfully long pause, she asked: "Who?"

Lord Ballcock had been creeping along a dark, dank passageway under the house, illuminating his way with his gas-company issue torch. He still felt cheated by the fitter and his mate, charging five hundred pounds for the loan of their van and clothing for a couple of hours.

"*Woo-oo-oo*," Hegarty made a ghostly noise behind him.

Lord Ballcock spun round and shone his torch up under the miscreant's chin. He found himself staring into Rummidge's face. He screamed.

Daisy sat up, alarmed. "What was that?" she squeaked.

269

"Sounded like somebody screaming." Fred's Mum looked visibly shaken. "Around this place, I'm hardly surprised."

Self-consciously, Boadicea climbed down out of Fred's Dad's arms. "Was that scream any of you?" she quavered.

"No. Was it you?"

"Don't think so." Boadicea shook her head quickly. "This place is still too creepy for my liking," she said in a small voice.

Rummidge looked on with polite interest as Hegarty patted Lord Ballcock's hand. "Are you all right, Sir? Speak to me, Sir." Hegarty was beginning to panic.

Lord Ballcock opened his eyes and glared at Hegarty. "Hegarty, you idiot. Are you trying to give me a heart attack? Where did you get that hideous mask?"

"That er... That wasn't me, Sir." Hegarty thumbed over his shoulder and Rummidge loomed out of the darkness.

"Can I help you, gentlemen?"

Lord Ballcock scrambled to his feet. "We're... ah... looking for a reported gas leak."

"Indeed, your Lordship?" Rummidge raised a bushy eyebrow. "Master Frederick would be surprised to find you moonlighting as a gas fitter."

"I thought we were with the water company," Hegarty looked stunned.

Lord Ballcock deflated. The butler had seen right through his disguise. He reached into his pocket and took out a wad of 20 notes. "You're...?"

"Rummidge, the late Professor's manservant." Rummidge bobbed graciously.

"Rummidge, you haven't seen us." Lord Ballcock held out the wad of money.

Rummidge took the money in white gloved fingers. "Seen who, Sir?" he rumbled.

Fred and Daisy hurried down the stairs, expressions of relief that they had not found anything upstairs to worry about most evident. "Nothing up there to account for it," Fred reported. The rest of the group were standing in the hall, having searched the ground floor. "That just leaves the cellar."

"And the laboratory," Daisy reminded him.

Fred wished she had not. He jumped violently as Britannia gave a squawk of fright. One of the many false panels in the walls had slid open, revealing a secret passage, and worse - Rummidge. "Did you see anybody down there, Rummidge?" asked Fred. "In the cellar or the lab?"

"Yes, Sir," confirmed Rummidge. "Lord Ballcock and his assistant Mr Hegarty have effected a burglarious entry of the property and are in the process of exploring the laboratory." He had decided to nail his colours firmly to Fred and Daisy's mast.

Lord Ballcock shone his torch around the laboratory, the beam glinting on the glassware of the experiment. He stopped suddenly and Hegarty crashed into his back. He staggered forwards and rounded on his associate. "This is ridiculous!" he growled. "Switch the light on."

"Right you are, Sir." Hegarty looked around vaguely. "Er... Where's the light switch?"

"Where do you usually find light switches?" asked Lord Ballcock.

Hegarty's features collapsed into a frown. "If I'd known you were going to ask questions..."

"By the door, moron!" shouted Lord Ballcock. He winced and looked around furtively in case anyone had heard.

"Sorry, Sir." Hegarty wandered over to the door and shone his torch around. There was a switch on the wall. He gazed at it thoughtfully. "Sir," he whispered. "Is this it?"

Lord Ballcock turned to see what he was raving on about now and his eyes widened in horror as he saw Hegarty about to pull a huge, high-voltage switch attached to the wall. "Hegarty! Wait!!"

The laboratory was lit up with a blinding light and suddenly the entire room seemed to be filled with blue-white sparks as the experiment in the middle of the room exploded with a deafening bang. Lord Ballcock ducked as he was showered with bits of broken glass.

"Now that definitely came from the cellar." Daisy looked suspicious. She started towards the Library, where the most direct route to the laboratory was. She was just about to step through the door when two figures burst out of the room, trailing blue smoke, shot out the front door and raced off down the drive. She stared after the figures bemused.

CHAPTER TWENTY-THREE:

In Which Fred Enjoys A Night On The Town

And Daisy Admires Knuckles' Knees

Boadicea stepped out of Knuckles' blue Rolls-Royce and gazed up at the impressive frontage of the flagship nightclub and restaurant of Knuckles' business empire. The entrance of '*La Cuiller Graisseux*' was a huge, neon and fibreglass pineapple, pulsing yellow and blue. It was said that the planning committee at the local council had approved the alterations to the building retroactively after the head of the department had suddenly and mysteriously resigned his post and retired to one of the Greek islands. Her sister followed her out of the vehicle and they stood under the canopy that sheltered the entrance. As Daisy and Fred disembarked from the back seat of the Rolls, Boadicea could not help noticing lurid, colour photographs of various unclad young ladies framing the doorway, protected by glass. "Ooh, Fred, is this a strip club?" she enquired mischievously.

Fred had not been paying much attention to where they were going, as the car had been full of distractions, most of them Daisy. As he stepped from the car, he attempted to straighten his ill-fitting dinner jacket without much success, and turned to admire Daisy once more. As usual, she looked like a million dollars, and he had the greatest difficulty in not just standing there and gawping at her. She was wearing an understated little black number with a micro mini-mini skirt that showed off her long, long legs. It looked very respectable until she turned round to reveal a back scooped to within millimetres of her intergluteal cleft. Boadicea and Britannia were glittering expensively in matching, long, sequinned gowns with bodices which showed off their best points. Boadicea was in scarlet and Britannia in ultramarine. Fred could not help thinking that life was a profusion of riches these days. Boadicea's query threw him completely. "P-p-pardon?"

Daisy eyed the photographs around the doorway uncertainly. "What are we doing here?" she asked. "I thought we were going to a restaurant." She pulled the piece of paper that Knuckles had sent out of her handbag. "This is the right address," she pondered. "The best night out the town can offer, Mr Knuckles said. And the sign *does* say restaurant and nightclub."

It was very generous of Mr Knuckles to treat the three of them to a night on the town after the unfortunate misunderstanding at the golf course, thought Daisy. She could quite understand why Mr Knuckles had been at the end of his tether, though. Being a high-powered businessman and entrepreneur had to be hard on the nerves. He had even sent a chauffeur driven Rolls to pick them up and take them to the most expensive restaurant in Stretcham.

"It doesn't exactly inspire confidence, does it?" sniffed Boadicea. "I don't mind the restaurant bit, it's the nightclub part that bothers me."

"I... I... I think there must be some mistake," gurgled Fred, going bright red. He had regained his bearings and made the discovery that their destination was the selfsame nightclub where the staff of St. Norbert's had taken him for his stag-night.

Britannia sensed his discomfiture and smirked mischievously. "Is something the matter, Fred?"

275

"Who, me?" squeaked Fred. "No."

"Do you think it'll be anything like that time we went to see the Chippendales in Warmhampton?" mused Daisy, peering at the photographs around the door in fascination.

Fred looked startled. "The Chippendales?" If that was Daisy's idea of masculine perfection, then he was dead meat.

Daisy nodded cheerfully. "That was a lot of fun," she chortled. "Boadicea helped oil one of them. Bit off his g-string with her bare teeth."

"Don't knock what you haven't tried," sniffed Boadicea. She beamed at the hulking, dinner-jacketed bouncers on the door. "I've never been to a *real* strip-club before. Come on, then," she chirped and led Daisy and Fred through the garish entrance.

Past the two smartly-attired monsters on the door, they moved through a beaded curtain into the club proper. The atmosphere assailed them immediately. The smell of cheap cigars and something not quite identifiable, but undeniably exotic. The lighting was a dim, sultry red that provided plenty of dark nooks for the patrons of the club to lurk in. Between the low stage and the bar, which filled the entire wall opposite the stage, there were cosy booths, designed for discreet liaisons; tables with candelabra centre-settings to hide behind.

A large, balding man in an ill-fitting dinner-suit sauntered over, a white cloth over his arm. He offered them a low bow. "Are you a member of our establishment,

Sir?" he enquired of Fred disapprovingly. His eyes flickered and Fred could sense the threatening presences of the two bouncers coming in behind them.

"I...er..." Fred's mouth stopped working properly. The Maitre D' flared a single nostril. Fred prepared to be forcibly ejected from the club by the two sartorially-perfect gorillas behind him.

"That'll be all, Geraldo." Knuckles appeared behind the Maitre D' and offered his guests a charming smile.

Daisy's eyebrows raised when she saw that their host was wearing a kilt. "You have great knees, Mr Knuckles," she commented.

"Thank you, my dear," Knuckles bowed graciously. "They're not a patch on yours."

Fred knew what he meant. They were what had struck him the most when he first met Daisy. He smiled to himself as she went bright pink.

"Do you have Scots roots, then, Mr McCallister?" enquired Boadicea with her usual mischievous glint.

"That's correct, Miss... ah..."

Fred realised that Knuckles had not been introduced to the third and fourth members of the team. He hastily made the introductions.

"Yes, Miss - sorry, *Ms* Ballcock. My grandfather came from North of the Border, and I still have relatives up there. I'm proud to wear the clan tartan."

"It's always puzzled me why Scotsmen wear kilts," pondered Daisy.

For a moment, Knuckles was stumped by that one, but he rallied round magnificently. "It proves what a man you are," he replied. "You have to be tough to wear a kilt."

"I can imagine," said Daisy.

"Is anything worn under the kilt?" asked Boadicea.

Knuckles smiled. She had walked right into that one. "No, it's all in perfect working order," he deadpanned.

Boadicea's eyes narrowed dangerously. She hated being the straight man.

"Nice place you've got here, Mr Kn... er... Mr McCallister," commented Fred hastily. He realised he had better change the topic of conversation before things got nasty.

"*La Cuiller Graisseux*," said Knuckles proudly, rolling the words around on his tongue like a fine wine. "Private nightclub and dining club. Just one of my little enterprises. Sounds classy, eh? The mother came up with the name. Said it was a joke, but I liked it so much, I had the sign made as a surprise for her."

"I can imagine it was," Fred replied faintly. The name was anything but classy. It was the French for 'The Greasy Spoon', but Fred was not going to tell him that, and neither probably was Mrs Knuckles.

"Is this place a strip club, Mr Knuckles?" piped up Boadicea, still intrigued by the whole notion.

"The club is a discreet and intimate venue offering a four-star restaurant with a floorshow." Knuckles sounded as if he had memorised a chunk of the publicity material. "I prefer to call it an adult revue. I got the idea from seeing the shows in Las Vegas. You know, high-class, tasteful yet *risque*." Daisy nodded. She knew exactly what he meant.

"The next show's about to start." Knuckles led them to a booth about half-way between the stage and the bar and seated them. The Maitre D' reappeared, smirking obsequiously. He addressed himself to Knuckles. "Would you care to order your drinks, Sir?" he asked.

The expression on Knuckles' face was one of sheer, sickening self-satisfaction. "My special reserve," he growled. The Maitre D' bobbed and moved away, and Knuckles leaned forwards towards Daisy, putting a hand on her knee. "A little drinkie of something special to start with. I had this stuff imported specially from Bulgaria."

One of the waiters arrived carrying a tray with four of the dinkiest little sherry glasses on it. Daisy eyed the glasses unenthusiastically. "When you said a little drinkie, you weren't kidding."

"My special reserve," Knuckles beamed. "Balkan Oloroso. Nectar." He handed out the glasses to Daisy, Fred and Boadicea and sat back in his chair. He sniffed the bouquet ecstatically. Daisy put her nose to the mouth of her glass. Her eyes started to water. Boadicea wiped a drop of sherry off the end of her nose and glared at Fred for jogging her arm. Britannia had knocked hers back in one and had gone very quiet. Knuckles held his glass up to the light to admire the colour. Fred held his glass up to the light, half-expecting to see a goldfish swimming around in it - at least that was what the smell had indicated to him. Knuckles sipped his sherry appreciatively.

Fred, Daisy and Boadicea looked at each other. There was no way to postpone the awful moment. Fred put his glass to his lips and mimed a sip. Boadicea treated hers like a glass of nasty medicine and knocked it back in one like her sister. She pulled a face as it went down like a depth charge. Daisy took a cautious sip and grimaced. "I'd have that horse shot if I were you," she commented. She reached over to pour herself a glass of water from the carafe in the middle of the table to get rid of the taste. As she was pouring, one of the waiters bustled past, jogging her arm. The contents of the carafe sluiced across the table and into Knuckles' lap. He leapt up with a profanity that shocked the nightclub into silence.

Daisy gazed at his dripping sporran. "Oh, I've got your dangler-thingy wet," she gasped apologetically and wrung it out for him. Knuckles winced and sat down again.

"That's quite all right," he mumbled.

Daisy turned to look at the stage as a spotlight came on, and the heavily perspiring band in the corner in their white tuxedos struck up a lively dance rhythm. Her expression of polite interest turned to one of incredulity as the young woman on stage proceeded to divest herself of everything she was wearing - which had not been a lot to start with - while gyrating and spinning around a brass pole attached between the stage and the ceiling above.

Fred didn't know where to stick his face and settled for gazing fixedly at Daisy, who appreciated the attention.

"Mr Longfield." Knuckles flashed Fred a mouthful of alarmingly sharp-looking tombstone teeth. Daisy jumped. Under the table, he was resting a hand with quite unnerving familiarity on her knee. No prizes for guessing what was on *his* mind, thought Daisy. "Perhaps we could discuss the matter of your Uncle's formula," he continued.

Fred offered Knuckles a queasy smile. How was he going to tell him they had burnt the only copy of the formula? He turned to Daisy for support and jumped, as she was staring at him with the intensity of a rabbit caught in the headlights of speeding traffic.

"I hope we can come to some kind of agreement." Knuckles gave his famous axe-murderer smile.

"How much were we discussing for the formula?" piped up Boadicea, tearing her eyes from the stage.

"Bouncy??!" exclaimed Daisy.

"Ah yes. Money," Knuckles mused. "The amount under consideration was one million pounds sterling. That's a one with six noughts after it," he added.

"I know." Boadicea's eyes had glazed over.

"Now just a second!" Fred came into the conversation. He was not sure what kind of dangerous game Boadicea was playing; they no longer had the formula to sell.

"I can arrange transfer of the funds to a bank of your choosing in the form of ten lumps of one hundred thousand pounds." Knuckles had taken the dirk out of the top of his sock and was paring his nails with the point of the blade.

The Maitre D' edged over and bent his balding pate to Knuckles' level. He whispered something in the master-criminal's ear and Knuckles nodded, gesturing him away with a flick of his freshly manicured nails. "We can finalise the transaction away from all these distractions later," he beamed. "I have a small matter to sort out. If you'll excuse me." Knuckles stood up from the table and melted into the crowd.

Fred and Daisy both rounded on their raven-haired friend. "Bouncy, what the hell are you trying to do?" hissed Fred, in case he was overheard by the hovering Maitre D'. "Get us all killed? We don't have the formula any more. We burned it. We've got to tell Knuckles before things get out of hand."

"Shush, Fred, I know what I'm doing," whispered Boadicea.

The Maitre D' swooped back to the table in the company of a waiter with an ice bucket and a bottle of champagne. Glasses were placed in front of them and the waiter deftly opened and poured the champagne. "What's this?" Fred looked like a startled owl.

"Champagne, Sir," replied the Maitre D'.

"I can see that," said Fred. "We didn't order it."

"I know, Sir," the Maitre D' smiled obsequiously. "M'sieur McCallister apologises, but he has a small matter to attend to. He will join you again later, and in the mean time, he hopes you will accept this bottle of champagne. Enjoy." He bowed before hurrying away.

"That was generous of him." Fred was staring at the label on the bottle.

A round of polite applause greeted the end of the

perky blonde's act on the stage. "I must say," opined Boadicea, sipping her champagne, "this is a lot more civilised than going to see the Chippendales. No baying or howling or throwing knickers on the stage..." She looked slightly disappointed.

Daisy watched the dancer leave the stage carrying her costume. "Huh," she muttered. "I could do that."

"Go on, then," said Boadicea. "I'm sure Fred would like to see that."

"Don't drag me into this," cautioned Fred. "I'm saying nothing that might incriminate me."

Daisy held out her champagne glass. "Maybe after a couple more glasses I might reconsider my position," she smiled.

Fred wondered if by the end of the evening he was going to have a twitch.

-oOo-

CHAPTER TWENTY-FOUR:

In Which Daisy Starts A Fight

And Boadicea Makes A Confession.

"More champagne?" asked Fred. He and Daisy were drinking alone. For once in their lives, Boadicea and Britannia had got the message they were playing gooseberries and had wandered off towards the bar in search of new friends.

Daisy gazed reflectively at her glass. It was one of the old-fashioned, wide-bowl champagne coupes from the days before they discovered a fluted glass stopped the champagne going flat. "You know something," she remarked conversationally. "They say the shape of these champagne glasses was based on Marie Antoinette's breasts." She drained the last drop and held the glass against her person. "Just goes to show what advertising hype can do for a girl," she observed. She held the glass out for Fred to refill it.

On the other side of the night-club, one of the members of a party of computer programmers attending a convention nearby had spotted Daisy and taken a fancy to her. The gentleman in question was in a state of some inebriation, although his taste was obviously unimpaired. This accounted for his trying to attract her attention by throwing peanuts at her from the bar. Most missed their mark by a wide margin.

Daisy looked in surprise at the peanut that had landed on the table in front of her. She looked around for the source of the peanut and spotted the drunken computer programmer in mid-throw. Seeing he had caught her attention, he popped the peanut into his mouth instead of throwing it and waved cheerily at her. Daisy looked away hurriedly. Another peanut hit her in the back of the head.

"Is it my imagination or is it raining peanuts?" she asked, trying to make light of the incident. A peanut ricocheted off her glass with a *ping*. She started and turned to glare at the drunk.

"Ignore him, perhaps he'll go away." Fred refilled her glass and raised his in a toast. "What shall we drink to?" he asked.

"Excess," replied Daisy.

"That sounds good enough to me," Fred raised his glass.

The drunk looked around for something else to attract Daisy's attention with, as he had run out of peanuts. He spotted a dish of cocktail cherries and grabbed a handful. He started propelling them one after another in Daisy's direction.

Daisy sipped her champagne and started as a cocktail cherry landed in her glass and sent a spray of bubbles up her nose. She put down her glass, grabbed a stuffed olive from the dish on the table and went to hurl it at the drunk. Fred relieved her of the olive and attempted to calm her.

The drunk, seeing that more drastic action was required, lowered himself from his bar stool and grabbed a ice cube from the ice bucket on the bar. He lined up the shot and threw the ice cube at Daisy. The ice cube bounced off the back of Daisy's chair and landed on the floor. A passing waiter stood on the ice cube and the pina colada he was carrying on his tray shot down inside the back of Daisy's little black dress. She leapt up with a squeak of distress as the slice of pineapple slid unimpeded down her intergluteal cleft.

The drunk followed the ice cube with a more deadly missile, an ashtray off the bar. He pitched the missile with a singular lack of accuracy at his target and hit a waiter, who happened to have the misfortune to wander into range, in the back of the head. The missile was propelled with such force and velocity that it instantly rendered the waiter deeply unconscious. He toppled to the ground and the large bowl of fruit punch he was carrying emptied itself all over Fred.

A couple of other waiters rushed over to the aid of the fallen waiter while the Maitre D' hovered around Fred and Daisy making sympathetic clucking noises as Daisy picked bits of sliced fruit off Fred. Four other waiters threw themselves at the drunk, and after a brief struggle managed to frogmarch him off backstage. From beyond the double doors came the sounds of a bitter and bloody battle. The doors burst open again and the drunk strolled nonchalantly back into the night-club, straightening his tie. He was grabbed in a flying rugby tackle by one of the surviving waiters and dragged back through the double doors.

The Maitre D' bit his thumb after the drunk and inadvertently flipped the top set of his false teeth out. The dentures landed in the mint julep being drunk by the wife of a moderately successful company director. The unfortunate woman leapt up from the table with an ear-splitting shriek. Her husband, seeing his wife being attacked by something nasty in her drink that was trying to bite her, grabbed the candelabra from the centre setting of the table and went to batter the foreign object in his wife's glass with it. The Maitre D' rushed over to the table and managed to calm down his two alarmed customers. As they watched nervously, he deftly picked the false teeth out of the glass and popped them back into his mouth. This set the woman off screaming again. He attempted to smile reassuringly at the man, which was not easy, as he had inadvertently put a mouthful of mint that had garnished the drink in with his dentures. The company director helped him get the greenery out of his mouth by punching him in it.

Daisy and Fred ignored the fight that was developing. Daisy slid round to sit next to Fred and picked a lemon slice out of his breast pocket. She was very close to him. He could smell her perfume. She dropped the lemon slice into her empty glass and put her arms around his neck. Slowly and very deliberately, she kissed him.

Knuckles emerged from the meat-locker with a self-satisfied smile on his face. It wasn't a Good Friday, but Mickey the fence was going to find the next twenty-four hours very long indeed. The view of the meat-locker floor was singularly uninspiring, and all the blood rushing to his head would give him a dreadful migraine, but that was what you got for crossing Raymond McCallister.

Knuckles frowned. He had heard muffled bangs and crashes coming from the club while he had been attending to business, and coming out of the meat-locker, the noise was even worse. He strode across the kitchen, flung open the door to the club and staggered as one of his patrons slammed a roundhouse blow to his chin. He picked the miscreant up and threw him through the door to the

287

ladies' loo.

Both Fred and Daisy had realised things were
getting out of hand when the girl on the stage had to leap
out of the way of a flying chair. The fight had escalated to
riot proportions while they had been engrossed in each
other, and already the grand piano in the orchestra pit was
well ablaze. "Fred, I think we'd better make our excuses
and leave," opined Daisy nervously. "If we stick around
here, we're liable to get killed!"

"What about Boadicea and Britannia?"

"They probably started this," replied Daisy
dismissively. "They're big enough to look after
themselves. Follow me." She slid gracefully under the
table and scuttled under an adjoining table. With a last,
desperate look around, Fred followed her.

The woman sitting at the adjoining table leapt up
with a shriek as she felt something rub against her leg. She
resoundingly slapped the face of the large, florid
businessman she had been sharing drinks with. The man
fell off his chair and landed on the floor. He found himself
face to face with Fred. Preceding the lunge with a stream
of abuse, the florid businessman threw himself at Fred,
seizing our hero by a handful of trousers as Fred attempted
a strategic withdrawal. Fred struggled desperately, hearing
seams popping, and resigned himself to abandoning
trousers. He released the belt and waistband clasp, and his
attacker went over backwards clutching the garment.

Fred staggered to his feet. His moment of freedom
was short-lived. He was whirled round by another attacker
and caught a glimpse of Knuckles' maddened

physiognomy.

"Fred!" A brunette tornado in an expensive frock threw herself through the air. Boadicea landed on Knuckles' back and the three of them fell on to a table, which collapsed under their combined weight. Rolling across the floor, Fred landed a blow on their host's chin that felt as if it had broken his hand. Knuckles gave a bellow like a wounded bull and Fred resigned himself to being beaten into a pulp.

Rescue came suddenly as Britannia snatched up an empty champagne bottle and smashed it over Knuckles' head. He flopped to the floor in a spectacular swirl of tartan that left the entire club in no doubt what a Scotsman wore under his kilt.

"Frilly ones too." Boadicea shook her head in disgust.

Fred looked around frantically for Daisy. He spotted her on the stage, battling the dark-haired stripper who was obviously irate at having her act interrupted. The girl grabbed a handful of the front of Daisy's dress. There was an expensive ripping noise and Fred suddenly realised how Daisy had achieved such a sleek silhouette in such a tight- fitting dress. She gave the stripper a hard shove and tumbled off the stage into Fred's arms. He swept his jacket around her shoulders to rescue her modesty. "Let's get out of here!" he shouted over the din of battle.

Boadicea winced as a chair sailed over her head and crashed into the band in the corner of the room, flattening the double-bass player. She craned her neck and spotted Daisy and Fred. "Come on, chaps, this way!" she exhorted.

Fred gave the Maitre D', a second person who

seemed to be intent on killing them, a shove that bowled over a party of Japanese businessmen as he landed on them. Fred propelled Daisy after Boadicea and Britannia through the doors that led backstage. "Where are we going?" yelped Daisy.

"Out!" shouted Fred succinctly. They were in a dimly lit passage backstage, littered with packing cases and discarded costumes. With Boadicea leading the way, they hared past the various dressing rooms, past girls dressed in a stunning variety of skimpy costumes. There was a squeal of fright behind them. Fred looked back to see Knuckles shove one of the strippers out of his way. Daisy skittered to a halt and dragged a laundry basket into his path.

"This way!" Fred propelled Daisy ahead of him through the door and braced it shut with a packing case of party hats. They were in a supply room. Fred looked around in alarm. "How do we get out?" he yelped as he realised the room had no other exits.

Daisy had clambered up on a packing case. "This way," she said. Fred followed her gaze and saw a small window high on the wall. It would take some squeezing through, but it was a way out. Boadicea took off her shoes and hoisted up the tight skirt of her dress, swarming up beside her friend. Britannia was right behind them, and as Fred heard Knuckles throw his bulk against the supply room door, he scampered after them.

Fred looked around the flat, asphalt roof of the club in confusion. "What are we doing up here?"

"Trying to escape," retorted Boadicea. She winced at a clatter from the small window in the wall behind them.

Knuckles and his thugs would soon be after them. "They say confession's good for the soul." Boadicea was dithering in the chill wind blowing in from the Down. "I have something to confess."

"Can't this wait?" asked Fred.

"Not really." Boadicea bit her lip. "This is really important, and I don't know how to break it to you."

"Just come straight out with it," suggested Fred.

"We've still got the formula."

Fred stared at the statuesque brunette. "What do you mean? We saw you burn the formula. So did Sir Roland."

"Well, you see the papers I burnt weren't *exactly* the formula," Boadicea admitted sheepishly.

Fred gripped Boadicea by the arms, a look of horror on his face. "You mean we've still got all of the notes - intact?"

"I just couldn't bring myself to destroy them," Boadicea apologised. "I thought they might come in handy some time, so I photocopied them just in case."

Daisy scurried over to the edge of the roof and peered over. "There's a drainpipe here." She swung a long leg over the edge of the roof. She glared at Boadicea. "We'll discuss this at length when we get back to the house."

In a matter of moments, the four friends were hurrying along the alley at the back of the club, towards the main road. Daisy looked down at herself. She thought she was carrying off wearing nothing but Fred's tuxedo jacket rather well. "That was a novel experience," she commented.

"I'll say one thing for you, Fred," grinned Boadicea. "You certainly know how to show a girl a good time!"

Fred looked at Daisy and they both burst out laughing.

Britannia raised an eyebrow. "Come on, you three," she exclaimed. "The night's far from over!"

-oOo-

CHAPTER TWENTY-FIVE:

In Which Knuckles Decides From Now On It's No More Mr Nice Guy

And Rummidge Scares The Wits Out Of Him

Knuckles surveyed the wreckage of his beautiful nightclub with the expression of a man in deep mourning. He looked up to see the fire engine pull away from the kerb and accelerate away down the street.

"Well, we'll leave you to tidy up now, Sir," said the Police Superintendent. He signalled to his men to put away their riot shields and banged on the side of the black maria for the driver to take most of Knuckles' clientele for that evening off to the police station. "You'll be coming along to the station later to prefer charges, Sir?" he asked.

"Yes, thank you, Bill," Knuckles offered his old friend a peculiar handshake. "See you at the lodge on Saturday?" The Police Superintendent was racked by a fit of theatrical coughing and looked around to make sure nobody had overheard. He saluted Knuckles and strode away to count the number of tear gas grenades his men had used that night.

Llewellyn patted Knuckles consolingly on the shoulder. "Never mind, Boss, you can always claim on the insurance." He tried to sound optimistic.

"We're not covered for acts of civil war," growled Knuckles bleakly. He righted one of the few chairs that remained intact and brushed fire-fighting foam off the seat before sitting down. His eyes narrowed as he took in the broken chairs and tables, the charred remainders of the tablecloths and the shattered glasses littering the floor.

"This formula business is costing too much!" He punched his fist into the palm of his hand, making Llewellyn jump.

"Boss?" Llewellyn looked confused.

"First I'll have to pay for new windows and a new carpet for the club house at the golf course." Knuckles gritted his teeth. "Not that it'll do me any good - I've been black-balled by the members!"

Llewellyn winced. "That sounds painful, Boss," he said sympathetically. "But what's that got to do with that formula?"

"That Longfield bloke and the Chayne bit have been behind it all," growled Knuckles. "I nearly get blown to bits when that weird butler of theirs comes round to tell me about the formula. When we go round to talk to them I nearly get poisoned with ink!"

Llewellyn took a step backwards out of striking range in case Knuckles remembered he was responsible for the episode with the pen.

"And this place will probably have to be pulled down," continued Knuckles. He banged his fist down on the edge of the stage and winced as he further bruised his hand. "I'll tell you something, this is the last camel that broke the straw's back! We're going to get that formula off our Mr Longfield. We've tried fair means and now we're going to try foul. Then we'll make sure some harm comes to him, and his little friends too. I'm fed up of being a pillar of society. From now on, it's No More Mister Nice

Guy!"

"What's a pillock of society, Boss?" asked
Llewellyn. "And this Nice Guy, is he that dodgy cousin of
Sledgehammer O'Riley's?"

Knuckles gave him a long, simmering look and
strode over to the car, where Bert was dozing. He
clambered into the back and punched Bert in the back of
the head to wake him up. Llewellyn hopped into the car
beside Bert and looked quizzically at Knuckles. "Are we
going home, Boss?" he asked.

"No," growled Knuckles. "We're going on a job."

"Oh, goody, a job," chortled Bert. "It's a long time
since we done that. What kind of job?"

"We're going to do a little bit of good, old-
fashioned breaking and entering," said Knuckles. "We're
going to get that formula my way..."

-oOo-

Britannia paid off the taxi that had brought the four
friends back to the old house, as Fred had his hands full.
The old house looked surprisingly inviting. Fred's
handiwork had finally sorted out the wiring, and the lights
were all working. She and Boadicea levered the heavy
front door open and held it to permit Fred and his burden to
pass.

Fred had slung Daisy over his shoulder like a sack
of potatoes after the night air had hit her. She was giggling
merrily to herself, humming and la-la-ing tunelessly. "I
thought you said she could hold her drink!" He jumped as
she slid an inquisitive hand into the waistband of his boxer

shorts. They had made a strange foursome in the snug of the Pig and Thistle - him trouserless, Daisy in his jacket, and Boadicea and Britannia in their posh frocks.

"Her capacity for alcohol is inversely proportional to her height." replied Boadicea.

"I'll have you know I can hold my drink," protested Daisy, peering back over Fred's shoulder. She pointed past Fred's nose at a lissom thigh on a level with Fred's face "See these legs?"

"Can't take my eyes off them," replied Fred.

"Hollow."

"That would explain a lot," opined Fred. Since leaving Knuckles' club, between them Daisy, Britannia and Boadicea had shifted the best part of a bottle of Pernod, mixed with orange juice and he was surprised Daisy was still conscious.

"Take her upstairs and sling her on the bed," suggested Boadicea. "I'll bring up the cocoa."

"Choc-choc," giggled Daisy, giving an excellent chicken impression. Fred sighed and started up the stairs with her. Daisy regarded the world passing her by upside-down. Boadicea smiled as she heard Daisy say distinctly, "Ooh, this is interesting."

-oOo-

Tiptoeing so as to make as little noise as possible, Knuckles crept along the gravel drive up to the old inventor's house. It was four in the morning and the first rays of daylight were beginning to show in the east. He beckoned Llewellyn and Bert to follow him and winced as Bert dropped the gas-fitter's toolbag he had found in the bushes with a loud crash.

"Ssh!" hissed Knuckles indistinctly through the fishnet stocking he was wearing over his head. Tiffany - Mrs Knuckles - would probably be livid when she found he had borrowed her best pair, but that was the least of his problems. He pulled the stocking up to glare at his two accomplices. Llewellyn and Bert recoiled in horror at the waffle-like aspect his face had taken on. "We'll try the door," whispered Knuckles. "No sense in making a lot of work for ourselves." He beckoned them to follow him and crept over to the huge doors at the entrance of the big house. "Gimme the lock picking kit," he whispered.

Bert dumped the toolbag down on the stone step with a clatter and started to rummage through it. He had put the lock-picking kit in there, he was sure. The bag was full of all sorts of useful tools for house-breaking - crowbars, screwdrivers, even a blowtorch. The contents of the bag made a noise like a medieval tournament as he stirred them around. Knuckles clapped his hands to his ears and aimed a boot at Bert's proffered backside as he bent over the bag.

Bert straightened up, rubbing his bruised fundament and handed the small, lock-picking kit to Knuckles.

"Now, don't make a sound!" spat Knuckles. He crouched by the doors and inserted the lock-pick into the key hole.

The left hand door swung open, apparently of its own accord. The butler's nightmarish physiognomy was eerily illuminated by the light of Knuckles' torch. "Can I help you, Sir?" enquired Rummidge quietly. Knuckles fainted dead away at the ghastly apparition.

"Gentlemen?" Rummidge called after the fleeing figures of Llewellyn and Bert. He watched them skitter to a halt and beckoned for them to come back. "I'm afraid that Mr Knuckles appears to have had a slight accident," intoned Rummidge.

Even a couple of complete idiots like Llewellyn and Bert could understand that. They eyed the unconscious Knuckles, perplexed.

"Is he dead?" Bert wrung his hands anxiously.

"No such luck." Llewellyn bent over the body and was rewarded with a foul exhalation in the face. "We can't leave him here, though," he whispered, taking charge. "You take his feet."

Bert nodded and took Knuckles' ankles. Llewellyn levered their employer up into a sitting position, and holding him under the armpits, tried to lift him. "Bloody hell, he's heavy!" muttered Llewellyn.

"Let's just drag him," suggested Bert.

"Good idea." Llewellyn gave him the thumbs-up. They took an ankle each and dragged Knuckles into the entrance hall. Rummidge closed the front door behind them.

"Might I ask what you gentlemen are doing here?" asked Rummidge.

"We came for that formula," grunted Llewellyn. Even dragging Knuckles' bulky figure was difficult.

"I see, Sir." Rummidge nodded, his neck clicking alarmingly. He regretted telling Knuckles about the formula in the first place. "I too have been searching for the late master's formula, also with no success," he lied consummately. "I don't believe that the formula is anywhere in the house. I suspect that young Mr Longfield has lodged it with his bank."

"What do we do now?" asked Bert.

"I suggest you take Mr Knuckles upstairs to one of the guest rooms," said Rummidge. "He can recover in there."

"Right," Llewellyn grunted. They started up the stairs, trailing Knuckles behind them.

Bump went Knuckles' head on the first step.

Bump went Knuckles' head on the second step.

Bump... bump... bump... bump... bump bump bump bump... bump.

"He's going to have a heck of a headache when he wakes up," observed Bert apprehensively.

"I don't think we'd better be around when that happens," cringed Llewellyn.

Directed by Rummidge, the two thugs carelessly tossed their unconscious boss on to the bed in the 'Scarlet Death' room. The room was sufficiently distant from the bedrooms of Master Fred and Miss Daisy and the Mizzes Ballcock that there shouldn't be any unnecessary interaction between the parties, reasoned Rummidge.

A moment after Knuckles's head hit the counterpane, the bed had tipped up and Knuckles had disappeared through a hatch in the floor. "Ah," said Rummidge, a hint of embarrassment in his voice. "I was certain Master Fred and I had fixed that one."

"Where's he gone?" squeaked Llewellyn, panicking.

"All the booby traps in the house lead to the sea caves, Sir," replied Rummidge, emotionless.

"Booby traps??" exclaimed Bert. "Sea caves?"

"Grisley End was once a centre of smuggling on this stretch of the coast, Sir," said Rummidge. "The cliffs are riddled with sea caves and tunnels that were used to smuggle contraband into England. Many of the rooms here were booby-trapped against agents of the Revenue and Customs. It's only a seventy foot fall straight down into the sea. Providing Mr McCallister is a proficient swimmer, I'm sure he'll have survived." Rummidge offered what he hoped was a reassuring smile.

-oOo-

Knuckles woke the moment he hit icy sea water. He floundered, disoriented, in the waves. He had swallowed what felt like a gallon of water and was chilled to the bone. Doggy-paddling to the side, he clambered out of the water on to a set of stone steps. Pausing to orient himself, he discovered he was in a high-vaulted natural sea cave under the solid rock of Grisley Point. Between him and the entrance to the sea cave, a deep pool and around the edges several man-made places where contraband could be unloaded from small boats. All were illuminated by electric bulkhead lights. Close to the opening to the sea was the largest landing, a wooden jetty with a winch and beyond that a stone slope that led upwards. A little closer was little more than a doorway that led to a stone spiral staircase, the foot of which descended directly into the water. He was standing on the third landing point, a ledge with a cobbled surface and inset narrow-gauge railway tracks that led away to a tunnel to the side. Pulling his torch out of his pocket, he switched it on and was relieved to see the beam shine out up the tunnel. He squared his shoulders and started out along the tracks.

-oOo-

Llewellyn and Bert raced down the stairs to the entrance hall, making a noise like an avalanche in hobnail boots. They arrived just in time to see the doors of the Library burst open and the saturated form of Knuckles emerge.

"Are you all right, Boss?" exclaimed Llewellyn, solicitously. "You're all wet!"

"Ssh!" Knuckles frantically put a finger to his lips.

"Sorry, Boss," whispered Llewellyn. "It's a long time since we did this before, and I keep forgetting what to do."

Knuckles gave him a hard, gimlet-eyed look. "What's there to forget about breaking and entering, for gawd's sakes?" he muttered. "All you've got to do is keep quiet and remember not to leave any fingerprints!"

"I knew I should have worn my gloves," said Bert.

Knuckles rolled his eyes skywards. He beckoned Rummidge closer. "Now where do you think Mr Longfield might hide this formula-thing?" he whispered.

"Boss?" hissed Bert. He had spotted the Sylph, standing off to one side of the entrance hall, pending removal to the laboratory of some other convenient place of storage. Getting no reply, he raised his voice. *"Hey, Boss!"*

"What??" hissed Knuckles exasperatedly, his voice a good octave higher than normal. From where he was standing, Rummidge thought that Knuckles was in serious danger of bursting a blood vessel.

Bert pointed at the Sylph. "Do you think this might be it?"

Knuckles crossed to the device and walked around it pensively. He looked over to Rummidge. "Well?"

Rummidge shrugged expansively. "I haven't been privy to Master Frederick's experiments," he confessed. "However, the contraption would appear to be of some scientific nature."

Knuckles looked thoughtful. "We'll have to come back with a box van to shift this thing. In the mean time we still need to find the formula and the instruction book for this… whatever it is." He headed back to Rummidge threateningly. "Any ideas?"

"You… ah… you might try the Library, Sir," the retainer suggested nervously.

"Good boy," rumbled Knuckles, patting the butler on the head. He turned to say something to the others and

Rummidge took the opportunity to make a strategic withdrawal. He slipped through the third panel between the Drawing Room and Dining Room doors and had vanished by the time Knuckles turned back.

Flustered, Knuckles beckoned for his associates to follow him back into the Library. He shone the torch around. A load of old books. The beam fell across a painting on the wall. That looked a little more promising. He crossed the room and ran his hands round the frame. Bingo. He hinged the painting aside. It was hung on a panel concealing the faceplate and door of a wall safe. He rubbed his hands together gleefully.

He put a hand to his mouth, and taking the tip of a soggy gloved finger between his teeth, drew the glove off. Stripping off its partner, he wiggled his fingers. Time to get to work. He took a matchbox out of his pocket and buffed the fingertips of his right hand to sensitise them. Putting an ear to the cold, grey steel door of the safe, he started to turn the dial of the combination lock, listening intently for the soft click of the tumblers falling into place.

Llewellyn shone his torch around the hall, feeling at a loose end. Standing at the foot of the stairs was a suit of armour, leaning casually on a broadsword. He hinged open the visor and jumped back as the armour collapsed in an avalanche of scrap metal.

Knuckles had leapt a good couple of feet into the air. He darted over to the door and glared murderously at Llewellyn. Llewellyn was standing on the other side of the hall, staring fixedly at a painting of a horse on the wall.

"Be quiet!" Knuckles rasped. "Berk!" He ducked

back into the library to start cracking the safe again, grousing quietly to himself. He applied himself to the safe door, listening to the tick-tick-tick as he manipulated the lock.

This took him back to happier days. Rich pickings in the stockbroker belt, before he started to concentrate on his more legitimate businesses. Back in those days, all he had to worry about was dodging the old bill. Now it was a different kind of bill he had to dodge; wages, stamp contributions, sick pay, bills for food and drink at the club, cleaning; the list seemed endless. It was no way for a man once described as the 'Terror of Stretcham' to carry on.

He heard a sound on the stair. Someone coming! He closed the picture over the safe and threw himself to the floor behind the settee.

Boadicea Ballcock skipped down the stairs, wearing nothing more than a teddy that set the hearts of the onlooking thugs fluttering. She had been having a restless night, and she knew exactly what was the best remedy. She went into the library and headed straight for the small table by the settee where the decanter of Napoleon brandy was. She tossed on to the settee the soft toy she had been clutching to her bare frame, and poured herself a generous measure of brandy into a balloon glass.

Knuckles, staring up at the vision of unclad loveliness before him, suddenly gave a soft squeak of pain as the high heel of one of Boadicea's slippers speared the back of his hand. A little whimper popped out, his eyes watering, and he went to bang his other fist down on her toes. Suddenly the pressure went off and he tried to jam his injured hand into his mouth.

Boadicea tucked the teddybear under her arm and strolled out of the room, sipping her brandy. The sight of her posterior wiggling fetchingly up the stairs made Knuckles forget the pain. He gave a heartfelt sigh.

Once he was sure she was out of earshot again, he stood up, wafting his aching hand in the air. He returned to the painting and hinged it aside to get at the safe again. He just might be able to get the safe open by noon, the way things were going. He gave a whine of frustration as Bert, who had wandered into the library after him, dropped and smashed a small ornament he had been admiring from the mantelpiece.

"QUIET!!" bellowed Knuckles. He clamped a hand over his mouth, his eyes like saucers as he realised what he had done.

"Ssh!" Bert put a finger to his lips. He made a strategic withdrawal from the room at speed as Knuckles went for him, brandishing his torch threateningly.

"Berk!" Knuckles stared at the safe. One last try, then it was down to dynamite, and plenty of it. He was astonished to be rewarded after only a few seconds' twiddling, with a loud click. He put a shaking hand to the handle of the safe and pulled it down. It turned with a satisfying metallic *clack* and the door swung open. Knuckles found himself staring at bare bricks where the interior of the safe should have been. His bottom lip started to quiver, tears stinging his eyes.

Llewellyn and Bert turned as Knuckles stormed out of the library, shining his torch around. The beam fell across the lower steps of the grand staircase. "This way,"

Knuckles grunted, and led the way up the stairs.

"Boss," Bert ventured.

"What?"

"Where are we going now, Boss?"

Knuckles rounded on Bert, looking ready to throttle him with his bare hands. "Upstairs," he rasped.

"Why?" asked Bert.

"I'd have thought it was bloody obvious!" growled Knuckles. "They haven't left their precious formula lying around downstairs, have they?"

"Ah," Bert's voice was full of admiration. "It's no wonder we call you Boss, Boss."

"Belt up and follow me," whispered Knuckles. He beckoned his two hefty associates after him and continued on up the stairs. Reaching the upper landing, they looked around at the doors leading off.

Bert put the toolbag down with a clatter. "Which room, Boss?" he asked. "Ow!"

Knuckles opened a door and peered in. He pulled the door to again. "Check the other rooms," he whispered.

Llewellyn gave Bert a concerned look. "I'd get a bit of steak on that before it swells up." Bert nodded and wandered through another doorway.

Knuckles emerged from the first room and looked around, puzzled. "Where's Bert?" Llewellyn pointed to the door that Bert had gone through. Knuckles went over and tried the handle. "It's locked."

"D'you think he's found it, Boss?" Llewellyn looked hopeful.

The sound of flushing water came though the door, then it was opened by Bert, pulling up the zip of his flies. Knuckles glared at him. "I needed that," Bert confided. "Ow!"

Knuckles opened another door and looked inside. He was greeted by snoring from within. He smiled to himself and turned to the other two. "Wait here," he hissed. "And don't make any noise!" He moved cautiously into the room, shining his torch around. In the bed, Fred was snoring like a faulty road drill. Knuckles moved over to the bureau in the corner of the room and hinged down the lid. He started to rifle through the papers within.

The bureau was filled with dog-eared sheets of yellowing paper covered in arcane formulae scribbled in a spidery script. Knuckles examined the papers with a rising sense of excitement. Had he found the formula? He tossed the sheet of paper he was examining to one side as he decoded the phrase "2 lbs Brussel Sprouts." A hand tapped him on the shoulder. Slowly he turned and came face to face with Rummidge, who offered a friendly smile.

Knuckles let out a hearty shriek of fright and hit the floor running. Rummidge, Llewellyn and Bert hared after him as he sprinted off down the drive.

Fred stirred momentarily in his sleep, while Daisy, Britannia and Boadicea slept on.

CHAPTER TWENTY-SIX:

In Which Knuckles Gets The Wrong Experiment

And Daisy Takes A Shower

The doorbell rang and Daisy stepped out into the hall. "I'll get it," she shouted. She skipped over to the door, hitching her blue silk pyjama trousers up periodically as they showed a marked tendency to descend round her ankles. She opened the door and took a step back in alarm. Standing on the step were Llewellyn and Bert and three other heavies she did not recognise, all looking less than appealing. "Mr Llewellyn, Mr Bert, what an unexpected pleasure!" Daisy tried to be jovial. "What brings you gentlemen round here?"

"Mr McCallister would like a word with you and Mr Longfield, Miss Chayne," said Llewellyn curtly. He and his entourage brushed past her into the hall. "If you would please fetch Mr Longfield."

Daisy knocked anxiously on the bathroom door. It was opened by Fred, his face half-obscured by shaving foam. "Fred, there's a whole bunch of Knuckles' friends in the hall," she twittered fearfully. "It looks like a Rentamob convention down there."

Fred provided the voice of cool reason. "Stop panicking, Daze. There's probably a simple explanation for all of this."

"Knuckles is going to kill us for the formula!"

Fred put a hand on her shoulder, almost holding her down, as she gave every impression of being ready to take off like a gazelle. "I'll go down and have a word with them."

"You'd better wipe your chin first," said Daisy. "You look like Father Christmas."

"Ho ho ho, Merry Christmas." Fred laughed hollowly and squirted his can of shaving foam into the air, producing a miniature blizzard.

Fred strode down the stairs into the hall with the measured tread of a gunslinger at High Noon, Daisy trailing behind him nervously. He regarded Llewellyn, Bert and the rest of the thugs calmly, although inside, he was ready to turn tail and run. "I believe Mr McCallister wants a word with us."

"He'd like to sort out this business about the late Professor's formula, Mister Longfield," growled Llewellyn.

"But we haven't agreed whether I would sell it or not," said Fred.

"I'm afraid it's no longer a matter for you to decide." Llewellyn signalled to his men and they moved forwards menacingly to seize Fred and Daisy.

-oOo-

"La Cuiller Graisseux" had been completely renovated at some speed in the hope of a grand reopening that evening. Some of the tables still sported plastic dust sheets, and over by the bar, two stepladders supported a plank upon which "Anaglypta" McGurk – an old schoolchum of Knuckles who had turned to housepainting following his last spell at Her Majesty's – was balancing precariously to touch up the ceiling.

Bustling noises were evident from the swinging doors leading to the kitchen, and two sweet trolleys laden with confectionaries ready for the evening's diners had been parked at the side of the stage. On the stage, illuminated by a spotlight, one of Knuckles' dancers was gyrating energetically around a brass pole between floor and stage in her birthday suit.

Fred and Daisy had made the trip from Grisley End in the back of Knuckles' luxurious Rolls-Royce, but had been troubled by muffled noises coming from the boot.

"Mister Longfield! Miss Chayne! Marvellous to see you again!" Knuckles strode towards them, the picture of bonhomie, and shook Fred's hand warmly. "I trust you had a pleasant trip."

"As pleasant as could be expected under the circumstances," interjected Daisy icily.

Knuckles looked chastened. "Do I detect a rebuke?" he asked. "All I want to do is put a simple business proposition to you."

"Who are your friends, Pookie?" Knuckles was interrupted by the young woman who had been rehearsing on the stage. She was now enveloped in a peach-coloured silk robe. Big hair, platinum-blonde, high cheekbones, glossy red lips. Barely contained by the robe, a body sufficiently augmented to technically make her a silicon-based lifeform.

"You haven't met the memsahib? My darling Tiffany." Knuckles kissed the dancer's fingertips fondly.

"Charmed, I'm sure," Tiffany smiled thinly. She regarded Daisy with a degree of suspicion.

"Mr Longfield and Miss Chayne are here to discuss a business proposition, my Angel," smiled Knuckles. "Nothing to worry your pretty little head about. Now run along - man talk."

Both Fred and Daisy spotted the flash of annoyance that crossed Tiffany's face. Composing herself, Tiffany offered them another insincere smile. "'Scuse me then. Toodles." She edged past them and Daisy distinctly heard Mrs Knuckles muttering to herself: "I gave up a PhD in Physics for *this?*" The woman wiggled off backstage, her aft aspect the centre of all male attention in the place.

"What's this business proposition, then?" asked Fred. He had a feeling he did not really want to know.

"Ah yes." Knuckles smiled to himself. "You give me the Midas formula, and I don't kill you."

The colour drained from Fred's face. "That sounds quite reasonable to me," he croaked.

"It's not exactly a business proposition," Daisy opined brightly. "I much preferred the deal you were discussing earlier. You know, the one involving a million pounds and various profit-sharing rights."

"Ah well," Knuckles sighed. "The million pounds was never really a viable proposition, and in any case, I'm in a much stronger bargaining position now than before."

"How do you mean?" asked Daisy.

"It's no longer a question of our making a deal for the formula," he smiled. "It's more that Mr Longfield here will set up the process and then he can show me how to run it, in exchange for your continued wellbeing." Knuckles offered a smug smile.

"And where does the bargaining part come into it?"

"I'll have you here all the time, so that Mr Longfield here won't try anything silly," Knuckles replied as if the answer were obvious.

Fred did not like the way their genial host's mind was working. However, he was not going to let himself be intimidated by a third-rate thug like Knuckles McCallister. He was going to call Knuckles' bluff and see how much of a tough-guy he was. "What makes you think I'll set up the Midas Experiment for you?"

"Because if you don't, I'll be forced to do Miss Chayne some irreparable damage." Daisy stared at Knuckles with saucer-like eyes.

"Now, there's no need to resort to threats!" exclaimed Fred indignantly.

Daisy regarded Knuckles coldly. "It's all right, Fred, I can fight my own battles." The simmering look in her eyes said it all. Forcing herself to smile sweetly, she edged cosily up to Knuckles. "Now, Mr Knuckles. You wouldn't want to hurt me, would you?" She ran a finger down the opening of his shirt and gripped a tuft of hair on his chest between finger and thumb. "Would you?" she asked through gritted teeth and tugged.

Knuckles let out a banshee-like howl and clutched his hands to the bald patch on his chest like a startled topless bather. Daisy dusted off her palms and he eyed her nervously. "I knew you'd see reason." Daisy stepped back to Fred's side to put a little distance between them. She did not see Knuckles signal surreptitiously to a couple of uncredited goons until it was too late. The two thugs grabbed her arms in vice-like grips. She struggled valiantly, stamping on one's toes until his colleague stamped on hers. *"Ow!"* She hopped up and down in pain.

Fred took a step to defend her, but was shoved roughly back by Knuckles. The look on the hoodlum's face said it all. He might not like hitting ladies, but rearranging Fred's features would not bother him in the least. He took a deep breath. "Look, Mr McCallister," he admitted. "We tried the formula, but it doesn't work. The gold produced by the process is unstable at an atomic level. The bonds between the protons break down over time, or if they receive a shock. Nothing we managed to create lasted longer than a couple of days. Most of it broke down much quicker. Not just turning back to its original form but breaking down as coherent matter. *Poof!*"

Knuckles' eyes narrowed. "I expected you'd start making up some cobblers like this, Mr Longfield." He beckoned Llewellyn over. "Bring in the other bargaining chips," he growled.

Llewellyn strolled out of the room, a sardonic smile on his lumpy features. He returned moments later with two heavily laden but anonymous goons. Both goons had a large, lumpy, hessian sack slung over his shoulder as if he were delivering the coal. They dropped the sacks in turn to the floor in front of Fred and Daisy. Both sacks landed with a heavy thud and a pained exclamation. "Sorry,"

Llewellyn offered the first sack as he untied the knot securing it. A familiar mane of raven hair appeared, framing a winded and extremely cross face.

"Bouncy!" exclaimed Daisy in horror.

Boadicea Ballcock allowed Llewellyn to assist her in extricating herself from the sack. Her abbreviated nightwear was filthy. The sack had only recently contained coal. She indignantly looked down at herself and then kicked Llewellyn in the shins, bruising her toes more than doing him serious damage. "What's the meaning of this outrage?! What am I doing here?!" she berated Llewellyn, backing the big man into one of the booths. "How dare you abduct me?!!"

Britannia emerged from the other sack, similarly dishevelled. "Bouncy!" Daisy struggled in the half-nelson Bert was holding her in. Her free hand was keeping up her pyjama trousers. "What happened to you?"

"One minute I was in my bed, zizzing peacefully, the next minute somebody had stuck me in a coal sack," Boadicea's voice was shaky. She glared at Daisy. "I might have known you were behind it all!"

"Me?" squeaked Daisy. "Don't blame me! Blame Knuckles!"

"If it's got anything to do with you, Daisy Chayne, it's always your fault."

"Now come on, arguing between ourselves won't get us anywhere." Fred assumed the role of the voice of reason.

"Ah, put a sock in it, Fred!" growled Boadicea. She

was definitely in a mood and no amount of reasoning would change that. "If we ever get out of this mess alive, Daze, I'm going to kill you!" she promised.

"No, that would be my privilege." Knuckles' smile was that of a crocodile contemplating a bather in the Nile. The nuances in his voice were chilling. Boadicea, Britannia and Daisy stared at him in horror. He let that information settle in, then smiled genially again. "I'm sure there's no need for animosity," he continued. "Why don't we wait for my colleagues to bring the Midas Experiment over from Grisley End? Ideally over a glass of champagne."

-oOo-

Tiffany had emerged from backstage again and was disporting herself on the stage in a fresh, indecently abbreviated costume that was roughly ten percent cloth and ninety percent bare skin. Knuckles clicked his fingers imperiously and two waiters darted forwards to place champagne flutes in front of the five people in the booth. The flutes were expertly filled without ending up half-full of froth. "To a short wait," Knuckles rumbled ominously.

Daisy, Boadicea and Britannia drained their glasses and held them out for refills. Fred sipped his more cautiously, desperately trying to think of a way out of their predicament.

Four or five refills later, Daisy was increasingly relaxed, to the point that she was wriggling fetchingly to the beat of Tiffany's backing track on the booth seat next to Fred. "This brings back memories," she observed offhandedly.

"Eh?" said Boadicea, Britannia and Fred

simultaneously.

Daisy looked coy. "I took a year off between reading Astrology at UCLA and Management at Warmhampton University," she confided. "My sister Bluebell was already working there, and she got me a summer job dancing at the Lido de Paris." She noticed the thunderstruck expressions on her friends' faces. "You know - those huge headdresses, costumes made of ostrich feathers and dental floss... It was a riot."

"I can imagine," said Boadicea faintly, and Fred realised that there were some of Daisy's secrets that even her best enemies were not privy to. Boadicea rallied with an effort and frowned at Daisy. "That explains a lot about our holiday in Skiathos. I had a feeling you'd done that kind of thing before when you were dancing on the bar." She turned to Fred. "You should have seen her." She rolled her eyes.

Fred was unsure what the most politic reply might be.

"Well, if you ask me nicely, I might give you a personal performance," said Daisy lightly. Fred's mouth went dry. He took a healthy swig of champagne and came to a decision that was mostly alcoholic bravado. She stood up. "I can do that," she announced blithely, indicating Tiffany's onstage gymnastics. To prove her point, she clambered over Fred out of the booth. Fred tried to stop her and stared after her with an expression of alarm.

"She's drunk!" Fred rounded on Knuckles indignantly. He pointed an accusatory finger at Daisy, who was happily spinning around the brass pole.

"*Pish tush!*" Knuckles wagged a finger airily,

attempting to be reassuring. "Fine champagne does not intoxicate, it merely relaxes." He poured himself another glass to demonstrate, but his eyes were on Daisy and he nearly managed to miss his mouth.

"In that case, she's as relaxed as a newt!" Fred retorted. He folded his arms and gave Daisy one of his famous jaundiced looks.

Daisy was oblivious to the argument. She mounted the polished stage of the night-club and as Tiffany rotated past on the axis of the pole, linked arms with Mrs Knuckles and sent the dancer spinning uncontrollably across the stage. Tiffany sailed over the edge and landed with a tremendous crash, demolishing the aforementioned sweet trolley parked at the side of the stage.

Boadicea and Britannia burst into spontaneous applause.

Tiffany surfaced from the ruins of the sweet trolley, unhurt but for her dignity. A large, Black Forest Gateau had broken her fall. She liberated a large bowl of sticky rice pudding from the sweet trolley and, interrupting Daisy in mid-rotation, managed to pour it down the front of Daisy's pyjama trousers. Daisy gave a squeak of alarm.

Daisy gave an angered growl and poured a jug of cream down the other girl's cleavage from the sweet trolley that Tiffany had not demolished. Tiffany gazed indignantly down at her bosom and gave Daisy a hefty shove. Daisy skidded on the gooey mess on the stage and grabbed the girl for support, breaking the clasp of Tiffany's flimsy top. She sat down heavily in a large bowl of yoghurt, which splattered everywhere. Tiffany crowed triumphantly as Daisy struggled to pick herself up off the floor. The bowl was jammed tightly on her hips. Daisy wriggled uncomfortably as yoghurt ran down her legs to join the pool of rice pudding on the stage. She gripped the bowl with sticky fingers and pushed hard. It parted company with her anatomy with an audible plop. She put a foot against Tiffany's shapely rear and shoved. Tiffany skidded on the pool of yoghurt and milk pudding on the stage and spun spectacularly into the second trolley. She stood up, indignantly scraping the remains of a sherry trifle off her person and advanced on Daisy.

Rice pudding squelched between Daisy's toes as she backed away from the girl. Tiffany had two large handfuls of whipped cream. She stalked Daisy, a cruel smile on her face. Suddenly she leapt on top of her, ensuring that every inch of bare skin was covered in cream. Daisy squealed as her feet shot out from under her and she found herself sprawled on the polished, slippery stage of the nightclub. Covered in a layer of viscous cream and rice pudding, Daisy started to wonder if this pole-dancing idea had been all that hot. Her long, blonde hair was plastered back against her head, covered in more of the sticky stuff. She tried to get up, but Tiffany was upon her again in an instant, slapping a handful of sticky trifle into her face. She gurgled as what felt like half of it went up her nose. It provided just enough of a distraction. Daisy suddenly found herself pinned to the stage as Knuckles and his goons cheered 'the Memsahib' on.

Daisy attempted to retire from the match, but Tiffany was having none of this and attempted to grab Daisy's legs in a flying rugby tackle. Daisy squealed as her pants were skinned violently down her legs. Tiffany sank her teeth into Daisy's upturned behind.

-oOo-

A subdued and rather sticky Daisy had rejoined her friends in the booth with Knuckles. She had salvaged her pyjamas from the battlefield and was sitting with her arms folded and rice pudding in the most peculiar places.

"It's here, Boss." Llewellyn had spotted one of the goons who had been assigned to the box van. As a precaution against damage, they had taken a slower route back to Stretcham and the nightclub than Knuckles' Roller.

Knuckles turned breezily to Llewellyn. "Wheel it in, Taff." Fred looked up and his eyes widened in alarm as Llewellyn and Bert wheeled a wardrobe-sized object covered in tarpaulin on to the stage. Two pipes and an electrical cable snaked offstage behind the object, which had been mounted on castors for ease of transport. Knuckles stepped up on to the stage and whisked away the tarpaulin with a flourish. "The Midas Experiment," he beamed triumphantly. "Already plumbed in and ready to go."

Fred found himself staring at the Sylph Home Spa.

Before he could do anything, Daisy had given a woozy squeak of recognition and clambered on to the stage. She prodded the external controls and Knuckles took an apprehensive step backwards as the contraption gave an enormous shudder and started to vibrate, gurgling and whooshing like a time machine about to head for the Jurassic Era. To the consternation of all present, she then proceeded to divest herself of every stitch she was wearing and stepped inside the cubicle. A couple more key presses to start the built-in hi-fi blaring out the old J Geils Band classic "Angel In The Centerfold" and dispense a handful of shower gel and oblivious of her surroundings, Daisy proceeded to soap herself. All over.

Knuckles flopped into the booth seat beside Fred. "That. Isn't. The Midas Experiment." Fred pointed at the Sylph.

"No problem." Knuckles was transfixed by what was going on in the cubicle.

Tiffany stood on the sidelines, completely upstaged once more. Her gaze switched rapidly between Knuckles and Daisy's impromptu ablutions and back again. Knuckles was regarding the proceedings in the Sylph with an expression not dissimilar to that rabbits reserved for oncoming juggernauts. His lips were forming a mute, but distinct "ooo..." that Tiffany regarded as her personal property. With a feral growl, she hurled herself into the cubicle, which rocked under the impact. Daisy gave a bleat of distress as she found herself under attack once again.

Fred went to stand up, but Boadicea pushed him back into his seat, shaking her head. Daisy and Tiffany should settle their argument between themselves.

A pool of foam was spreading out from the base of the Sylph, dripping on to the newly-laid carpet and ruining it. Tiffany was battering Daisy about the head with a loofah, partially blinded by shower gel which was erupting periodically from the now-jammed dispenser. Daisy was doing her best to defend herself with a couple of sponges.

Boadicea nudged Britannia. A look passed between the two young women. Nobody did that to *their* Daisy. They sprang to their feet and leapt to her defence.

Knuckles and Fred sat transfixed by the scene unfolding on the stage. Fred cocked his head on one side trying to figure out whose leg Boadicea was trying to bite. He could not tear his eyes away from the sight, even when Knuckles tapped him on the shoulder.

"Tell you what, Mr Longfield," rumbled Knuckles, somewhat absently. "You can forget the Midas formula. If you can just persuade Miss Chayne and her friends to re-enact this twice nightly…"

-oOo-

CHAPTER TWENTY-SEVEN:

In Which Fred Becomes A Reluctant Alchemist

And Knuckles Learns The Ropes

Daisy woke and gave a luxurious stretch. She had slept like a baby in the huge, Emperor-sized bed, although for some mysterious reason she had felt distinctly queasy - almost seasick. She levered herself up on her elbows and looked around herself muzzily. The world seemed to be undulating beneath her. Her mouth tasted as if something had crawled in there during the night and died. Her brain, she suspected, had been surgically removed, jumped up and down on, and jammed back into place the wrong way round. She rolled over to go back to sleep and came face to face with Fred.

She woke him with a light kiss to the end of his nose. "Good morning," she chirped playfully.

Fred smiled and they indulged in a little early morning smooching, but before they could graduate to anything more biological, Boadicea Ballcock had peered over Fred's shoulder.

"Is this a private party, or can anybody join in?" she enquired.

Daisy gave a squeak of fright and fell off the edge of the bed. She staggered to her feet and discovered she and Fred had been sharing the bed with both Boadicea and her sister Britannia. She also discovered they were in strange surroundings - a large, modern master bedroom with a view overlooking the river.

She cradled her head in her hands. That was the last time she let herself be plied with champagne by organised criminals, she vowed silently. She was also wearing the top of a man's pair of flannelette pyjamas, and she *knew* for a fact that Fred didn't possess such an item of nightwear in his wardrobe.

"I feel like I've been resurrected," she whimpered, sitting down on the edge of the bed.

"Is it me, or is this bed... *sloshing?*" enquired Boadicea delicately.

Fred sat up slowly. "Water bed."

"Thank goodness for that," breathed Daisy. "I thought I was having a nasty turn."

Fred unsteadily got out of bed and made the discovery that he had been sleeping in his suit. Pulling on his shoes, he went over to the door to see if it was locked. To his surprise, he found that it was unlocked. Daisy, Boadicea and Britannia joined him, and Boadicea, being the bravest of the three of them, cautiously opened the door and peered out into the passage outside. It was deserted, so she tentatively stepped out of the room and crept along to the end of the passage. Daisy, Fred and her sister followed her trepidatiously and in that order. They came out on to the landing above the modest entrance hall and gazed down the staircase towards the front door. One of Knuckles' henchmen was posted by the door, and as he saw them, he pointed grimly towards one of the doors leading off the hall.

Knuckles' home was a palatial building in one of the more fashionable suburbs of the town. Counting millionaire businessmen and a minor rock star as his neighbours, the house stood on top of a hill, sloping away to the river. The interior was even more impressive than the exterior. The rooms were filled to overflowing with objets d'art and antiques. Fred wondered vaguely how much of it had featured on Crimewatch UK on television.

As they reached the bottom of the stairs, they could hear the sound of voices coming from the doorway the thug had indicated, which was slightly ajar. Fred moved over to the doors and peered through into the room beyond. His eyes widened at the sight that met him. Knuckles, his wife Tiffany, Llewellyn and Bert were sitting down to a hearty breakfast at the long dining table. At the head of the table, Knuckles was sitting behind a copy of the morning's paper.

Fred suddenly found himself sailing through the doors having been given a tremendous shove from behind. He landed sprawling on the carpet with Daisy and the Ballcock Sisters on top of him. Two huge shot-putter types, who had been responsible for pushing them, followed them into the room and picked Boadicea and Britannia up off the floor. They hoisted Boadicea over the back of one of the chairs at the table and sat her down facing Llewellyn. Britannia was seated opposite Bert. Fred was positioned next to her, and Daisy sat down demurely at the end of the table, opposite Knuckles.

"Ah, Miss Chayne, Mr Longfield, the Mizzes Ballcock," said Knuckles with a most charming smile. "So glad you could join us. What would you like for breakfast?"

Daisy was speechless. One of the two shot-putters put a bowl of breakfast cereal down in front of her and poured on some milk. The other poured her a cup of black coffee. Daisy shrugged to herself, realising she'd had nothing to eat since the previous night, and tucked into the cereal.

The only sound in the dining room was that of spoons against china until the bacon and eggs were served, and then Boadicea spoke.

"Would somebody mind telling me what's going on here?" she asked.

Knuckles folded his newspaper and offered her a charming smile. "Nothing for you to worry your pretty little head about, my dear Ms Ballcock," he said condescendingly.

Boadicea glared at him. She hated being patronised.

"All young Fred here has to do is get the Midas formula working - in its entirety - to my satisfaction."

"Then you'll let us go?" asked Daisy.

"Ah, that's the catch." Knuckles looked regretful. "I'm afraid I can't afford any loose ends."

"I've never been called a loose end before!" Boadicea looked affronted.

"I've told you the formula's useless," Fred stared at Knuckles exasperatedly. "I explained the problem last night."

Knuckles stood up and moved round the table to Fred's side. He leaned on the table, putting his face a matter of inches from Fred's. "If you don't make the formula work, you'll regret it for what little is left of your life," he rumbled.

Fred swallowed audibly. He broke the silence. "Well, we can't waste time sitting around here all day," he opined briskly. "I've got to dismantle the experiment and get it set up again in the garage."

-oOo-

Everything that had stood in the laboratory that had anything to do with the Midas experiment had been dismantled and carefully packed away in tea chests full of straw for the journey across town to Knuckles' place. Fortunately, little damage had been caused by the mysterious explosion that had coincided with Lord Ballcock's visit. What glassware had shattered had been easily replaced. Fred ticked off the last items on his inventory list and looked forlornly round the laboratory. It looked more like a wine cellar than the lair of a mad scientist now. "Well, that's everything." He picked up the sheaf of Great Uncle Plum's notes and formulae. "Not forgetting the most important thing."

"Jolly good." Llewellyn and Bert grasped him by the elbows and escorted him up the stairs from the laboratory and out of the house. Fred made no attempt to struggle, as he knew the two thugs could take him apart with their bare hands. He simply hung between them, his feet dangling in mid-air.

Llewellyn and Bert carried him over to Knuckles' Rolls-Royce Corniche that had brought them back to the house. Knuckles was proudly polishing the Spirit emblem on the bonnet with his handkerchief.

The pantechnicon that had accompanied them to transport the equipment pulled out of the gates of the house as Llewellyn and Bert released Fred and shoved him forwards. Knuckles took the sheaf of notes out of Fred's hands and leafed through them, a beatific smile on his brutish features. "Thank you, Mr Longfield," he beamed.

The hieroglyphics on the pages were as indecipherable as ancient Greek to Knuckles, but the important thing was that he had the formula in his hands. He pushed Fred into the back of the car where Daisy had been waiting patiently.

Daisy stared at Fred in abject disappointment. "Oh, Fred!"

"There wasn't a lot I could do, was there?" Fred sounded completely defeated.

"There now, that wasn't too much of a chore, was it?" enquired Knuckles cheerily, sliding in beside them. He patted Bert on the shoulder as the thug slid in behind the wheel of the Rolls. "See if you can get us home before the lorry."

"Righto, Boss." Bert gunned the engine, kicking up gravel from the wheels and sped down the gravel drive.

"Oi! What about me??" Llewellyn shouted after the car as it shot through the gates in a plume of dust.

-oOo-

Knuckles ushered them back into the house. Fred was pushed roughly by one of Knuckles' henchmen into the Chesterfield settee in the lounge. Daisy landed beside him and they huddled close together as Llewellyn and Bert perched themselves on the arms of the settee. Knuckles sat down opposite them in his favourite, big, comfy armchair.

The door opened and a large woman with a fake

suntan, suicide-blonde hair and a marked resemblance to a chipmunk bustled into the room with a trolley piled high with cucumber sandwiches and cups of tea. "I thought you might like a drop of tea."

Knuckles smiled patiently. "Thank you, Mother."

The woman regarded Fred and Daisy curiously with dark, beady little eyes. She slapped Knuckles reproachfully in the arm. "Aren't you going to introduce us, then?" Knuckles remembered his manners and made the introductions. He introduced the woman and Mother Knuckles extended a pudgy hand to shake Fred's and Daisy's. "I hope Raymond's treating you well," she smiled. "Don't mind his manner, he might sound a bit gruff, but he's just a soppy old pussycat under it all."

Knuckles rolled his eyes. Undermined by his own Mum! How could he cultivate an image as a hard man when his mother went around telling everybody he was a pussycat. At least she had not told them about the crocheting.

"D'you like the antimacassars?" Mother Knuckles squawked amiably. "Raymond did those. It's his hobby." She gave him an affectionate hug, her considerable bulk putting a strain on the arm of the chair. "He's a clever old bugger when he wants to be."

Knuckles' eyes boggled in horror. *"Mu-um!!!."* He rapidly composed himself again, going from outraged five-year-old having a spit-wash in front of his mates to Warmhamptonian gangster in a blink of an eye. His voice took on the quality of a cat snagging its claws in silk. "These young people and I do have some important business to discuss."

"Oh, *excusez-moi*," Mother Knuckles sounded sarcastic. She could take a hint, though, and sauntered out of the room, her nose in the air.

Once the dreaded Mother Knuckles had left the room, the son turned his attention back to his unwilling guests. "Now, Mr Longfield, we are going to get this experiment sorted out," he growled dangerously. "And this time, no funny tricks, or..." He released Fred and drew a finger across his throat with a suitably disgusting accompanying sound effect. Fred stared at Knuckles. That he would carry out his threat had been implicit.

-oOo-

Knuckles led Fred into the garage like a naughty schoolboy, an ear tweaked viciously between thumb and forefinger. To accommodate the considerable power demands of the apparatus, Knuckles had enlisted the services of the gang's electrical and electronics expert, "Sizzling" Norman Collings to rewire the garage with that in mind. Collings, a tall, twitchy individual with short hair that was always standing on end - and occasionally smouldering - made the final connection and sucked a singed finger as the new fuse box spat out a shower of sparks as he threw the main switch. "There you are, Guv," Collings beamed, twitching alarmingly. "Two sixty amp lines straight through from the mains. That should do." He started to collect his tools together, tossing them into a metal toolbox that looked as if it had recently been in a fire. The last item was a bare lightbulb. It flickered into life as he picked it up. Fred and Knuckles looked at each other nervously.

Fred made the last connection and stood back from

the experiment critically. He had numbered every part of the complex, three-dimensional jigsaw of glassware, but he could still not be one-hundred percent sure he had got everything in the right place. He shrugged to himself. Only time would tell. He pulled on a pair of heavy rubber gloves and started pouring chemicals from the bottles he had brought from the old house into the various reservoir retorts around the experiment. He watched as the multi-coloured fluids started to make their way round the experiment, mixing and changing as they went.

Knuckles was looking on like a five-year-old with his nose pressed to the toy shop window. The burly goon was almost bouncing up and down with impatient excitement.

Finally, Fred mixed up the last of the strange substances detailed in the notes - the most important ingredient, the sticky green glop that the other chemicals finally distilled down and mixed with. The twin platinum electrodes that energised the final part of the experiment sank slowly into the stuff. Fred attached the high tension cables from the power supply unit that had been set up in the corner of the garage. It was plugged into the house mains via a trailing flex. Boadicea, Britannia and Daisy were sitting beside the device, watching him dejectedly.

"That's it," Fred breathed. "Although I don't know if the standard mains will provide enough power."

"You'd better hope it does," growled Knuckles. "Or I might think you're up to something."

"I thought the deal was you'd let us go now!" exclaimed Fred.

Knuckles shook his head, making sarcastic tisk-tisk

noises. "Now, whatever would have made you think that?" He walked round the experiment thoughtfully. "When can we try it out?" he asked.

Fred shrugged. "Straight away, if you like."

Knuckles beamed as if he had won the pools. "I'll just get something to try it out on." He hurried out of the garage.

"You sold us out!" Boadicea stared at Fred as if he had betrayed them.

"He didn't have much choice." Daisy leapt to his defence, but Fred could tell she too was disappointed.

"Knuckles has the formula. There's no telling what he'll do with it!"

"Not quite," said Fred quietly.

The two women stared at him. "What did you say, Fred?" Boadicea looked surprised.

Fred looked around furtively, then leaned in close to his two friends. "Knuckles hasn't got *all* of the formula," he confided. He pulled a single sheet of paper out of his inside pocket. "This is the formula for that green gunk in the centre beaker," he whispered. "Without this, the experiment won't work." He quickly slipped the paper back into his pocket as Knuckles returned carrying a paperweight.

"Will this do?" asked Knuckles, presenting the object. Fred took it off him and examined it. It was a piece of sea-rounded sandstone, and on the surface, someone had roughly inscribed with a ball-point pen: *'Souvenir of Little*

Bispham - July 1975'.

"Fine." Fred picked the stone up with a pair of tongs and lowered it into the reaction vessel. Handing around goggles, he went over to the power supply unit and set the dials, then he rested his hand on the knife-switch that would set the process in motion. "Mind your eyes!"

A dull electrical hum vibrated the garage, shaking rust from the iron roof members. Electricity arced around the reaction vessel and a distant voice bellowed from the house: "Raymond? What the hell are you doing in that garage? Me Hoover's packed in!" Knuckles stuck his head out of the door, and told his mother in no uncertain terms what she could do with her Hoover.

Fred snapped off the power and approached the reaction vessel with some trepidation. He breathed a sigh of relief as he saw the familiar glint of gold. He fished the lump of solid gold out of the reaction vessel and dunked it in a bucket of water to rinse the chemical residue from it.

"Give it here!" Knuckles was eager to hold the object.

"Careful, it's still warm," cautioned Fred. He dropped the lump of gold in Knuckles' hand. Knuckles juggled the object like a hot potato, an inane grin on his face.

-oOo-

Daisy had problems of her own. To ensure that she, Britannia and Boadicea would not (and could not) escape, Knuckles had delegated the dreaded Mother Knuckles to lock them in the guest bedroom again. Boadicea was sitting dejectedly on the bed. "Come on, bird-brain." She glared at Daisy. "Think of a way of getting us out of here!"

Daisy paced up and down the room like a caged tiger. Sitting around there doing nothing was against her nature. However, there were Knuckles' compatriots outside to stop them going anywhere. She moved over to the window and pressed her aching forehead to the cool glass as she realised there was nothing she could do. Below, in the garden, she could see the garage, lights flickering in the window as Fred battled with his Great Uncle's formula. She turned away from the window and sighed.

-oOo-

Fred was exhausted. He had run the experiment more than twenty times for Knuckles. All the items he had converted lay in a golden heap on the far side of the garage, but so far none had done the disappearing trick. He knew the weakening effect of the transmogrification would eventually cause all of them to implode with a pop and a shower of pixie dust, but he had not been able to convince Knuckles of the fact.

The greed in Knuckles' eyes was more than evident as they reflected the golden glow of the spanner in the reaction vessel. With shaking fingers, he extracted the spanner from the centre of the experiment and dipped it into a beaker of fresh water to rinse away any last traces of chemicals. He turned to Fred. "D'you think you could scale this up to a proper industrial process?" he asked.

-oOo-

Daisy lay on the bed, her hands folded behind her head, staring at the ceiling in the hope of divining some inspiration from the mirror tiles. Her reflection stared back at her with a blank look that didn't inspire her with confidence. She could see a certain appeal in having a ceiling covered in mirror tiles, but she doubted whether she would put any up at her flat.

Her eyes narrowed. There was something peculiar about one of the tiles. That one there. There was a slightly wider gap around three sides than the other tiles and the reflection it gave was distinctly different to its neighbours. It wasn't, she surmised, flat to the ceiling and no decorator or glazier or whoever would stick up mirror tiles would leave a flaw that apparent in a job unless they were hopelessly slapdash and not bothered about their kneecaps.

"Bouncy," she said thoughtfully. "I think that's the hatch into the attic."

Boadicea followed her gaze, standing up from the edge of the bed. "You might be right, Daze. But what good does it do us?"

"There might be a way out on to the roof," replied Daisy. "Or something up there that might help us get out of here." She bounced to her feet.

Boadicea looked around the room. The house had very high ceilings and the mirror tiles were well out of reach of both of them. There was little furniture in the room that they could use to climb up to the opening. "How do we get up there?"

Daisy slipped off her shoes and stepped up on to the bed, wobbling slightly as the bed undulated under her. "Why don't Britt and I give you a bunk-up?" she suggested.

"As the actress said to the bishop."

"Behave." Daisy made a stirrup with her hands. "Come on, I want to get out of here." Britannia clambered on to the bed beside her and knitted her fingers together to provide a second stirrup for her sister.

"Why is it always me that gets to do the dangerous things?" asked Boadicea.

"All right, cleverclogs," retorted Daisy, "Why don't *you* give *me* a bunk-up?"

"Just don't drop me." Boadicea swarmed up on to the bed and planted a foot in Daisy's proffered stirrup. Putting her hands on Daisy's shoulders, she put the other foot into Britannia's hands and on the count of three, was boosted aloft by them both.

"Why didn't you take your shoes off?" grunted Daisy, wobbling as Boadicea scrabbled at the mirror tile above them.

"Didn't think," replied Boadicea. "You know something, I don't think this is a way up into the attic."

Daisy looked up. "What? Ooops! Oooo! Ah!"

For what seemed like an eternity, they wobbled precariously, then tumbled to the counterpane. Daisy bounced once and landed on her back on the floor. Britannia was in a similar predicament on the other side of the bed. Boadicea found herself standing up to her ankles in cold water as her high-heels went straight through the heavy waterproof covering of the water mattress. Water fountained up around her knees, splashing down on to the white sheepskin rug.

Daisy leapt to her feet. "Are you all right, Bouncy?"

"A trifle wet."

Daisy regarded the spreading pool of water as the mortally wounded water bed evacuated itself all over the floor. "Mr. Knuckles isn't going to be pleased about this," she ventured.

Boadicea stepped off the bed, having spotted something out of the window. She looked down into the garden below. Mrs Knuckles, the marmoset-like mother of the gangster, was returning from a shopping expedition, driven in the Mercedes by Llewellyn. Mother Knuckles and Llewellyn came inside the house to put down the boxes and bags they were laden down with. She flinched as there was a screech from the living room.

Britannia was standing at the door, an ear to it, listening intently. "I think someone's coming!" she hissed.

"Well, get away from the door!" exclaimed Daisy. Outside the door, there was a series of shouts, and the handle rattled as someone tried it.

On the other side, Llewellyn was trying to shoulder the door open, feet splashing in the water pouring from underneath. Behind him, Mother Knuckles was jumping up and down, screeching like a banshee, effing and blinding. Something about a key. She darted forwards and turned the key as he hurled himself at the door again. The door burst open and he tumbled into the room, landing with a terrific splash on the bed. At that moment the floor under the bed decided to collapse and Llewellyn disappeared into the void.

Daisy sprang towards the door, Britannia in close pursuit. "Come on, Bouncy!" she exhorted.

"Where d'you think you're going?" Mrs Knuckles, a meat cleaver in her hand, was blocking their way.

-oOo-

Knuckles sat on the waterlogged settee, holding his head in his hands, wondering how much water could possibly fit into one water bed. The ceiling of the living room had fallen in and every stick of furniture in the room was ruined. No amount of cleaning would repair the damage. The carpet, plaster ground into it, was a write-off. The tv and the video had exploded. As for his collection of stolen objets d'art... He ground his teeth noisily. Llewellyn, carrying a mop and bucket and wearing rubber gloves and a pinny, hurried past apologetically. Knuckles turned at a noise behind him. It was Bert, who had Daisy and Boadicea in matching arm-locks. Daisy was squirming.

Bert thrust the two women to stand with Fred by the fireplace, under the armed guard of "Sledgehammer" O'Riley who had brought Britannia down. "What shall we do with them, Boss?" asked Bert.

"Shoot them," suggested Mother Knuckles, staring around the ruin of her beautiful home.

"Now now, Mother dear," growled Knuckles. "We aren't savages. We can't go around shooting people."

Daisy and Boadicea looked at each other in relief.

337

"We have to make it look like an accident," added Knuckles. He turned to Llewellyn and Bert. "Bung 'em in the boat house."

CHAPTER TWENTY-EIGHT:

In Which Fred And Daisy Nearly Have Their Hopes Sunk

And Knuckles' Experiments Come To An Explosive Conclusion

The boat house stood at the far end of the croquet lawn to the rear of Chez Knuckles, a small jetty sticking out into the river where Knuckles' pride and joy, the pleasure launch "*Smashangrab*" was moored. The boat house itself was a run-down and dilapidated structure of worm-ridden timber, neglected by previous owners, but which Knuckles intended eventually to get round to renovating. Llewellyn and Bert shoved Fred, Daisy, Boadicea and Britannia inside.

Daisy was singularly unimpressed by their surroundings. "Ugh!" she exclaimed, ducking under a gargantuan spider's web that had obviously taken its owner months, if not years to complete. Ropes, cans of paint, tools, old chairs and various bits and pieces were stored in the boathouse, strewn carelessly around. A thick layer of dust covered everything, as Daisy discovered when she put her hand down on the old rocking horse in the corner.

Fred was more concerned about having his hands tied behind his back by Bert. The rope dug into his wrists painfully. He looked over to see Daisy being similarly trussed. Then they were pushed face to face and lashed together to one of the posts supporting the upper floor of the boathouse with what seemed like miles of rope. The operation was over in a matter of moments and Llewellyn stood back to admire his handiwork. "There. Ropes not too tight, are they?"

"No, thanks," Daisy replied brightly. "Very comfy."

"Perfect," confirmed Fred. "Cheers." He and Daisy were so close they had to be careful not to bump noses. They gazed into each other's eyes.

Boadicea eyed them uncomfortably. "You're not going to tie me up with those two, are you?" she asked. "Two's company, four's a crowd and all that," she observed lightly.

Llewellyn dextrously tied Britannia to another of the posts and turned to Boadicea. "Now it's your turn."

"Oh well, there's no need to put yourselves out on my part." She started to edge towards the door. "I'll be on my way, if it's all the same to you."

A look passed between Llewellyn and Bert. They moved to flank her. "Oh no, Ms Ballcock, you're not putting us out," leered Llewellyn. He grasped her arm in a painful grip.

"Let go!" Boadicea aimed a painful kick at his shins.

Llewellyn winced. "You're going to regret that," he growled.

Boadicea regarded him imperiously. "Oh yes?"

It was all over in a flash. Boadicea dangled limply from the beam nearest the door by her wrists, trying to work out how she had got there. Llewellyn gave her a little shove so that she swung backwards and forwards on the end of the rope that secured her. Chuckling to himself, he strolled out of the boathouse with his hirsute colleague.

-oOo-

"We can't raid Knuckles' place without a search warrant, Sir Roland," the Superintendent explained slowly. "And we need a good reason to raid a place before we can get one." He looked to his superior, the Chief Constable, for support. The three men were standing in Sir Roland's study at the Manor, the two police officers called in for a council of war.

"No no," smiled Sir Roland amiably. "I wasn't suggesting we *raid* Mr Knuckles' house. I was merely suggesting we drop by on a friendly visit. He might not know anything about where my daughter and her friends are." He had dropped by Grisley End that morning and found the place not only unlocked, but no sign of Fred, Daisy, the Ballcock Sisters *or* the Sylph.

The Chief Constable was dubious of Knuckles' innocence in any matter, and the idea sounded logical to him. "We could always try out that new police launch your river boys keep going on about," he suggested to the Superintendent. "Knuckles' gaff backs on to the river, so if there's anything funny going on, we're bound to see it."

"Fair enough." The Superintendent turned to Sir Roland. "Mind if I use your 'phone, Sir?"

-oOo-

Daisy gave a desolate sigh and looked around the boat house. Her eyebrows shot up as she spotted something on the workbench just beyond Boadicea. "I spy with my little eye," she began.

"That's it," growled Boadicea. "Daisy's gone bananas. For goodness' sakes, Daze, those ugly beggars are going to kill us! Do you really want to play some stupid game?"

"Oh, come on." Fred leapt to Daisy's aid as usual. "It'll keep our spirits up. And at the moment, I reckon they're in need of keeping up."

"As a matter of fact," Daisy sniffed, "I was going to say I spy with my little eye, something beginning with K." She inclined her head towards the work bench to emphasise the point.

Boadicea sighed bleakly and shook her head. Fred, however, had followed Daisy's gaze and spotted what she had seen. "Oh yes," he grinned. "Something beginning with K."

"Have you gone soft in the head too, Fred?" Boadicea's eyes narrowed. "Kite? Kookaburra? Kumquat?" she suggested sarcastically.

"Knife!" shouted Daisy. "K-N-ife!"

"Where?" asked Boadicea.

"Behind you," replied Daisy. "Twit!"

Boadicea swung her legs to rotate herself on the end of the rope. She spotted the knife immediately. "Oh yes." She slowly spun back round to face them.

Daisy stared up at her friend expectantly. "Well, what are you waiting for?"

"Okay, you get that point," conceded Boadicea.

"No, stupid," Daisy glared at her friend. "Try and untie yourself. If you can get the knife, you can cut us free and we can all escape."

"I know," Boadicea chided. "I was going to do just that."

Fred could see through the boathouse window, and alternated looking out for Llewellyn and Bert with watching Boadicea's progress. Suddenly, Boadicea's contortions paid off and she dropped out of sight with a cry of surprise and a muffled thud. She surfaced from behind a pile of ropes, dusting herself down. She quickly untied her sister from the post securing her.

"Don't just stand there, cut us loose!" hissed Daisy urgently.

Fred had been looking out of the window again and had spotted Llewellyn and Bert approaching from the house, carrying a large bag of B and Q cement between them. "They're coming back!" he exclaimed. "Don't try to untie us, just go and get help!"

"I'm not Lassie, you know." Boadicea hurried over to the door that led out on to the jetty. Britannia followed her.

"Be careful!" called Daisy.

Fred could see that Llewellyn and Bert had seen Boadicea and her sister slipping out of the boathouse. They dropped the bag of cement, which burst with an explosion of fine dust. Llewellyn charged after the escaping women. "Not so fast!" he shouted.

343

Boadicea gave a squeak of alarm as Llewellyn appeared behind her, blocking one escape route. Bert was racing round to cut off her other route. Llewellyn grinned idiotically as he advanced on her. This time he was not going to let her escape again. The last thing Boadicea wanted to spend the afternoon doing was dangling from a beam in the boathouse while Llewellyn and Bert mixed a bucketful of concrete for her to stand in. She looked around for any avenues of escape, but only one presented itself. She rocketed a shapely right foot into Llewellyn's groin and folded him in two. Britannia made the perfect dive into the river. Bert made a grab for Boadicea, and only just stopped himself falling in the water as she followed her sister into the water.

-oOo-

Fred stared bleakly out of the grimy window of the boat house. Outside, he could see Llewellyn and Bert mixing a large tin bath, full of quick setting concrete. The door opened again and Knuckles stood in the opening, Fred's labcoat stretched across his bulky frame. He regarded the two prisoners with a derisive smile on his face. "I wouldn't be too concerned about your little friends the Misses Ballcock. Muscles and the boys have an eye out for them, and there's every possibility that they're already at the bottom of the river."

"You... you..." Daisy struggled for an adequate word, but her vocabulary was not up to it.

"Ratbag; snake; creep; bastard; molester of hamsters," suggested Fred, whose vocabulary was up to it. His ears sang as Knuckles batted him across the back of the head with a rubber gloved hand.

Knuckles stripped off his rubber gloves and reached

into a pocket. "Watch what you say, Mr Longfield." He grinned sardonically. "I was going to say you might live to regret it, but you won't." He took a Swiss Army knife out of the back pocket of his trousers and folded out the largest blade.

Fred swallowed. "I'm sure there's no need for any unpleasantness."

"Oh, there's always a need for a little unpleasantness," growled Knuckles, a particularly nasty smile playing across his lips. He placed the blade between Fred's shoulder-blades, and cut the thick coil of rope that bound the two captives together. Fred and Daisy staggered apart as the rope tumbled around their ankles. Knuckles pushed them both to sit down on the workbench under the window and checked the rope securing Fred's wrists and ankles. With a grunt of satisfaction, he moved over to Daisy. "I'd hoped to be able to witness your demise personally. However, the timing of the tides necessitates your both leaving immediately for the estuary. I don't want to delay my experiments with the formula, or wait for the next tide, so I'm leaving the actual disposal in the capable hands of my colleagues Llewellyn and Bert. I came to say goodbye." Knuckles stood in front of Daisy, crouching down to be on a level with her face, his frequently-broken nose a matter of inches from hers.

"Goodbye?" Daisy looked at him with big eyes. "That sounds awfully final. Couldn't we make it *au revoir*?"

Knuckles shook his head.

"I'd settle for farewell, or even toodle-oo," suggested Daisy.

345

"I'm afraid when we part company in a short while, it will be permanent," Knuckles reassured her. "It comforts me to think I'll never see either of you two crackpots ever again."

"Charming," grunted Fred.

"Well, if that's how you feel." Daisy's tied-together feet lashed upwards in a deadly arc.

"Did you say something, Llew?" asked Bert, looking up from the tin-bathful of concrete he was mixing. Llewellyn's gaze was in the direction of the boathouse, and he followed it to see Knuckles staggering out of the ramshackle construction, both hands clutched to his groin.

"Everything all right, Boss?" Llewellyn called.

Knuckles gave an uncharacteristic high-pitched squeak in response and limped off up the path. Llewellyn shrugged and turned his attention back to the bath of concrete. He slapped his head. "You know something, Bertie? We're going about this completely the wrong way."

Bert was crouching over the concrete, using a dessert spoon to ladle water into the mixture to keep it workable. He looked up at Llewellyn in annoyance, as he took his concrete mixing very seriously. "How's that then, Llew?"

"We'll only strain something important carrying this thing inside to stick their feet in, then we'll have the added problem of getting them out and on to the boat once it's set round their ankles."

Bert thought about it and had to admit that Llewellyn had a point there. "What do we do, then?" he asked. "We can't throw away all of this concrete, after all the care I took mixing it!"

"Steady on, old chum," Llewellyn reassured him. "We can save a lot of sweat by just lifting this on board the boat. Then we get them to come out on board and stick their feet in it. All we have to do when we get out into the estuary is *hup*, over the side and watch the bubbles."

"Brilliant," breathed Bert. "I wish I had a scientific mind like you."

Llewellyn wagged a finger. "You're an artist, old son, not a scientist."

Bert sprinkled a handful of cement over the sludgy mess and mixed it in with his Marigold-gloved hand. "True. Very true."

Daisy and Fred looked up as the door of the boathouse opened again and Llewellyn entered. Daisy craned her head round to see him. "Ah, come to your senses at last, have you?" she smiled.

"No," replied Llewellyn casually, untying the captives' wrists and ankles. "I just came to get you. We're ready for you now." He hauled Daisy to her feet and frogmarched her out of the door, Fred trailing in their wake.

"What do you mean, you're ready for us now?" demanded Fred indignantly. "You can't seriously think you can get away with sinking us in the estuary!"

"Oh yus we can," replied Llewellyn. He had marched Daisy out on to the jetty at the front of the boathouse and was assisting her cross the narrow gangplank on to Knuckles' pleasureboat, where Bert was waiting for them in the stern with the concrete.

Fred sat down next to Daisy on the rail of the boat, his back to the boathouse and Chez Knuckles. He looked at Daisy, who was staring at her tin bathful of concrete. He could feel the concrete, cold and wet around his own ankles as he pushed his feet into the grey, sludgy mixture under Llewellyn's watchful eye.

"This will ruin my shoes!"

Fred could hardly believe what she was saying. "Daisy, these maniacs are going to kill us!" he exclaimed. "You're chuntering on about your shoes, and they've got something distinctly permanent planned!"

"But they're my favourites!" pouted Daisy. She scooped up a handful of concrete and aimed it at Bert's head. He ducked and the gravel-laden sludge smashed the sliding glass door of the wheelhouse.

"Knuckles will kill you for that!" exclaimed Bert in horror.

"He's going to do that anyway," smirked Llewellyn, strolling nonchalantly into the wheelhouse to start the engine.

"Take your shoes off, then they won't get messed up," suggested Bert.

Daisy thought about it and conceded it was the best option under the circumstances. She slipped off her high heels and stuck a toe experimentally into the concrete. Wrinkling her nose in disgust, she lowered her feet into the tin bath, grimacing as the mixture squidged between her toes. If there was one thing she had hated when she was little, it was the feeling of wet sand between her toes on the beach. This was a hundred times worse.

We're ready to cast off," called Llewellyn.

"Whoopee," replied Fred sardonically.

"Don't worry, Fred," Daisy's tone was comfortingly self-assured. "They won't chuck us over the side. Those gorillas don't have the nerve."

"I don't think they have the nerve *not* to drown us," opined Fred bleakly. "I mean, they want to cover their tracks now Knuckles has got the formula."

-oOo-

Knuckles checked the instruction sheet that Fred had prepared. Jollop, reaction vessels, electrodes... He took the metal bar he was going to convert into a gold ingot and carefully lowered it into the large reaction vessel full of the slimy, green jollop. He frowned. The stuff had smelled different when Fred had mixed it up. He shrugged. He had followed the instructions precisely enough. He attached one of the high-tension cables to the bar and stood back. That was everything. All that was needed was the electricity. He moved over to the huge box of tricks with the dials on it that his boys had removed from the old house and checked the settings on the rheostats. He turned them up to full power. Taking a deep breath, he gripped the main switch in one gloved hand and yanked it down.

-oOo-

The thoughtful expression on Fred's face piqued Daisy's curiosity. "What's the matter, Fred?" she asked. "You look like a person who can't remember if he left the gas on at home."

"That's about the size of it," nodded Fred. "I can't help feeling I forgot to tell Knuckles something important about the formula."

"Well, that's his problem," sniffed Daisy. "We don't want to help him. After all, we know what he's got planned for us!" She stirred the sloppy concrete with her toes. Now she had got used to the sensation, it was not too bad.

Fred closed his eyes and offered up a silent prayer as the twin diesel engines of the pleasureboat thundered into life. In the wheelhouse, Llewellyn had donned Knuckles' Captain's cap and was using the throttles to manoeuvre the pleasureboat into the middle of the river. The estuary was only a dozen or so miles to the east, and they would be there in under a couple of hours. Then it was a one-way-ticket to the sea bed.

He and Daisy turned for a final look up at the well-appointed house on the hill. The grounds rolled down to the river bank, and they could see Knuckles' pride and joy, his newly-repaired, gleaming, Royal blue Rolls-Royce standing in the drive.

Fred clicked his fingers. "That was it," he nodded. "I was going to tell him to watch the power settings weren't too high, or the reaction might overload."

"Good, perhaps he'll blow himself up then." Daisy's voice was filled with unaccustomed rancour.

The explosion enveloped both the garage and the house, reducing both structures to ruins. It knocked Fred and Daisy off the rail of the boat and set their ears ringing, but not before they had seen a chunk of Georgian chimneystack the size of a refrigerator flatten Knuckles' precious Rolls. The garage had simply disappeared, possibly vaporised. The red, pan-tile roof of Chez Knuckles had lifted back like the lid of a music box and fallen into the front garden. Flames jetted high into the air, the blast scattering brickwork and broken glass all over the immaculately manicured lawn. Bricks, plaster, chairs and tables rained down out of the sky. Fred and Daisy ducked instinctively as the gaudy awning over the rear of the boat was tattered by falling debris.

A large, oak beam from the ceiling of the dining room came in vertically like a guided missile, punching through both the deck of the boat and the hull. Llewellyn stared at the water fountaining through the hole in horror. "Abandon ship!" he screamed, and vaulted over the side. Unfortunately, he leapt over the side closest to the bank and vanished with a spume of evil smelling black mud.

"I think those idiots have the right idea," Daisy whispered, extracting her feet from the wet concrete. She pulled Fred to his feet and they quickly lowered themselves over the other side and into the water.

It came in like a V2 rocket on its final approach, making an extraordinary racket as it trailed smoke across the sky. It plummeted into the water a couple of yards in front of them, and surfaced, red eyes glaring from a blackened face. "You!" exclaimed Knuckles, spotting Fred and lunging at him with the clear intention of doing him permanent damage.

"Now now, Mr Knuckles!" Daisy was attempting to soothe his nerves, without much success. Knuckles was wading after Fred, waving a piece of wood over his head. Fred had a slight advantage, having not just been blown two hundred feet into the air, and possibly twice that downrange. He was putting some distance between himself and the charred figure of Knuckles. He scrambled up on to the bank and raced off across the cratered lawn of Chez Knuckles with the lord of the manor in hot pursuit.

"Fred!" Daisy could hardly watch. She raced after the two men, intent on defending her man. Twice round the oak tree, down to the river again and back, Fred was running for his life, pursued by a snarling Knuckles. *"Ooof!!"* Knuckles had brought Fred down in a rugby tackle and was kneeling astride his chest, throttling him. Daisy snatched up a croquet mallet from the lawn and wound up a hefty swing.

"All right, McCallister, what the hell's going on now?" The voice was amplified by a megaphone, and even reached the dull recesses of Knuckles' brain. He released Fred and looked up to see a police launch coming ashore at the bank. On board were the Chief Constable, the Chief Superintendent, and a dozen or so plain clothes CID. Three vans full of Uniform Branch disgorged more rozzers than Knuckles cared to count.

In the prow of the police launch, like some kind of strange figurehead stood Boadicea, wrapped in a policeman's tunic, a helmet perched on her head which showed a tendency to slide down over her eyes. She pushed it back and grinned delightedly, waving at Fred and Daisy. Daisy dropped the croquet mallet and hugged Fred as he picked himself up from the lawn.

Knuckles ran straight at the Chief Constable, prompting the Armed Response Unit to cock their weapons, and threw himself at his feet, his hands out in surrender ready to be cuffed. "It's a fair cop, Ernie, lock me up," he wept. "I can't take any more."

The Chief Constable stared in acute discomfort at Knuckles, as the big man's tears were wetting his trouser leg. "Buck up, man, you're supposed to be the nastiest piece of work this side of the river since the Krays!"

"Who, me?" squeaked Knuckles. "I'm retiring! I can't take the stress of this business any more! I'm not cut out for this kind of thing. It was simpler in the old days. All you needed was a striped jersey, a mask and a crowbar. Now you have to have a degree in rocket science just to be dishonest. Well, I'm getting too old for any more of this! The most underhand thing I want to do in future is my crocheting!" He allowed himself to be led away by two nice gentlemen in white coats.

Fred had spotted the sheaf of Uncle Plum's notes where they had landed. The information had got them into a great deal of trouble, and it was time they did with the formula what his father had suggested at the outset. Joined by Daisy, Boadicea and Britannia, he fed the papers into the bonfire that had been Knuckles' garage.

The Chief Constable watched Knuckles' associates being rounded up and put into the waiting black maria. He turned to Daisy. "Are you all right, Daisy?" he asked.

"I'm fine now, Uncle Ernie," grinned Daisy as Fred set light to the last pages of the formula and watched the ashes blow away across the river.

THE END

of *Daisy and the Reluctant Alchemist*

Fred and Daisy Will Return in

Give Me Your Answer Do

About The Author
John Mark Oates is a Novelist, Humorist, Full-Time Carer and All-round Good Egg. Mark has been at the writing game since he was 16. He spent fifteen years as his mother's full-time carer and is now fulfilling the same role for his 85-year-old father. Mark has just broken into the self-publishing market and is now delving into his portfolio of past projects to put them out into the world.

About The Book
Schoolteacher Fred Longfield is possibly having the worst day of his life – his wedding day – then he meets scatterbrained heiress Daisy Chayne and things go steadily downhill from there.

Knocked into the park boating lake, assaulted by a series of people, dumped at the altar and fired from his position at the school, it ultimately turns out to be the luckiest day of his life.

-oOo-

Fred inherits his Great Uncle's country pile, which includes the formula and equipment for turning any other element into gold. Fred's real troubles begin when the local villain finds out about the formula and wants to make Fred an offer he cannot refuse...

Daisy and the Reluctant Alchemist is a romantic screwball-comedy adventure in the style of *Bringing Up Baby* — where the Hero meets a possibly crazy Heroine who proceeds to wreck his life. In fairly short order, he realises she is the Best Thing to have ever happened to him and they live happily ever after.

Daisy and the Reluctant Alchemist is one of my favourite

legacy projects. It was relegated to the shelf in mid-revision, a little while after its first draft in 1991, for personal reasons. In spite of those connections, I have always been fond of the characters of Fred and Daisy. I've given the story a major spruce-up for its publishing debut. I hope to start publishing further works as soon as I can complete them.

Printed in Great Britain
by Amazon